WITHDR

Radical Feminism Today

Books are to be returned on or before
the last date below.

- 8 OCT 2002

1 0 NOV 2002 03 02 0

0 2 MAY 2003

- 4 NOV 2003

JAN 2004

2 0 MAY 2005

LIBREX —

Radical Feminism Today

Denise Thompson

SAGE Publications
London • Thousand Oaks • New Delhi

First published 2001

SAGE Publications Ltd
6 Bonhill Street
London EC2A 4PU

SAGE Publications Inc
2455 Teller Road
Thousand Oaks, California 91320

SAGE Publications India Pvt Ltd
32, M-Block Market
Greater Kailash - I
New Delhi 110 048

British Library Cataloguing in Publication data

A catalogue record for this book is
available from the British Library

ISBN 0 7619 6340 5
ISBN 0 7619 6341 3 (pbk)

Library of Congress Control Number available

Typeset by SIVA Math Setters, Chennai, India
Printed in Great Britain by The Cromwell Press Ltd,
Trowbridge, Wiltshire

Contents

Introduction

The general tenor of the arguments in this book is that radical feminism is not one form of feminism among others, but simply feminism 'unmodified' (MacKinnon, 1987: 16), and that the common practice of qualifying feminism with any of a variety of pre-existing frameworks serves to disguise the core meaning of feminism. In the 1970s, those frameworks tended to be summed up under the headings 'liberal feminism', 'socialist feminism' and 'radical feminism'; subsequently, they have multiplied into a plethora of 'feminisms' which defy enumeration. But such a characterization disguises the relations of power involved. What has been happening is not a struggle over the meaning of feminism between equally matched contenders, but a stream of attacks powered by allegiances to varieties of malestream thought, against what is labelled 'radical feminism'. This labelling serves the ideological purpose of opening a space within feminism for other 'feminisms', thus providing a platform for attacking it from within.

This present work is an investigation of one of the most influential sites of the process of dismantling feminism from within, what I have come to call 'academic feminism'. By 'academic feminism' I do not mean everything produced in universities under the heading 'feminism'. Still less do I mean all feminist work which is academic in tone and format, since I regard my own work as academic in this sense. What I am referring to is that work, self-identified as 'feminist', which either ignores feminism's central problematic of opposition to male supremacy, or which actively sets out to pillory genuinely feminist work. The meaning, value, truth and reality of feminism, as I shall be arguing at length, is its identification of and opposition to male domination, and its concomitant struggle for a human status for women in connection with other women, which is at no one's expense, and which is outside male definition and control.

Because academic disciplines are conventionally male-identified, it is hardly surprising that a feminism which exposes those interests cannot be allowed a place in the academic canon. That some feminist work in the academy has nevertheless been able to identify and to resist the coercions and seductions of malestream thought, is a tribute to its authors' commitment, persistence and dedication. There are many feminists within academe whose feminist politics is direct and unequivocal, and who have succeeded in conveying it to their students, but they are in the embattled minority like radical feminists everywhere. But in too many self-identified feminist texts emanating from academe, the signs of their origins are only too evident. The chief of those signs is equivocation on, or outright repudiation of, the question of male domination. While this may be inadvertent, it is none the less systematic. Constructs of 'cultural feminism', 'essentialism', 'puritanism', 'false universalism', 'political correctness', 'white and middle-class', 'ahistorical', etc., are typically directed against those feminist writings which most clearly identify male domination and its ways.[1]

Although the critique of academic feminism is one of my major concerns, I do not discuss postmodernism in any detail. This might seem a curious omission in light of the overwhelming influence of postmodernism on feminist theorizing in the academy in recent years. The omission, however, is deliberate. I do not discuss postmodernism as an identifiable framework because to do so, even as critique, would be to reinforce its position of pre-eminence. To focus attention, even critically, on postmodernism would be to award it credibility as a feminist enterprise, when from a feminist standpoint it is merely another ruse of male supremacy. As Mia Campioni put it:

> The white, male, middle-class intellectual response to this revolt [of the 'other'] has been to appropriate this claim to 'otherness' as its *own* revelatory experience. ... As a male theorist declared unilaterally: 'we have found that we are all others' (Paul Ricoeur, quoted in H. Foster, ed., *The Anti-Aesthetic*, 1983: 57). He forgot that he was once more speaking for all of 'us'. The noisy protests of others hitherto mute (or ignored/unheard) must have come as a huge shock to him. ... He could not understand these protests in any other way than by assuming this 'other' to be him again, or to be again there for him to appropriate as his own. (Campioni, 1991: 49–50 – her emphasis)

On the other hand, I do address many of the issues which have been raised under the postmodernist banner, and many of the texts I discuss are explicitly identified as 'postmodernist'.

The referent of the 'feminism' I will be alluding to throughout this present work is that 'second wave' of feminism, initially known as the Women's Liberation Movement, dating from the late 1960s and early 1970s. Feminism, in the sense of women defending their own interests in the face of male supremacy, is of much longer duration than the last three decades, and hence to call this latest manifestation a 'second wave' does an injustice to the long history of women's struggles on their own behalf (Lerner, 1993; Spender, 1982). (There is no 'third wave' – feminism at present is a clarification and holding on to the insights and gains of the Women's Liberation Movement in the face of the male supremacist backlash, and of those co-optations and recuperations which penetrate (pun intended) the very body of feminism itself. Still less have we arrived at any era of 'postfeminism', for the simple and obvious reason that male supremacy still exists.) But although 'feminism' has wider historical connotations than I give it here, my task is not to write a history of feminism throughout the ages; it is, rather, to engage in 'the self-clarification of the struggles and wishes' of the age I myself have lived through (to paraphrase an insight of Marx's).[2]

As I mentioned above, it is radical feminism which provides my own standpoint and which I regard as feminism *per se*. But although I will be arguing at length that much that is called 'feminism' is not, I have often allowed the designation 'feminism' to stand even while I argue against it. In other words, I use the term 'feminism' in a systematically ambiguous way. Sometimes I mean feminism *per se*, that is, radical feminism which identifies and opposes male domination; and sometimes I accept the self-identification as 'feminism' even while disagreeing with it. Which is which should be clear from the context. I have kept the ambiguity in the interests of open-endedness because it resides in the texts under discussion. It is sometimes the case that I criticize one aspect of a text which in other respects displays impeccable feminist credentials.

The texts which I use to exemplify this kind of academic feminism have been selected randomly. They are exemplary only, and not in any sense chief offenders in the issues I identify. They are intended to illustrate certain themes, and not to castigate individual authors or particular pieces of work. I could have chosen any number of other texts to illustrate those themes, which are endemic in academic feminist theorizing and not peculiar to particular authors.

My task is not to sort out who is a feminist and who is not. The issue of defining feminism is not a question of who is (or is not) a feminist. While it may indeed be the case that no one has the right to tell anyone else whether or not she is a feminist, that is not what is involved. To see it in that way can only impede the progress of feminism because it stymies the important project of self-clarification by placing a ban on saying what feminism is. It reduces politics to a matter of personal preference and opinion. The crucial question is not 'Who is a feminist?' but 'What is feminism?' This latter question can only be addressed with reference to the logic of feminist theory and practice. The meaning of 'feminism' needs to be radically contested and debated. But that cannot happen as long as feminism continues to be implicitly defined only in terms of anything said or done by anyone who identifies as a feminist.

As an exercise in radical feminist theory, this present work is somewhat unusual. Radical feminist writing has not on the whole tended to engage in explicit theory-making in the sense of building on, extending and engaging with attempts to say what feminism is. For if radical feminism has not been welcomed into academe, the feeling has been mutual – neither has radical feminism been eager to intrude upon the more arcane levels of theorizing. Arising as it does out of the practical politics of women's lives and experiences, and springing directly from the changed consciousness which is feminism, the theory has tended to *show* itself in the issues addressed and in the ways in which those issues are interpreted, rather than by being *said* outright.[3] In most cases feminist theory is implicit in feminist texts, rather than explicitly spelled out. By and large this has been a deliberate strategy on the part of radical feminist theorists. It has meant that radical feminism has remained tied to issues of real concern to women, rather than being enticed by the seductions of theory for theory's sake (Stanley and Wise, 1993). For the most part, radical feminism has focused on exposing the worst excesses of the social system which is male supremacy. The need to say what feminism is, however, has become urgent and pressing in light of the strength and influence of the anti-feminist backlash, a backlash which is increasingly masquerading as 'feminism' itself. This present project is a contribution to the debate.

The work is divided into two Parts. Part One is called 'Understanding Feminism'. In it I discuss what is at stake in feminist politics. In Chapter 1 I define feminism as a moral and political struggle of opposition to the social relations of male domination structured around the principle that only men count as 'human', and as a struggle for a genuine human status for women outside male definition and control. I also discuss what is involved in a feminist standpoint. Chapters 2 and 3 deal with the concept of ideology. Chapter 2 discusses some objections which have been raised to the use of the term, and argues that it is useful as a designation of the ways in which domination is disguised in order to justify it and make it palatable. In this chapter I also criticize arguments to the effect that truth is complicit with domination, and discuss the issue of comprehensibility in feminist theory. In Chapter 3 I investigate some of the ways in which ideology works, through the inculcation of pleasure and desire, and through interpreting relations of ruling as the personal preferences or attributes of individuals. Part Two is called 'Misunderstanding Feminism'. It is devoted to criticisms of a number of ways of characterizing feminism other than in terms of the opposition to male domination. Chapter 4 discusses the feminist reluctance to define feminism. Chapter 5 discusses a number of implicit definitions of feminism in terms of 'women', 'patriarchy', 'sexism', 'gender' and 'dichotomies', arguing that all these meanings have limitations as the chief designator of a feminist politics. Chapter 6 looks at the question of 'differences between the sexes'. In Chapters 7 and 8 I discuss in some detail the question of 'differences among women', and in particular the contentious issue of 'race' and the part it has played in feminist politics. In the last chapter, I use the early radical feminist insight that male domination is the primary form of social domination in order to suggest alternative ways of bringing a feminist perspective to bear on racism and imperialism.

Notes

1   For a critique of the concept of 'essentialism' and its unjustified use against radical feminism, see Thompson, 1991, Chapters 7 and 10.

2   'Letter to Ruge', Kreuznach, September 1843, in *Early Writings*, Penguin Books, 1975: 209.

3   The reference is to Ludwig Wittgenstein's distinction between 'showing' and 'saying': 'What *can* be shown *cannot* be said' (Wittgenstein, 1951: 4.1212). The distinction may be absolute in the case of logic. But a political commitment such as feminism must be able to identify explicitly the interests, meanings and values which determine both what feminism is struggling against and what it is struggling for. In that sense, any distinction between what can be said and what must simply be shown is provisional. It is tied to certain purposes and shifts according to the task at hand.

Part One   Understanding Feminism

1 Defining feminism

On Definition

Understanding what feminism is is not a straightforward task because there is a reluctance among feminist writers to engage in explicit definition. On the whole feminists tend, often quite deliberately, not to say what they mean by feminism. 'That word', wrote Alice Jardine, 'poses some serious problems. Not that we would want to end up by demanding a definition of what feminism is and, therefore, of what one must do, say, and be, if one is to acquire that epithet [feminist]; dictionary meanings are suffocating, to say the least' (Jardine, 1985: 20). Even compilers of feminist dictionaries are reluctant to engage too rigorously in definition. Maggie Humm, for example, said that it could only be 'misleading to offer precise definitions of feminism because the process of defining is to enlarge, not to close down, linguistic alternatives' (Humm, 1989: xiv).

These warnings against definition would have some point to them, were it not for the special circumstances of the current condition of feminist theorizing. There is little common agreement about what feminism means, even to the point where positions in stark contradiction to each other are equally argued in the name of 'feminism', with little hope of resolution as things stand at the moment. The need for clarity is pressing in a context where a great deal of what is called 'feminism' is not, where euphemisms and evasions abound, where the 'sponge words' (Mills, 1959) of postmodernism soak up all meaning, and the backlash against feminism masquerades as feminism itself. Definition, in the sense of the explicit assertion of meaning, has an important role to play in the feminist struggle.

To define feminism is to take responsibility for what one says about feminism. It is a way of situating oneself and clarifying the standpoint from which one approaches the feminist project. And it is not only the author who must decide on the accuracy or otherwise of her own definition, but also the reader. By defining feminism, the author is providing for the reader the opportunity to enter into debate. No discourse belongs solely to its author. Readers too participate in the creation of meaning. A definition sets up a dialogue, and it does that best when the author gives a clear and unambiguous account of what feminism is in the context of her own discourse. Definition is a clarifying device. Saying clearly what is meant by feminism is to make provision for challenge and debate. Definitions are tentative, open to challenge, must be argued for and substantiated, and can always be modified. Because the problem of dogmatism is a very real one, it is as well to remember this. Defining something is not to fix it irrevocably and for all time. A definition is not the essential and only true meaning. It is not authoritative, only more or less accurate for the purpose for which it is intended. Far from rigidifying meanings, definitions are devised in particular contexts for particular purposes. The context in this case is that of a feminism under attack from within, and the purpose is to clarify what is at stake in feminist politics. While a definition certainly closes down some alternatives, it also opens up others. Hopefully, the alternatives which are closed down by the definition I propose are those anti-feminist positions paraded as 'feminism', while the alternatives it opens up are those of a feminism which is truly in the interests of women.

What follows is a 'definition' only in the sense that it is an explicit clarification in the light of the special circumstances mentioned above. In fact it is rather more than a definition. It is an extended account of the ways in which the discourse of feminism makes sense. It is an account of how the term 'feminism' is used, but not just any usage will do. As I argue throughout, there are some usages of 'feminism' which either make no sense of the feminist project, or are actively antagonistic towards it. Hence, simply pointing to the way the term 'feminism' is used is insufficient for the purpose of clarifying the nature of feminism. To the extent that uses of the term 'feminism' contradict or confuse the ethical and political aims of feminism, they cannot be said to count as feminism.

Defining Feminism

The theme of 'social construction' runs throughout the literature of 'second-wave' feminism. ('Gender' is commonly used to denote this theme but, as I argue at some length later, there are grave problems with this usage.) This is intended to emphasize the fact that sex, sex differences, relations between the sexes, the very category of 'women' itself, are due to social arrangements and not to biological necessity, that these are questions of culture not nature. To insist that the situation of women is socially constructed, and not naturally given, is a necessary emphasis given the justificatory role still played by biological explanations for women's social subordination. But the idea of 'social construction' is not a new one, nor is it a peculiarly feminist one even in the weakest sense, that is, concerned specifically with women. It originated with sociology.[1] It is not even a particularly radical idea, since it can be found in the most conservative of sociological writings. Although it is an improvement on arguments from 'nature', it has a limited use for feminist purposes unless it is combined with an analysis of what kind of society it is we are talking about, and of the implications of that for feminist theory and practice.

From the outset, it should be obvious that feminism is a social enterprise, a moral and political framework concerned with redressing social wrongs. It is an ethical stance in that it starts from and continually returns to questions of value, of good and evil, right and wrong, of what is worthwhile and significant and what is not. Feminism is centrally concerned with judgements of what ought and what ought not to be the case, with what constitutes right action and the good life and with what operates to prevent that, with the nature of the human conditions within which we want to live and those which must be resisted because they are morally wrong. Morality is not just a private matter. Although it concerns what each of us decides about what constitutes the good life and how to live it, that does not mean that morality is an individualistic phenomenon in any sense which implies that 'individuals' are discrete entities, existing in isolation, prior to or somehow 'outside' social relations. Individuals can be nothing but social beings, and the moral beliefs which structure human life are collective. That does not imply actual universal agreement, because in that case there would be no decisions for people to make. But it does mean that morality must be shared and communicable, even when it involves an 'unpopular' stance taken in opposition to dominant beliefs.

The way in which feminism is political is not well served by the conventional meaning of 'politics', for example, as 'all that characterizes or touches upon the domain of public policy' (Montefiore, 1990: 201). One of the earliest insights of feminism was the recognition that the public/private distinction is an ideological construct which confines important aspects of the subordination of women to the domain of the 'private', and allows some of the most violent manifestations of the power of men over women to go unrecognized and unchecked. The feminist slogan 'The personal is political' both acknowledges and challenges that dichotomy. A feminist politics involves struggling to make the 'private' woes of women 'public'. It involves, too, identifying the numerous ways in which the 'public sphere' men value is dependent for its continued existence on the unpaid, unacknowledged and unreciprocated work of women. And it involves elucidating the ways in which the 'public' penetrates the 'private' – home, family, bedroom, and the individual psyches of women *and* men.

The public arena is, ideally, the domain of consensus, since it is not possible to reach agreement unless the debate happens out in the open. It is this ideal of consensus which feminism appeals to in its attempts to bring the wrongs done to women under public scrutiny. In this sense, feminism's claim to be political is similar to politics in the conventional sense, in that it aims to put women's interests on to the public agenda. But it is also different in that it insists that there are crucial dimensions of the 'private' sphere which ought to be matters of public debate and rectification. In so doing, feminism brings into question the split between 'public' and 'private' on which conventional politics depends. Feminist politics requires that the nature of politics in the conventional sense be radically changed if it is to include the interests of women. This requirement cannot be met by a tokenistic fitting of some women into positions which remain unchanged. Women cannot be 'equal' with men as long as there is no equality among men. In feminist terms, what women want is a human status where rights, benefits and dignities are gained at no one's expense, and where duties and obligations do not fall disproportionately on the shoulders of women. Such a project promises to transform politics altogether.

Politics is also concerned with social relations of power, and the relations of power which feminism identifies are those of male domination. Feminism aims to expose the reality of male domination, while struggling for a world where women are recognized as human beings in their own right. Using the unequivocal and adamantine terminology of 'male domination' and its synonyms does not mean men's absolute power and women's absolute powerlessness. It is used for the sake of clarity, in order to designate as clearly as possible what it is that feminism is opposing.

If it is feminism's peculiar genius to have uncovered the social reality of male domination, simply to appeal to 'social construction' becomes radically inadequate as a feminist strategy. If social reality is male supremacist, then what the 'social construction' thesis implies is that we are 'constructed' as the bearers of the social relations of male supremacy. But while this *is* a major implication of feminist theory, it is immediately countered by the existence of feminism itself. Feminism says that male domination constitutes the conditions under which we live, but that *it ought not to be so*. At one and the same time, feminism both exposes the existence of male domination and challenges it. Indeed, it is through exposing male domination *as* domination that feminism poses its major challenge, since social domination operates most efficiently to the extent that it ensures compliance by being disguised as something else, and not domination at all. It has been the task of feminism to tear away the masks behind which male domination hides its true nature, and expose it for the dehumanizing system it really is.

Male domination does not mean what one writer referred to as 'unrelenting male drives for dominance and mastery' (Hawkesworth, 1989: 543). It does not mean that all men are invariably oppressive to all women all the time, nor that women are invariably the passive, peaceable victims of a male will to power. It is a social system, a matter of meanings and values, practices and institutions. While social structures are maintained through the commitment and acquiescence of individuals, and can be eroded by the refusal of individuals to participate, they have a life of their own, and can continue to exert their influence despite the best efforts of the well-intentioned. The manifestations of male domination, although they are sometimes horrifically violent and degrading, are also subtle, mundane, ordinary, unremarkable, and, moreover, very deeply embedded in the psyches of individuals, and not just male individuals either. It constitutes the social environment of women as well as men, the 'mutual knowledge' of social actors (Giddens, 1984: 375) and part of the taken-for-granted ambience of everyone.

To insist on the reality of male domination does not mean that individuals are nothing but inert entities moved hither and yon by forces outside their control. Whether particular actions, desires, etc., maintain the social structure, or whether they erode it, is the responsibility of the individual agent to decide, a responsibility which remains even when evaded. Male domination is not some kind of monolithic and homogeneous system within which individuals are inserted without their knowledge and with no possibility of non-compliance. Any such assertion would be empirically false. It is not the case that individuals have no choice but to comply with dominant norms and the norms of domination. No regime can turn human beings into automata or reduce people's choices to absolute zero. Even the totalitarian regimes of the twentieth century, with their widespread brutality, murder, terror and lies, failed to crush all rebellion. At the same time, the extent to which people are kept in ignorance of where their real interests lie, are manipulated for purposes not their own, are prevented from controlling the conditions of their own existence by powerful vested interests, is the extent to which they are subjected to conditions of domination. It is this reality of domination which feminism resists with its commitment to the belief that human beings have the right to exist in freedom and dignity simply because we exist.

None the less, social systems are maintained and reproduced through people's commitment to their continued existence. 'Society' requires people's active participation if it is to exist at all; and individuals only exist within the social realities which supply them with ways of knowing, understanding, valuing, and recognizing self and other. Anthony Giddens put this in terms of the 'recursive' nature of human social activities, which are

> not brought into being by social actors but continually recreated by them via the very means whereby they express themselves *as* actors. In and through their activities agents reproduce the conditions that make these activities possible. ... The fixity of institutional forms does not exist in spite of, or outside, the encounters of day-to-day life but *is implicated in those very encounters.* ... Human societies, or social systems, would plainly not exist without human agency. But it is not the case that actors create social systems; they reproduce or transform them, remaking what is already made in the continuity of praxis. (Giddens, 1984: 2, 69, 171 – emphases in the original)

But while this account fills out the concept of 'social construction', it is still inadequate for feminist purposes because it says nothing about domination. In Giddens' account, the very possibility of the existence of social conditions of domination is argued away. He defines power in terms of human agency, as the capacity of individuals, singly or collectively, to get things done, to achieve outcomes, to make a significant difference in the world. He is fully aware that people do not have unlimited freedom of action. But he casts the issue only in terms of constraint and enablement, while providing no criteria for deciding which is which. He says that 'the structural properties of social systems are both enabling and constraining' (Giddens, 1984: 162). But if constraint is enablement (and vice versa), how do we distinguish between the constraints which enable, that is, which provide the basic pre-requisites for action, and those which 'enable' no more than people's consent to their own oppression? He also says that constraint operates 'through the active involvement of the agents concerned, not as some force of which they are passive recipients' (p. 289), and that 'all forms of dependence offer some resources whereby those who are subordinate can influence the activities of their superiors' (p. 16). But while this might be true, it takes for granted the very issues of dependence, subordination and superiority which feminism seeks to bring into question.

He also says that '"Domination" and "power" cannot be thought of only in terms of asymmetries of distribution but have to be recognized as inherent in social association (or, I would say, in human action as such)' (pp. 31–2). But if 'domination' is 'power', and 'power' is 'social association' or 'human action as such', there is no way of distinguishing between those dominating forms of power which serve the interests of some at others' expense, and those forms which everyone needs if we are to operate in the world. If 'domination' cannot be separated out from 'power' and confined to 'asymmetries of distribution', how do we distinguish power-as-capacity (including access to those resources which enable human action) from power-as-domination (including the monopolization of resources and their accumulation in the hands of the few) (Allen, 1998; Hartsock, 1974)?[2] On Giddens' account, there is no possibility of political struggle *against* relations of ruling and *for* the capacities of everyone to control the conditions of their own existence.

But for feminist purposes 'constraint' is not really the issue. Although women may indeed be 'constrained' under conditions of male supremacy, from the perspective of women constraints on the worst excesses of male behaviour are positively beneficial. The restraining powers of the state, for example, have sometimes been of benefit to women. The police and the judiciary have the power to protect women and children from violent men, and that power is sometimes used effectively, if too often reluctantly. The state also has the power to redistribute income, and that power operates in favour of the women and children who comprise a disproportionately large segment of the poor. That the state thereby constrains men, by imposing penalties for violence and by taxing the wealthy, is a positive virtue from the point of view of women. To couch questions of freedom and power in terms of 'enablement' and 'constraint' betokens a masculine ethos. This is the world view of those who already have the capacity to act freely because the world is made in their image and likeness, or who react violently if they are deprived of what they have been promised is theirs by right.

The political concern with 'power' is a concern with the sort of power which causes problems, that is, the domination which results in harm and misery. The *problem* with power is not that it achieves outcomes, but that it is exercised to prevent categories of people from achieving even the most basic outcomes necessary for their human dignity and respect. A liberatory politics like feminism is a stance taken against power in the form of domination and in favour of power in the form of the exercising of capacities at no one's expense. It requires knowledge of the ways in which power-as-domination is exercised, because those ways are not always overt and deliberate. It is a sociological truism that the social control of populations is most efficient when people control themselves, when they perceive the status quo as in their own interests and acquiesce more or less willingly in its maintenance and reproduction. Indeed, this commitment on the part of individuals is essential if the social order is to be reproduced at all. It is often the case that the interests of some people can prevail over and against the interests of others, without those others putting up any opposition at all. As Steven Lukes points out, power-as-domination is frequently exercised by control over sources of information so that people do not even get to find out that they have grievances, much less protest against or act to change oppressive conditions.

> the most effective and insidious use of power is to prevent ... conflict from arising in the first place. ... is it not the supreme and most insidious exercise of power to prevent people, to whatever degree, from having grievances by shaping their perceptions, cognitions and preferences in such a way that they accept their role in the existing order of things, either because they can see or imagine no alternative to it, or because they see it as natural and unchangeable, or because they value it as divinely ordained and beneficial? (Lukes, 1974: 23, 24)

Hence, people can willingly act to reproduce relations of domination and subordination without realizing that that is what they are doing, much less being in a position to resist. But Lukes is only partly right in his comment on relations of power between women and men, when he says that both are 'victims of the system, rather than one being held to exercise power over the other'. He is right to point out that it is 'not so much a question of men ... choosing to exercise power over women, through voluntary actions on the basis of modifiable attitudes', but rather 'a system of domination in which both men and women are caught up, albeit one serving the interests of the former at the expense of the latter' (Lukes, 1977: 10). But while it is true that both women and men can be complicit with relations of male domination, if the system operates in the interests of men and against the interests of women, they are not both 'victims' in quite the same way. It is misleading to refer to men as 'victims' of a system which ensures that their interests will prevail at women's expense, although it is true that the system is often unwittingly, and sometimes explicitly, maintained by both women and men. The system of male domination cannot be wholly identified with men's conscious, deliberate choices to subordinate women, firstly because the taken-for-granted nature of the system allows women's subordination to be effected through business as usual, and secondly because the actions of women can also serve to maintain the system as long as women remain unaware of their real interests. None the less, the question of women's liberation from male domination is a moral one, and, as such, it *depends on* 'voluntary actions' and 'modifiable attitudes' on the part of both sexes, but especially on the part of women, if the system is to be challenged and opposed.

To refer to 'male domination', then, rather than using the more neutral terminology of 'social construction', is not to refer to something monolithic and inexorable. No system of domination, even the most totalitarian, functions without contradictions, ambiguities and resistances. 'Domination' refers to a hierarchical social order wherein the interests of some prevail *at the expense of* the interests of others. It refers to social arrangements which facilitate the interests of elites to the detriment of categories of people excluded from access to the resources needed for even the most basic human dignity. It is maintained partly through ideological means to ensure the consent of the oppressed to their own oppression and to provide justifications for maintaining the status quo, partly through the threat, and periodic actual exercise, of violence. Male domination means that the male represents the 'human' norm at the expense of a human status for women. Men's interests and values are set up as universal 'human' interests, and genuinely human values like reason, virtue or courage are appropriated as exclusive to men. At the same time, male domination means that the female is regarded as subsidiary, subservient, ancillary to, or absent from, the 'human' norm, while the interests, values and rights of women are denied, trivialized or derided, and women's time, energy and attention are expropriated for men's use and pleasure. Under conditions of male supremacy, women are allowed, at best, a second-rate 'human' status acquired through relations of subordination to men; at worst, women's needs and interests are ignored, and women are treated as if we had no rights and no claim to be accorded human respect and dignity. As Simone de Beauvoir put it over 40 years ago: 'A man never begins by presenting himself as an individual of a certain sex; it goes without saying that he is a man. ... Representation of the world, like the world itself, is the work of men; they describe it from their own point of view, which they confuse with absolute truth' (Beauvoir, 1970: 15, 175).

Male supremacy, that view of the world which insists that only men be recognized as 'human', condones, permits, even at times recommends (as, for example, in pornography) harm to women. Because women are not human within the terms and under the conditions of male supremacy, they are not allowed access to the rights and dignities of being human. Because women are not recognized as human, they can be treated with contempt. What happens to them does not matter, their needs do not have to be considered, their interests can be trivialized and denied. Because women are not human, they become nothing but objects for men's use. This creates a contradiction at the heart of the world order that is male supremacy. The chief contradiction structuring and rupturing male supremacist conditions is the existence of women which continually gives the lie to the male as the standard of 'human' existence, a lie which is managed by acknowledging women only to the extent that they serve men's interests. It is not possible, after all, to deny women's existence altogether (although the instances where that happens are many and various and rarely commented upon). Moreover, women have many and varied strategies for resisting male domination. Some of these merely reverse the power hierarchy. Some are complicit with the meanings and values of domination while defeating a particular individual or individuals (male or female). Other strategies of resistance on the part of women radically undermine the belief in women's inferiority and availability to men, and manifest a power and capability far beyond anything permitted to women within the confines of the conventional female role.

Male monopolization of 'human' status dehumanizes everyone, for if women are not human, men cannot be genuinely human either. Tyranny corrupts. It corrupts the tyrannized by requiring of them the values of subservience, but (as Hegel pointed out) it is even more corrupting for the tyrant. By failing to recognize the humanity of his female other, the tyrant destroys his own human status. Because he will not allow her her own unique self, he deprives himself of anyone to recognize him. Because everyone's first 'other' is female, the mother, the process of dehumanization starts at once, from the beginning of each human existence, and hence 'humanity' under male supremacist conditions is flawed from the outset.

What feminism is fighting for is a world in which women have, and are seen to have, a fully human status. It is this aspect of the feminist struggle which has received the most attention, to the point where feminism has tended to be implicitly defined solely in terms of 'women'. This focus of attention is vitally important. It is necessary to rescue women from historical oblivion, to insist on women's human rights and dignities, to expose the injustices and harm done to women, to assert in a multitude of ways that women are human beings deserving of respect. But although many of the feminist enterprises devoted to women display insight into the social system of male domination even when it is not stated explicitly, focusing on women in and of itself says nothing about the male supremacist relations of ruling which makes this focus necessary. As a result, defining feminism only in terms of 'women' has given rise to a number of futile debates, about what is involved in the category of 'women', for example, or about whether women are the same as or different from men. It has also had the unfortunate political consequence of dividing women into a multiplicity of incompatible social categories. Hence, although defining feminism in terms of women is necessary, it is not sufficient as the unifying factor of feminist politics. It is the opposition to male domination which makes feminism relevant to women wherever they are situated, however differently they are excluded from recognition as human.

Because the male monopoly of the 'human' is still too little recognized, because it is still veiled by hegemonic meanings and values which authenticate maleness and depreciate femaleness, the creation of a human status for women requires that women seek recognition from each other, that women live in connection with women and recognize each other in ways which are outside male control and definition. It used to be argued that lesbianism was central to this project, as long as lesbianism was itself defined as women identifying with women, women loving women, women seeing each other as human individuals lacking nothing (Abbott and Love, 1972; Myron and Bunch, 1975). Lesbianism was seen as central to feminism, both as a challenge to male supremacy because of its challenge to the dominance of heterosexual desire, and as a redefining of the category of women, for women and by women and outside the male hegemony. This did not mean that all feminists, or all women, should be lesbians (any more than 'all women' should be any other one thing in particular). It meant that lesbianism, as mutual recognition between women, should be accorded an honoured place within second-wave feminism, so that it was available to women as a real alternative to defining themselves only in relation to men.

Initially, during the 1970s, it was argued that lesbianism was also central to feminism because it was a *sexual* practice and because of the kind of sexual practice it was, that is, sexual desire and activity without the penis, and hence a sexuality with a potential for equality rather than domination. But subsequent developments in the meaning of lesbianism have almost buried that feminist stance. One of those developments was the rise to prominence of lesbian sadomasochism, supported by a sexual libertarianism which defined sex only in terms of 'bodies and pleasures' and which demanded that sex be placed beyond political critique. It seemed that lesbian sex, too, could be hi-jacked for male supremacist purposes. This should have come as no surprise, since feminism had early identified the connection between sex and domination at the heart of male supremacist meanings and values. We had not, however, gone far enough in our analysis, and investigated the ways in which women, too, could be complicit with eroticized domination. Another development which rejected the feminist stance was the influence of a discourse of liberal tolerance whereby lesbianism was defined merely as a sexual preference, as the personal attribute of some (few) individual women. Although preferable to contempt or persecution, this attitude of tolerance ignored the social context of phallocratic reality within which sex is still embedded, and hence took the feminist politics out of lesbianism.

None the less the feminist point remains (marginalized and derided though it might be). The feminist point is that sex is central to women's oppression. It is through heterosexual desire that women are fitted, and fit themselves, into their subordinate roles in relation to men. Relations of domination function most efficiently to the extent that individuals consent to the status quo, rather than being overtly and forcibly coerced. People must accept the sphere allotted to them within the hierarchy and see it as the only reality. It is women's lot to serve men, to see no alternative to their subordinate roles in relation to men, to gain access to 'human' status only through men, and to embrace that as their own identity. Heterosexual desire puts the excitement and the reality into women's subordination to men (Jeffreys, 1992). Lesbianism within the feminist context was meant as a challenge to the exclusiveness and 'naturalness' of heterosexual desire as the only form of intimacy women are allowed. It was a refusal to serve or service men, a withdrawal of recognition from men as the only 'human' individuals, and a commitment by women to women's full humanity.

Lesbianism put the excitement and reality into separatism. It gave separatism its central focus and meaning by drawing on the power and energy of sex to bring women together. But we paid insufficient heed to the implications of our own analysis that sex derives its power and energy from the role it plays in reproducing the social relations of male supremacy. While the focus on sex accurately identified the problem, the ease with which lesbianism was reincorporated in the malestream, at best as a neutrally valued sexual preference, at worst as just one more pornographic scenario, indicates that the struggle is far from over.

Separatism is a continuum of feminist politics, involving a withdrawal of consent to male supremacist relations of ruling. It is not some kind of revolutionary end point. Rather, it is a constant strategic necessity as long as the male remains hegemonically the 'human' norm and male supremacist conditions require female compliance. Male supremacy not only excludes women – from 'human' status, and from highly valued forms of life, such as government, wealth, creative and artistic endeavour – it also *includes* women, in roles confined to the support and nurturance of males, as mothers, wives, receptacles for the penis, as the mainstay and support of masculinity, as the unrecognized recognizers of male subjectivity, required to silence their own interests in the interests of masculine importance, status and reality. It is this inclusion of women within male supremacist meanings and values which requires women's exclusion from those spheres men value, spheres which could not exist without the work women do in providing basic human necessities. Women's exclusion from positions of power and influence has a purpose – to keep the majority of women tied to men, promoting male interests, nourishing and fostering male subjectivities, doing the work and providing the ground from which men can launch themselves into those projects so highly valued within male supremacist conditions.

It is this inclusion which separatism contests. While separatism has been criticized for exacerbating women's exclusion from male dominated domains, in fact feminism has never been unequivocally in favour of women's equality with men. The public domain is hierarchical, exploitative, structured by invidious distinctions between categories of human beings, motivated by subjectivities domineering and contemptuous, or obsequious, ingratiating, envious and resentful. Women's entry into statuses and positions structured by the requirements of male prestige and power, does no more than set up among women the same hierarchies already existing among men, and reproduces current invidious distinctions among women. So feminism's challenge to women's exclusion is not unambivalent. Feminism's refusal of women's inclusion, however, as female auxiliaries to projects designed in the interests of men, as supporters and exponents of male supremacist meanings and values, is clear and unequivocal. It is in that sense, as this very refusal, that separatism is the chief strategy of second-wave feminism, not, however, as a refusal to have anything to do with men. Such an interpretation is not only unrealistic, it is also individualistic. It interprets male domination only in terms of men and their attributes, rather than as a system of meanings and values. It also rules out the possibility of important feminist projects which engage directly with male supremacist institutions (reproductive technologies, for example), with the aim of challenging them.[3] Separatism is a withdrawal of allegiance to these conditions. That may or may not involve withdrawing from some forms of relationships with men, crucially, although not only, sexual relationships. But because men are not the only bearers of the social relations of male supremacy, withdrawing from men (even if that were possible or desirable) is not sufficient as a withdrawal of consent to male supremacist meanings and values.

In the most general terms feminism is a struggle in the domain of meaning, in contrast to, for example, women violently overthrowing the present ruling classes, or taking over the means of production or the world's wealth. Given how little social power women have, such enterprises are wildly beyond our capabilities or resources. Meaning is everywhere because we are language users. To say that feminism is a struggle in the realm of meaning is not to say that feminism is, therefore, not concerned with mundane matters like rape, child care, equal pay, parliamentary representation, etc. It is simply to say that those matters have a different meaning from a feminist perspective than they do from any other. It is also to say that, because meaning is everywhere, so is the possibility of feminist struggle. It is to say that feminist politics is not confined to the kinds of issues conventionally defined as 'political', but that it can happen anywhere with whatever tools are closest to hand. It can happen in the deepest recesses of the psyche as well as worldwide, in the most intimate of personal relationships as well as nationally and internationally. It is to say that feminism is available wherever women are, and advances wherever women do. The gargantuan accumulations of wealth in the hands of a few men at the expense of the majority of people, the all-pervasive systems of propaganda pacifying whole populations with banal, misogynist stupidities, the mass starvation and destruction of the environment generated by international capitalism, the nation states legislating in the interests of the powerful and stockpiling lethal weapons sufficient to wipe out the human race, and everywhere men on the rampage, raping, maiming and killing – all this is far too much for anyone to cope with, even collectively. But that is not cause for despair. The struggle is also against the meanings and values of the world that is the case, and that struggle takes place within each individual committed to the task of refusing compliance. While individuals can often do very little about the facts of domination, we can all radically bring the meanings into question and refuse to embrace the values.

In defining feminism as the struggle against male supremacy and the struggle for a human status for women identifying with women, I am not making the weak claim that this is only 'my' definition, that everyone has her own definition, and that anyone's definition is as good as anyone else's.

I am making the much stronger claim that this is what feminism *is*. The definition is presented as *the* definition of feminism, the one which makes sense of the feminist project. It addresses the logic of feminist politics, theory and practice; and it is broad enough to include most of what is recognized as feminism, while being specific enough to allow anti-feminist arguments and assertions to be identified and excluded. It is true that I am a single individual making the claim, and that I speak on no one's behalf but my own. But that does not debar me (or anyone else) from saying what feminism is. This does not mean that the definition proposed here is unchallengeable and beyond argument. On the contrary, because it is argued for in the clearest possible terms, it is very much open for debate. Disagreements, however, cannot be resolved by means of well-intentioned decisions to respect our individual differences of opinion. Although polite agreement to disagree may sometimes be the only civilized option, it does not resolve the contradictions, but simply postpones them. While individual feminists are the participants in the debate, feelings and opinions are not sufficient referents for feminist theory, which must be argued through with reference to the logic and evidence of feminist theory and practice.

Neither is the definition I propose confined to one type of feminism. The tendency to refer to 'feminisms' in the plural is an evasion of the real and important contradictions between competing assertions made in the name of feminism. To the extent that arguments are mutually contradictory, the conflicts will never be resolved by separating the antagonistic positions and allocating them to different 'feminisms'. Respect for differences can be carried too far, especially when those 'differences' are not just differences but glaring incompatibilities. I intend that the definition I have proposed here will allow the conflicts to be addressed directly.

A Feminist Standpoint

What I have been arguing for is a feminist standpoint, although the sense in which I use the term differs crucially from the way it is already being used within feminist writings. I do not ground a feminist standpoint in women, women's experience, women's pain and oppression (Jaggar, 1983), women's life activity (Harding, 1986; Hartsock, 1985; Smith, 1972), women's empathy (Keller, 1983), women's more integrated (than men's) ways of knowing (Rose, 1987), nor in any postulated unique access women might have to caring (Noddings, 1984), or to peculiarly female forms of knowledge (Andolsen et al., 1987). The concept of a feminist standpoint could only have come from women, and it must not lose sight of women and women's interests. But women's social location alone is not sufficient guarantee of feminist commitment, *vide* women's embracing of right-wing, fascist, misogynist values, for example, and the myriad of ways in which women can embrace our own oppression because it is the only reality we know. And men are capable of understanding a feminist standpoint, although not capable of contributing to one, I would suggest for strategic reasons – men still tend to dominate wherever they are included, because male supremacy is still the way the world is and its patterns and habits are still too deeply ingrained.

A feminist standpoint, as I interpret it, starts from the question which is prior to any discussions about women's nature, women's abilities, women's life situations, etc. That question is: *why* are women and their concerns problematic? It is the answer to that question – because of male supremacy – which constitutes the revolutionary potential and actuality of feminism. A feminist standpoint is grounded first and foremost in acknowledging the existence of male domination in order to challenge and oppose it. This consciousness arises out of the social positioning of women because the problems of women's exclusion from 'human' status are more pressing for women (although in the long term everyone stands to gain a human status which is at no one's expense). But women's consciousness of their life situations does not become feminist until it develops into an awareness that women's social positioning is structured by male domination, and unless the male monopolization of 'human' status is resisted consciously, deliberately and continuously.

Most of the proponents of a feminist standpoint are aware that women's experience alone is insufficient for feminist politics, but they are vague on the question of how we get from 'experience' to theory and politics. How does a feminist consciousness arise out of 'women's life activity' when all women are not feminists, and some women are actively anti-feminist? What is it that has been achieved with the commitment to a feminist standpoint? What is it that is being struggled against and what is being struggled for? What is it that a feminist standpoint aims to liberate us from?

None of the feminist standpoint theorists unequivocally identifies engaging with male supremacy as the link which transforms 'women's experience' into feminist politics. They certainly recognize the existence of, and oppose, male domination. They also apply this recognition to their analyses. But they do so only implicitly or tangentially, while at the same time failing to acknowledge that it is this very challenge to male domination which provides the structuring principle translating a consciousness of women's lives into feminist politics. In the absence of any explicit naming of what the feminist political struggle is about, their task is confined to finding something intrinsic to women's lives which in and of itself leads to a feminist consciousness. But to the extent that they do find this 'something', they do so because their prior commitment to acknowledging the existence of male supremacy allows them to see it.

Nancy Hartsock, for example, states that 'women's lives make available a particular and privileged vantage point on male supremacy' (Hartsock, 1987: 159). She then proceeds to examine what she refers to as 'women's life activity' and 'the sexual division of labour' in order to find that privileged vantage point. But her account of 'women's life activity' is already informed by her commitment to opposing male supremacy. It is her feminist standpoint which enables her, for example, to perceive 'the sexual division of labour' as a political problem rather than a fact of nature, women's unpaid work and women themselves as appropriated by men rather than freely given by women, and, as Alison Jaggar put it, 'household labor ... as work rather than as a labor of love' (Jaggar, 1983: 384). Hartsock is not examining 'women's life activity' *per se*, in order to find a basis for feminist politics, as she herself interprets her task. She is presenting women's lives from a perspective which already includes a feminist commitment.

Sandra Harding explicitly refuses to place the opposition to male supremacy at the centre of the feminist political agenda (Harding, 1991: x). Her reason for doing so is her belief in a plurality of oppressions: '[Feminist] tendencies that focus on male supremacy and gender relations without giving equal weight to other important aspects of social relations can provide resources for Eurocentrism, racism, imperialism, compulsory heterosexism, and class exploitative beliefs and practices' (p. 11). But by couching the political problem in this way, she commits herself to confining oppressions within discrete and unrelated categories. In her account, male supremacy is not just something other than 'Eurocentrism', etc., struggling against it is antagonistic to any project of struggling against other forms of 'oppression'. Focusing on male supremacy, she implies, happens at the expense of other forms of political struggle. She does not consider the possibility that these other 'aspects of social relations' also have male supremacist aspects, and hence that struggling against male supremacy is also to struggle against all forms of relations of ruling. (I discuss these issues in more detail later in relation to racism.)

Harding's feminist project is to demonstrate that knowledge grounded in women's lives can give 'less partial and distorted' accounts of nature and social relations than knowledge produced by 'men of the dominant groups'. But whether or not feminist knowledge is less partial and distorted than malestream thought is not the issue. The main problem with ideologies of domination is not that they are partial and distorted, although they are both. The main problem is the question of whose interests their partiality serves, and the ways in which their distortions operate at the expense of those they subordinate. Feminism exposes as partial that which claims to be impartial and disinterested, not because feminism is less partial, but because it enters the discourse from another direction, the interests of women in opposing male domination. Harding herself is aware that knowledge cannot be disinterested and value-free, but she equivocates on the next logical step – explicitly characterizing feminism in terms of the struggle against the meanings, values, discourses and practices of male domination. As in the case of Hartsock's account, it is possible to characterize 'women's lives' in the way Harding does only because of her implicit acceptance of a framework which already identifies the manifestations of male domination, her disclaimers notwithstanding. Despite Harding's own attempt to jettison 'the focus on male supremacy', it is only that focus which gives her her feminist insights.

Alison Jaggar gives the most detailed account of the political limitations of confining what she calls 'a women's standpoint' to women's experience. She is clearly aware that appeals to 'women's life activity' are not alone sufficient for feminist politics. She says that 'the standpoint of women ... is not something that can be discovered through a survey of women's existing beliefs and attitudes' (Jaggar, 1983: 371), and that 'all aspects of our experience, including our feelings and emotions, must be subjected to critical scrutiny and feminist political analysis' (p. 380). She discusses the case of right-wing women whose thinking about their lives and experiences, far from leading to a feminist consciousness, has resulted in a militant anti-feminism. She concludes the discussion by saying: 'Simply to be a woman, then, is not sufficient to guarantee a clear understanding of the world as it appears from the standpoint of women' (pp. 382–3).

But although she is aware that it is political struggle which transforms women's experience into a 'women's standpoint', and although she is also aware of male dominance as one of the problems addressed by feminist politics, she does not identify the struggle against male dominance as the crucial defining factor of that politics. She acknowledges the insight 'that the prevailing culture is suffused with the perceptions and values of male dominance' as 'one of the main contributions of radical feminism'. But she seems to believe that this insight entails attempting 'to create an alternative women's culture' which is unrealistic, elitist and incomprehensible to most women. She says that it is only socialist feminism which 'is able to explain why this culture is dominant and to link the anti-feminist consciousness of many women with the structure of their daily lives', because socialist feminism is 'explicitly historical materialist'. But at this point male dominance drops out of her account – 'this culture' is simply 'dominant' – and we are left with nothing but 'women's daily lives' and a 'political and scientific struggle' which has lost its central focus (p. 382). Without male domination as the inimical adversary of feminist politics, there is no possibility of identifying the ways in which women's lives are imbued with the meanings and values of male supremacy, and hence no possibility of engaging in any political struggle at all. Jaggar eventually acknowledges this. She emphasizes the long and protracted nature of the feminist struggle to 'reveal the intricate and systematic reality of male dominance', and says that 'In the end an adequate representation of the world from the standpoint of women requires the material overthrow of male domination' (p. 384).

Nothing more than this acknowledgement is needed for a feminist standpoint, since to expose, name and describe male domination is already to acknowledge women's interests in opposing it. It is at this point, once the existence of male domination has been recognized, that all the really hard questions start: What counts as male domination? How do we recognize it? Is this particular phenomenon an instance of male domination or is it not? What does sexuality have to do with it? What is my responsibility? Can anything be done about it? Should anything be done about it? It is certainly part of the feminist enterprise to insist on the recognition of women's 'contribution to subsistence, and their contribution to childrearing' (Hartsock, 1987: 164). But to focus only on revaluing women's traditional activities, important though that is, is not what centrally defines a feminist standpoint.

Feminism is a thoroughgoing critique of male domination wherever it is found and however it is manifested. It is a working towards ending male impositions of whatever form, and the creating of a community of women relating to women and creating our own human status unencumbered by meanings and values which include women in the human race on men's terms or not at all. That can only be done from a standpoint which recognizes the existence of the social order of male supremacy which allows a 'human' status only to men, a standpoint which involves a struggle to reinterpret and rearrange the world so that women can be recognized as human too.

Notes

1   Martha Nussbaum locates the origin of the idea of social construction even earlier in history, in ancient Greek philosophy (Nussbaum, 1999: p. 5 of 12).

2   Allen suggests a third meaning of 'power', a concept of 'power-with' as a way of theorizing 'coalitions with other social movements' (p. 8). But this is already contained in the idea of power-as-capacity, Allen's 'power-to', since there is no implication that the power to achieve outcomes only happens in isolation.

3   I am indebted to Renate Klein for drawing my attention to this point.

2 Ideology – justifying domination

Domination is routinely maintained through the willing, albeit manipu-lated, consent of populations. That is not the only way it is maintained. Oppression is in no sense 'caused' by the consent of the subordinated; nor can it be abolished simply by withdrawing consent, although such a with-drawal is necessary if there is to be any challenge to relations of domination. Relations of ruling can operate without the consent of the ruled, through the use of violence, force and coercion, through the monopolization of wealth and information, through the confining of goods and opportunities to small, elite segments of the population, through policies and practices which benefit some at the expense of others. But the social conditions of male supremacy function most efficiently to the extent that women (and men) accept the reality of their position, embrace it as natural and unalter-able, desire its continuation and fear its destruction, and believe it is their own meaningful existence.

To the extent that we live under conditions of domination, that fact must be disguised. The term 'ideology' is useful for designating that form of sys-tematic meaning which functions to legitimate relations of ruling, as long as it retains the connotations Marx and Engels gave it, to mean that 'the ideas of the ruling class are in every epoch the ruling ideas' (Marx and Engels, 1974: 64).[1] In that sense ideology refers to systematic meanings which excuse, permit, legitimate and provide justifications for relations of ruling. As meaning, it is not simply a matter of 'ideas' separated out from some other level of existence, usually designated 'material'. Meanings permeate both 'theory' and 'practice', and they are both private and public. They can operate unconsciously, through feelings of desire or aversion. They provide values and purposes and reasons for acting, and operate on every level of human existence. Ideological meanings are whatever makes domination palatable or acceptable, or natural, real and unchallengeable.

There have been objections raised to using the term ideology in this sense. But none of them provides convincing reasons to abandon the concept as the designator of attempts to justify domination, chiefly because they fail to see the overriding importance of domination, and hence to recognize the need for a term to designate those forms of domination which are not overtly coercive. As a consequence, they fail to allow that there is a meaningful connection between ideology and domination. The arguments tend to insist that there is an inextricable connection between ideology and the Marxist 'economic base/ideological superstructure' construct, and that, because that construct is untenable, so is the concept of ideology. Michèle Barrett argues that the concept of ideology is not necessarily tied to the 'base/superstructure' model of society, but says that it is still a useful term as long as it refers to the idea of 'mystification' in general, rather than being confined to class. She argues that discarding class relations as the central defining characteristic of 'ideology' also means discarding all references to agents or interests (Barrett, 1991: 167). But to abandon the concepts of 'agents and interests' is to abandon politics. If there are no 'agents', there are no perpetrators and beneficiaries of relations of domination, and no one whose human agency is blocked by powerful vested interests. If there is no one who acts, there is nothing to be done. To delete any idea of interests is to abandon any idea of domination, and hence any possibility of challenging it.

There is no reason why a distinction between the ideological on the one hand, and the economic on the other, should be made in the first place, no reason, that is, outside the more arcane levels of disputation within (or with) Marxism. From the standpoint of a critique of domination, it is quite feasible to hold that relations of ruling are maintained both ideologically and economically (and politically and by force). The ownership and control of wealth is only one way in which relations of domination and subordination are maintained, and they are maintained most efficiently to the extent that their nature *as* domination, their operation at the expense of the subordinated, is hidden from those subjected to them.

Abercrombie et al. (1980) raise other objections to what they call 'the dominant ideology thesis'. They argue that it is not the case that the cohesiveness and stability of capitalist society depend on the 'ideological incorporation' of the working class into acceptance of the status quo. To the extent that there *is* something like a 'dominant ideology', they argue, its function is limited to maintaining cohesiveness and unity among the ruling class; it has no function 'in the explanation of the coherence of a society as a whole' (Abercrombie et al., 1980: 3). The quiescence of the working class, their failure to resist capitalist relations of domination, is sufficiently explained by the coerciveness of the political and economic control. People are often well aware of the nature of class society and their position in it, but they do not have the power to do anything about it. The authors say that 'workers may accept the economic order of capitalism and its class-based social organization at a factual level, as an enduring system'. But, they go on to say,

this factual acceptance need not involve any signs of normative acceptance or indoctrination. ... Compulsion is most obviously founded in the structure of economic relations, which oblige people to behave in ways which support the status quo and to defer to the decisions of the powerful if they are to continue to work and to live. (ibid.: 122, 154–5)

This is true enough as far as it goes, and it is important to keep pointing out that relations of ruling are essentially coercive. But it is not an objection to a dominant ideology thesis. It can be acknowledged that it is not possible to fool all the people all the time, without abandoning the thesis. There is plenty of evidence of systematic behaviour which works against people's own interests at whatever cost to themselves and others, and which upholds the meanings, values and structures of domination. For example, women marry men they know to be violent,[2] they remain 'faithful' to husbands and boyfriends convicted of the most horrendous crimes of violence against women, they excuse and justify the violence of the men they 'love', they write 'love' letters to convicted rapists and mass murderers. Such behaviours only make sense with reference to something like women's own embracing of the male supremacist ethic which requires that women subordinate themselves in the service of men.

A further problem with these authors' account concerns their reliance on a domain of 'everyday discourse, epistemology, or way of life' (p. 189) where people get on with the business of living uninfluenced by the world view of the rulers. But that is certainly not the case with women, whose personal lives are precisely lived within the male domain which reaches into the deepest recesses of the mundane. Male supremacist relations of ruling penetrate (the metaphor is deliberate) the most intimate levels of the everyday, damaging bodies, distorting minds, breaking hearts and deforming the spirit. What Abercrombie et al. have 'established' is nothing more than a reassertion of the public/private distinction which enables the maintenance of male power over women by keeping its more immediate manifestations out of the public realm of contestation and sanction, and by confining women to the private and the domestic where they have few rights and little or no public voice. The ideology of 'public' and 'private', however, is not espoused only by men, but also by women to the extent that they willingly embrace what operates against their own interests in, say, personal safety or economic independence. To say as much is not to hold women responsible for the oppressive situations they might find themselves in. But the fact remains, as feminism has been at some pains to point out, there is no sphere of personal life which escapes relations of domination. Unless, of course, the reality of that domination is acknowledged and opposed.

Michèle Barrett also rejected any concept of ideology which implied that the subordinated participated in their own oppression. She argued that feminist writings which regarded 'cultural phenomena such as soap opera, royalty or romantic fiction' as forms of ideological subjection of women failed to take account of 'the passionate enthusiasm of many women for the products of which they are alleged to be victims' (Barrett, 1991: 10). But 'passionate enthusiasm' is the way ideology *must* operate if it is to operate at all. To assert that women get pleasure out of romantic fiction, say, is not to argue against its nature as ideological, but, on the contrary, to acknowledge the way it works *as* ideology, the way it has effects and is effective.

These effects do not have to be total for it to be identified as ideology. That women willingly embrace something is not a sufficient criterion for judging that it is therefore not ideological. It does not rule out the possibility of ambivalence, or that the pleasure might exist alongside doubt or a critical attitude. The only criterion for judging whether or not something is ideological is whether or not it reinforces relations of ruling.

Many years ago, at the beginning of this second wave of feminism, Shulamith Firestone exposed the ideology of romantic love as a crucial mechanism for ensuring women's subordination to men. 'A book on radical feminism that did not deal with love', she said, 'would be a political failure. For love … is the pivot of women's oppression today' (Firestone, 1981: 126). The problem with 'romantic (heterosexual) love' was the unequal power relationship between the sexes, the way 'love' was constituted at women's expense. Through 'love', women were excluded from the public realm of culture and confined to personal life, so that women's creativity, energy and emotional work could be used in the service of men. The contradiction between men's need for emotional nurturance from women on the one hand, and women's utter irrelevance to anything men define as important on the other, tended to remain hidden from men. Men managed the contradiction by elevating one member of the subordinate class of women above all the rest in order to dignify her as a worthy recipient of his affections. Firestone felt that women tended to be more realistic: 'in their precarious political situation, women can't afford the luxury of spontaneous love. It is much too dangerous' (p. 139). While both sexes needed emotional security, women also had their economic security and sense of identity and personal self-worth at stake. Despite their more realistic appraisal, however, women could not resolve the contradiction. The most they could do was to 'make the best of a bad situation' (p. 145). And for many women, even the realistic appraisal made no inroads on their desire.

It could be argued that Firestone's account is culturally specific, that it only applies in cultures where 'romantic love' has a meaning. And it is true that, to the extent that the economic coercion of women into marriage is close to absolute, when women's very lives depend on getting married and they have little choice in the matter, an ideology like that of 'romantic love' would be less important as a means of securing women's compliance. None the less, even the most coercively controlled social environments require pacifying ideologies. Such constructs as 'female chastity' and 'male honour', 'wifely duty', 'filial piety', 'maternal instinct', etc., are also ways of managing women's consent to their subordination to men. Like the ideology of 'romantic love' they, too, channel women's desire and commitment in ways detrimental to women's well-being. At the same time, there is a sense in which they are merely a gloss on the actual structures of social power. Sometimes, even the most aware woman has no choice because she is not provided with alternatives.

Perhaps the most famous exponent of an anti-ideology thesis is Michel Foucault, who provided a neat summary of the main objections:

> The notion of ideology appears to me difficult to make use of, for three reasons. The first is that, like it or not, it always stands in virtual opposition to something else which is supposed to count as truth. ... The second drawback is that the concept of ideology refers, I think, necessarily, to something of the order of a subject. Thirdly, ideology stands in a secondary position relative to something which functions as its infrastructure, as its material, economic determinant, etc. For these three reasons, I think that this is a notion that cannot be used without circumspection. (Foucault, 1980: 118)

But Foucault's objections are otiose, not surprisingly, given that he makes no distinction between power and domination, a tendency which he shares with most social theorists. While much of what Foucault said about power is accurate, his account is limited by his inability to recognize domination and hence to conceive of alternatives. None the less, he does clearly state the main objections to the concept of ideology. To take his third point first: as I pointed out above, using the concept of ideology does not necessarily entail any commitment to a 'base/superstructure' model of society. It is not intrinsically tied to the idea of an 'economic base' outside ideology and which determines it.

Foucault's second point – that the concept of ideology necessarily implies 'something of the order of a subject' – is correct. But rather than being an objection to using the term, that implication is one which should be retained. While it is politically important to challenge the ideology of individualism, not all references to individuals are ideological, and unless there is some idea of what it is to be human there can be no politics and no morality. Accepting the need for 'something of the order of a subject' does not entail accepting the other connotations which Foucault appears to believe are inextricably tied in to the idea of the individual (Foucault, 1980: 98, 117). It is possible at one and the same time to acknowledge that 'the subject' is historically constituted, *and* that each of us is a locus of moral choice and responsibility. To leave the account of 'the subject' where Foucault does, as both constituted by power and its vehicle (ibid.: 98), is to leave us trapped in domination, with no choice except inert subjection, active compliance, or magnanimity on the part of the powerful. While there may not be any 'source of all rebellions, or pure law of the revolutionary' (Foucault, 1985: 96), it is possible to refuse complicity, not always or once and for all, but over and over again, and wherever it *is* possible. And those refusals, sometimes tentative, sometimes adamant, sometimes partial, sometimes absolute, sometimes negotiable, sometimes permanent, are made by individual human beings who live with the consequences. Hence, the notion of ideology does require 'something of the order of a subject', although not one existing outside any system of meaning at all, but one capable of actively choosing among alternatives to the extent that alternatives are available and recognizable.

To come finally to Foucault's first point: that the use of the term 'ideology' necessarily stands in opposition to something identified as 'truth'.[3] In the sense in which I use the term, 'ideology' is not one special kind of discourse among others (using 'discourse' in the broadest sense to mean a system of meaning). Rather, it is, as Jorge Larrain says, 'a level of meaning which can be present in all kinds of discourses … [and which] may well be absent' (Larrain, 1979: 130, 235 n. 2). It is not the case that we are always in ideology. What we are always 'in' are systems of meaning. Whether meanings are ideological or not depends on whether or not they are used in the service of domination. That cannot be decided from a position of neutrality. Domination can only be seen from a position which involves a willingness to see it. Without such a position, manifestations of domination can always be interpreted as something else, as isolated instances, exceptions, idiosyncrasies, personal pathologies or trivia, or even as something they are not – pain as pleasure, for example, or degradation as fun, humiliation as pride, oppression as freedom.

Because ideological meanings can appear anywhere, there is no need to posit an alternative to ideology, a discourse of truth with which to counter lies, falsehoods and distortions, the usual contender for this status being science. The distinction between what is ideological and what is not, is not always a distinction between falsehood and truth. Although questions of truth and falsity are not irrelevant in deciding what is ideological and what is not, they are not the same question. Given that relations of domination constitute the status quo, ideological beliefs are often true (at least in the referential sense) rather than false. Whether or not any particular ideological practice is true or false depends on the standpoint from which it is viewed. From the standpoint of immersion in the male supremacist status quo, it is true, for example, that the only form of adult intimacy available to women is a sexual relation with a man, that women's lives revolve around 'getting and keeping a man'. Women (and men) believe it, act upon it, make choices based upon it, run their lives according to it. From a feminist standpoint, it is a lie. It involves a calculated falsehood which suppresses consciousness of alternatives, which obliterates the knowledge that women can also be intimate with women, as friends, lovers and kin, with children as human beings rather than as burdens or jailers, with men simply as friends, and that women can live happy and fulfilled lives without sexual relationships with men.

By and large, ideology is not stated in testable form. The generalized belief that only men are 'human', for example, is never stated in these terms. Indeed, to say it aloud is already to undermine its efficacy because it can only operate as long as it remains hidden. Saying outright that male supremacist conditions allot a 'human' status only to men, exposes the contradiction between the ideology and the fact that women are human too. Instead of being openly acknowledged, belief in the male as the 'human' norm shows itself in a myriad of disparate contexts, the connections between which only appear from a feminist standpoint. It frequently operates through what might be called the phenomenon of female 'non-existence'. There are those occasions of everyday social life where women are habitually talked over and ignored, where matters of interest to women are either never raised or are dropped as quickly as possible, where men talk to each other as though there were no women present, where at best women are listened to briefly while the message is conveyed that their right to speaking-time is strictly limited. There are the literary productions of famous men which contain no female characters and that fact is never remarked upon. There are the pages of daily newspapers where the doings of men are writ large and women hardly ever appear.

The contradiction between the ideological belief that only men are 'human' and women are not, on the one hand, and the actual existence of women on the other, is not just a matter of logic. The belief that women are not quite, or not at all, human gives men permission to manage the contradiction through violence against women. Men bash women because they can, because women have no redress, little or no access to the means for protecting themselves or asserting their human rights. Individual incidents of exceptional violence will usually be overtly deplored. But they will also be covertly condoned by being trivialized, turned into jokes or argued away. There is a variety of ideological tactics for hiding the systematic nature of violence against women, for denying the function it serves in keeping women subordinate to men by demonstrating to women that their right to safety and security of person can be withdrawn at any time without warning.

Sometimes the violence is denied outright. Take rape as an example. Sometimes the violence is denied by blaming the victim. It is said that she 'asked for it', that she deserved to be harassed, raped, bashed, even murdered. It is said that she nagged him, provoked him, criticized him and undermined his masculinity. It is said that she is a whore, a slut, or any one or more of a number of nasty names women are called. It is said that she dressed invitingly, walked on the streets or caught a train at night, or accepted a lift home. It is said that she didn't say 'no', or didn't say 'no' often enough or loudly enough, or said 'no' and meant 'yes', and anyway, she didn't struggle so how was he to know she didn't want it. Sometimes the denial takes the form of excusing the offender. It is said that he was drunk and didn't know what he was doing. It is said that he had a hard life, that his mother didn't love him, that his wife refused to have sex with him. More generally, the perennial and systematic male violence against females is explained away by accounting for it in terms of isolated, unconnected (and regrettable) incidents, perpetrated by admittedly nasty individuals, who could be of either sex but just happen to be male on each particular occasion.

It is certainly true that men who rape, bash, harass, violate, degrade or murder are grossly deficient human beings, whether their violence is directed against women and children, or against other 'inferior' males, such as homosexual men or Aboriginal men, or against each other in defence of slights to their masculinity. But that deficiency is not just a personal failing (although it is also that too, and they can be held responsible for their actions). Men's violence is a product of a phallocratic reality which constructs masculinity as something which has to be defended at someone else's expense. That someone else is always initially a woman, whom the burgeoning masculine persona must come to hold in contempt because she does not possess a penis, the only symbol of 'human' status allowed under conditions of male supremacy. Violent and arrogant males are those who have learned that lesson only too well, who have managed to continue denying the evident humanity of women, and whose own sense of 'humanity' extends no further than their genitals. The violence and arrogance express a subliminal awareness of the paltriness of the only justification they know for their own existence. The consequence for women is a permanent reign of terror, subdued most of the time, but always there curtailing our freedom of movement and action.

When the existence of women is acknowledged, it is interpreted in terms favourable to men. To be a woman under male supremacist conditions means to be the helpmeet and nurturer of males. To be a woman is not to exist in her own right. If she settles for her conventional role, she is confined to the constricted sphere of domesticity, financially deprived, emotionally and economically exploited, isolated from other women, restricted by the ever-present needs of the children, subjected to the whims of an individual man, her quality of life dependent on whether or not he is good to her, on his decisions, not hers. Women have developed countless stratagems for retrieving some sense of dignity and self-respect, or alternatively some modicum of power and domination, despite the limited domain within which they are allowed to operate. And caring for and relating intimately to children is a worthwhile and dignified project in itself, despite the low valuation it is given in phallocratic reality. But what it means to be a woman under conditions of male supremacy is to be expected to service men and children, preferably male.[4]

For the purposes of feminist politics, whether any particular ideological pronouncement is true or false is not the main issue. What a feminist politics has to decide is whether the meanings which structure people's lives reinforce relations of ruling by reinforcing the interests of the dominators and suppressing the interests of the subordinated, whether meanings can be used to challenge or undermine domination, or whether they have to be changed or discarded altogether. These are decisions which cannot be made once and for all, but which will continue to need to be made as long as male supremacy lasts. But such decisions cannot even be made unless the existence of male domination is seen in the first place.

Truth and Domination

The question of truth is not, however, irrelevant to feminist politics. Although it is not often addressed in feminist writings, there are some writers who are explicitly opposed to the idea that feminism can make claims to truth, on the grounds that such claims are inherently complicit with domination.

This is the position Jane Flax takes, for example (1990: 222–3). She asserts a direct connection between truth and domination, and asks: 'What *are* the relations of knowledge and power? Does all knowledge necessarily inflict violence on things, ourselves, and other persons?' (p. 236, her emphasis) – a question she has already answered by equating 'a claim to truth' with 'a will to power' (p. 12). For Chris Weedon, too, claims to truth are inexorably implicated in domination:

> 'Truth' is by definition fixed, absolute and unchanging. It is the final guarantee of the way things are. ... It is in making claims to truth that discourses demonstrate their inevitable conservatism, their investment in particular versions of meaning and their hostility to change. (Weedon, 1987: 131)

Although there is a real problem being alluded to by arguments like these, involving ideological versions of reality and the suppression of counter-hegemonic versions, that problem is not addressed by dispensing with claims to truth altogether, since any claim to be heard is also a claim to truth. Apart from the inherent absurdity of the argument, the demand to abandon any claim to truth whatsoever can only weaken the cause of those who have no right to be heard under conditions of domination, including the cause of feminism. Truth may not be the ultimate arbiter of the rightness of the feminist cause, given the tendency for dominant interests to define what counts as real. None the less, a strategic retreat from making claims to truth is a strategy which can only weaken the force of feminist arguments. In the truth stakes, the status quo may win much of the time. But that is not a good enough reason for withdrawing from claims to truth, even though what counts as true or false cannot be decided without prior commitment to certain kinds of meanings.

Truth is not a function of domination. Might is *not* right in any sense which entails that those who dominate monopolize the truth, or that only the dominant have access to the truth, or that truth is what serves dominant interests. Whatever 'truth' might mean, and however it is established, the fact remains that it is possible to make judgements of truth and falsity. Those judgements are not 'fixed, absolute and unchanging' (as Weedon claimed), neither do they have 'eternal value' (Grosz, 1989: 110). They are always justified in some way, although those justifications are probably never based on those necessary and sufficient conditions required by (some forms of) philosophy. Such judgements may indeed not 'set us free' (Flax, 1990: 42), but no emancipatory project is conceivable without them. Judgements of truth and falsity can be made anywhere, at any time, by anybody. And something remains true (or false) whatever anyone may say, whatever anyone wants (or does not want), whatever force or arguments are brought to bear. Nothing and no one can make something false if it is true, or true if it is false. There is always the possibility of being wrong, that is, of fallibility. There is always the possibility of lies, mistakes, deceptions, delusions, and it may not be possible to know on any particular occasion whether or not something is true. But truth is truth and not some other thing, and so is falsehood.

Unless it is possible to judge whether or not something is true, it is not possible to judge whether or not it is false either. There is a logical connection between truth and falsehood in the sense that the meaning of each is dependent on the other. It makes no sense to talk about 'falsehood' without a concomitant idea of 'truth'. Both are judgements about what is asserted. Unless both are possible, neither is, because the basis for the judgement, the existence of an alternative, has vanished.

The problem of domination is not a problem of truth at all, or not in the sense that those who challenge relations of domination must eschew all claims to truth. Far from being complicit with domination, truth claims on the part of feminism are a crucial aspect of its political opposition to male domination. The advent of 'second-wave' feminism was accompanied by a sense of outrage at how we had been lied to and deceived. If we were to expose lies and deceptions, we had to claim to be speaking the truth, and to identify the states of affairs which verified our claims and falsified the claims of male supremacist ideology. The question is not whether or not feminism should make, and be seen to be making, truth claims. The problem is how to get the truth uncovered by feminism heard, how to get feminist truth on to the public agenda and into the arena where the wrongs done to women can be addressed and rectified. The problem is how to bypass, undermine or overthrow male supremacist ideology and its ownership and control of the means of information distribution. Feminism exists under hostile conditions where it so often cannot even make itself heard, much less be understood and its truth claims evaluated.

Meaning and Understanding

It is not through its monopolization of truth that domination operates, but through what might be called the control and manipulation of meaning. Domination is control over systems of meaning, as well as over wealth, resources, populations, etc. It is *control over* (which is never absolute), in the service of vested interests, in any sphere. Domination must include control over meaning if relations of ruling are to be purveyed as in the interests of all. It is *meaning* which can be complicit with domination, not truth.[5] Meaning is logically prior to truth in the sense that it is not possible to decide whether or not something is true unless what it means is understood in the first place. Questions of truth and falsity cannot even arise unless what is said is comprehensible. And yet control over meaning operates as much through familiarity as through incomprehensibility. Ideology presents itself as familiar in the domain of the everyday world-taken-for-granted; while in the prestigious sites of knowledge, the universities, it presents itself as a scarce commodity, available only to the initiated few.

Comprehensibility has been an issue within 'second-wave' feminism from the beginning. The issue has largely been addressed in the form of complaints about the difficulty and elitism of 'feminist theory' emanating from the academy. For example:

> To me, feminism means the personal is political, however, this is totally opposite to the ethos of Academia. Academia means being detached, objective,

theoretical, impersonal, non-political and abstract. ... By theorizing feminism I feel removed from the day to day reality of women's oppression. (Nanette Herbert, 'Letter', *Trouble and Strife*, 25, Winter 1992)

Such complaints are not new. In 1976, some women criticized aspects of the Patriarchy Conference, held in London in that year, as 'intimidating and mystifying' (Dalston Study Group, 1978). They said that certain papers presented at the conference were no different in kind from those presented in 'a male academic environment'. The organization of the sessions did not allow the listeners to intervene or contribute; the language within which the ideas were expressed was 'the impoverished depersonalized analytical language of intellectuals', which bore no relation to 'day to day language', and which 'had the effect of *making* large numbers of women feel inadequate, stupid or angry'; and the papers made no reference to debates within the women's movement on the very issues those papers were supposedly addressing.

They suggested that the problem was partly a result of the paper-givers' failure to make their theoretical framework clear and accessible to those who were not acquainted with the particular theoretical constructs being used; partly a result of 'the isolated social position of radical intellectuals *vis à vis* the groups ... whose interests their theory seeks to represent and sharpen'. They themselves were not opposed to theoretical work *per se*. But they felt that theory needed to be linked to 'struggles and strategy' and to 'controversies within the movement', that arguments needed to be stated as clearly as possible and terms not in everyday use explained, and that the theorizer should incorporate her own process into her theorizing, clarifying her agreements and disagreements and acknowledging her own confusions.

The problems identified by the Dalston Women's Study Group remain unresolved over 20 years later. If anything, they have worsened under the influence of postmodernism. The inaccessibility of academic feminist theory was a problem then, and it is still a problem now, because the original problem has not been overcome. The original problem is the requirement that feminism subordinate itself to malestream thought, within either the traditional academic disciplines or whatever intellectual fashion is current.

There is a sense in which combining feminism with already recognized academic disciplines is a reasonable endeavour. Feminism did not start as an academic discipline, but as a groundswell of discontent arising out of women's changed perceptions of their own experience. This discontent was inchoate and untheorized, sometimes confused and confusing, sometimes prematurely closed off to debate. Already established academic disciplines seemed to promise intellectually rigorous ways of organizing and managing the changing consciousness of the world and women's place in it. But as the members of the Dalston Study Group pointed out, those best placed for doing the theorizing failed to stay in touch with the women's movement and their own experience of feminist politics. They allowed themselves to be seduced by the intricacies and sophistication of what they encountered in the institutions of 'higher learning'. They failed to take adequate account of the complicity of malestream intellectual traditions with the 'Man of Reason' paradigm identified by Genevieve Lloyd in the context of Western philosophy (Lloyd, 1984). This does not mean that there is an irrevocable incompatibility between feminism and academe. It does mean that there needs to be far more clarity and decisiveness about what feminism is, and constant watchfulness against inadvertent support for ideology.

To insist that theory, like truth, is inevitably dominating is to see theory as some kind of private possession of the ruling class, and not something that women who are concerned about oppression ought to do, because it sets up invidious distinctions between women and privileges some women over others. This kind of argument contains a grain of truth. Systems of formal education, especially university education, favour the economically privileged, and it is difficult to get access to formal education without money. None the less, theory is vital if feminism is to clarify where it has come from, its meanings, values and aims, and if it is not to become bogged down in dogma, infighting, irrelevance and eventual silence.

Demands for instant comprehensibility rest on this belief that theory is inherently dominating, that difficulties in understanding are invariably the result of powerful vested interests. But they fail to take into account the possibility that what is well known and easily understood may also be complicit with domination. As Sneja Gunew and Anna Yeatman have pointed out, 'it is hegemonic discourses which tend to define the familiar' (Gunew and Yeatman, 1993: xx). Appeals to the familiar are typically couched in terms of experience. The difficulty of theory is criticized on the grounds that it does not relate to women's experience. But such a criticism rests on the assumption that experience is some kind of realm of authenticity, a safe and secure haven which provides all the answers as long as we remain true to it (and to ourselves). Such appeals to experience ignore the fact that it is already constituted within the meanings and values of the social order into which we are born. Given the prevalence of domination, the familiar will tend to be that which operates in its service. That tendency is not inevitable. No system of domination, even the most totalitarian, is monolithic and inexorable, without conflict, contradiction, ambiguity, resistance and refusal. The very existence of feminism is evidence that challenging domination is possible. But if the challenge is to be sustained, appeals to experience need to be couched in terms which clarify what is at stake morally and politically.

The choice is not between theory on the one hand, and experience, the familiar, the already known and easily grasped, on the other. Rather, the choice is between different forms of theorizing, between familiar and largely automatic and unconscious categories, meanings, values and reality on the one hand, and deliberate structuring and restructuring of the world in accordance with a feminist morality and politics on the other. Experience, that which feels most our own,[6] is already theory-laden by interests which alienate us from the potentialities opened up by feminism. To suggest, as some theorists have (Trebilcot, 1991: 49), that we substitute 'stories' for theory allows no way of deciding between stories which reinforce the meanings and values of domination, and those which illustrate the meaning of feminism for women's lives. It is to ignore the fact that the experience which generates the stories is already theory-laden. Simply telling stories without any analysis or critique threatens to allow free rein to those meanings and values which already constitute experience as real. To fail to acknowledge the social conditions within which experience is already embedded is to reduce the political to the personal, to a matter of opinion with no way of adjudicating between conflicting accounts of the way the world is. This outcome is entirely functional in maintaining the dominant status quo. If conflicts cannot even be addressed, because everyone is simply entitled to her own opinion, they cannot be resolved. Theory is what provides the moral and political meaning, purpose and value of experience. If the theorizing is not done deliberately, it happens anyway; and since structures of domination operate most efficiently through the acquiescence of subordinated populations, opposition to relations of power requires constant vigilance if they are to be challenged and complicity avoided. Theory in this sense is vital to the continued existence of feminist politics.

Feminism gives rise to certain kinds of questions, names the kinds of things it names, uncovers certain kinds of facts, and interprets the world in the way it does, because of its prior moral and political commitment to opposing male domination in the interests of women first, a priority made necessary in a world in which women are placed last or nowhere at all. The feminist project involves both meaning and truth. It is feminism's politics and morality which give it its meaning, that is, the ways in which feminist understanding happens and the world makes sense from a feminist standpoint. The truth of feminism arises out of its system of meanings, in the sense that, with the advent of feminism, certain questions could be asked, certain facts appeared, and certain answers became possible, which were previously inconceivable. Feminist knowledge acquires its meaning through its political understanding of relations of power, and through its project of re-interpreting and changing reality in order to create possibilities for women to control the terms of our own existence, a project which proceeds at the expense of men only to the extent that men remain committed to a 'human' status acquired at women's expense. Feminism uncovers certain facts about the world, and in that sense can lay claims to truth. But although feminist theory is an empirical endeavour, concerned with discovering facts about the world and organizing and explaining those facts, the empirical content of feminist theory is not its most important aspect. Given the social power of the forces of male supremacy, the facts will frequently be against us anyway.

Since feminist knowledge is explicitly neither value-free nor disinterested, the knowledge which it generates is based on, and productive of, identifiable interests and values. It is formulated in the interests of women, in particular women's interest in seeing an end to male domination, and in opposition to those vested and powerful interests which maintain the male as the 'human' norm, and which enforce the interests and 'human rights' of some individuals at the expense of others. The moral values which feminism espouses are those of a genuinely human status available to all. The primary feminist value is a commitment to the ideal of human dignity, of the right of every human being to a dignified standard of human existence. The question of human dignity is an ethical one, not an empirical matter. That the ethic of human dignity is constantly violated in fact does not invalidate the moral judgement that people *ought* to be treated with respect. This commitment starts from the standpoint of women, because the exclusion of women from human rights and dignities is the most systematic and widely distributed of all human exclusions, because men have too much to lose, namely their masculinity defined at women's expense (although everything to gain), and because women already provide a model of the human unencumbered by the rapacious demands of the phallus. Women can be complicit with the meanings and values of male supremacy, and men can resist. But women's lack of the supreme value of phallocratic reality, suggests that women also lack the chief barrier to connecting with other human beings as unique and valuable ends in themselves, and provides a starting point for a revolution in the terms and conditions of human existence.

Notes

1 To use the term in this way is to confine it to one of its many meanings (Eagleton, 1991). Any meaning which deletes the connotations of domination, however, bowdlerizes the word and deprives it of its political import.

2 The question of why women *stay* with violent men is an ideological one, as is the 'explanation' that they stay because they like being beaten. Both question and answer ignore the structural constraints of economic dependence and male possessiveness which marriage still imposes on women. It also ignores the fact that many of the women killed by the men they have been intimate with, are killed after they leave, that is, they are killed *because* they have left.

3 Or 'science'. For a discussion of the science versus ideology debates, see Larrain, 1979.

4 It is a fascinating exercise to ask oneself what is the sex of the 'children' portrayed in the public media – films, television, newspapers, advertisements, novels. They are almost invariably male, especially if the child is active and adventurous.

5 Interestingly, Jane Flax concludes her book with a distinction between meaning and truth. She suggests the possibility of 'displac[ing] truth/falsity with problems of meaning(s)' (Flax, 1990: 222). She does not discuss in detail what that might involve, and she is doubtful about its feasibility. 'Perhaps it is better only to analyze desires for meaning and to learn to live without grounds', she says (p. 223). However, having located domination wholly on the side of truth, she does not perceive that questions of meaning, of how the world is known and understood, of communication, clarity, intelligibility and accountability, also involve questions about domination.

6 This is a variation on a statement by Catharine MacKinnon: 'Sexuality is to feminism what work is to marxism: that which is most one's own, yet most taken away' (MacKinnon, 1982: 1).

3 Ideology – 'enabling' and disguising domination

Pleasure and Desire

Above all, ideology is intended to be made true. One of the chief ways in which consent to oppression is managed is through the cultivation of desire, the constitution of subjects who embrace relations of domination because they want to, because it is pleasurable to do so. Pleasure and desire 'enable' the continuation of the social conditions of male supremacy. This cannot be left to chance or nature, but must be constantly reinforced and endlessly reiterated.

The medium which expresses male supremacist desire most clearly, without apology, equivocation or adornment, is pornography. In what follows, I locate the pornographic imagination with men because what I am criticizing is the ideological construction of sex around the penis. As such, pornography and its practices operate in the interests of men in complicity with the belief that 'humanity' depends on penis-possession. But although the primary motivating force and *raison d'être* of pornography is the eroticizing of men's domination of women, the pleasures and desires of domination are restricted neither to the male psyche nor to heterosexuality. The purpose of ideology is to purvey the interests of the dominators as the interests of all, and it serves its purpose to the extent that anyone can be complicit with the pornographic imagination. The meanings and values of domination, while they originate in the phallic mandate that women service the penis, can be, and are, generalized to any human interaction whatsoever. Women can be complicit with the ideology of pornography to the extent that they accept a second-rate 'human' status for themselves and eroticize their own subordination. This is exemplified in conventional heterosexual relations where women believe that they cannot live without a man, that they are empty and unfulfilled unless they are in a relationship with a man, and who structure their lives around that desire. Alternatively, women can also be complicit to the extent that they strive to be like men, finding value only in men, holding women in contempt, and accepting an erotics of domination as their own desire. The latter is exemplified in lesbian sadomasochism. Although in lesbian relationships there is no actual penis present, sadomasochism is phallic desire. Not only are sadomasochistic practices the acting out of desire for domination and subordination, the penis is frequently present in effigy, as a dildo (Jeffreys, 1993: 28–30). Gay male sexual practices, too, can be complicit with phallic desire, even though there are no women present, to the extent that those practices are sadomasochistic; and again, women are frequently present in effigy, as 'drag'. Both lesbian and gay male relationships can mimic heterosexuality. None the less, although the ideology of pornography reaches beyond the male psyche and the heterosexual context, I have confined it to that context in order to show the central significance of pornography most clearly and succinctly.

The central symbol structuring male supremacist desire is the penis-as-phallus. Because the following discussion focuses on those social conditions under which the penis *is* the phallus, that is, the chief value structuring the social conditions of phallocratic reality, I use the two terms, 'penis' and 'phallus', interchangeably. Used in this sense, 'the penis' is not simply 'anatomy'. I am not referring to it as some kind of 'in itself' biological organ, since such a usage (to the extent that it makes any sense at all) would mean that phallic domination is inevitable and unchangeable. Rather, what I am referring to is the *meaning* the penis carries under male supremacist conditions, a meaning which can be changed without doing any damage to the organ in itself. As should already be obvious, I believe not only that the penis *can* be severed from its role as primary symbol of domination, but also that that separation must be a present possibility (rather than a future hope), otherwise it would be inconceivable. But although it is already possible to conceive of the penis as just another bodily organ, possible on the part of both sexes although more possible for women because they have less at stake in the hyper-valuation of the penis and more to gain by reducing its significance, there is a great deal of feminist work still to be done before the penis-as-phallus is abolished and a genuinely human status becomes available to all.

The chief meaning and value of male supremacist conditions is that penis-possession stands for 'human' status (Dworkin, 1981; Thompson, 1991). Those who have penises are automatically 'human'; those who do not, are not, although that 'lack' can always be contested and frequently is. Because the penis is the central symbol of 'human' status under conditions of male supremacy, the chief pleasures and desires of those conditions centre around the penis. Because the penis means sex, the chief pleasures and desires of male supremacist conditions are those of sex.[1] The ideology of 'the natural' operates to keep sex out of the domain of the moral and the political, to render it beyond questioning and debate (unless it goes too far, in which case its excesses are located with isolated pathological individual men, or blamed on women). Under the ideological imperative of penis-possession, sex is the last bastion of the natural and men are its bearers. Although for most purposes male supremacist ideology equates women with nature, because both must be dominated by men as resources to be mined to fuel male power, within the ideology of phallic sexuality it is men who are entirely natural. That ungovernable 'male sex drive' must be allowed to operate at any cost because it is nature, only nature and nothing but nature. It is men's nature, therefore it is 'human' nature. It is beyond investigation, beyond political and moral critique. It exists and the lives of everyone must be structured around it. The problems resulting from its unchecked impetus – rape, prostitution, world over-population, AIDS, enforced pregnancy, for example – can only be managed, not abolished, because the penis must never be hampered in its progress. Men cannot help themselves because the penis has a life of its own and is not subject to the conscious will. What the penis obeys is nature, its desire and activity a direct and automatic result of the effect of hormonal secretions on the male body. Hormones are natural, penile activity is caused by hormones, male sexual activity is governed by the rule of nature.

From a feminist standpoint, however, this is nothing but male supremacist ideology. Far from being 'natural', phallic sexuality is a moral and political activity. Men do have a choice and they can be held to account when they exercise their freedom to choose at women's expense. Men's sexual behaviour is not caused by hormonal dictates. It is because the penis serves the ideological function of symbolizing 'human' status that it is so heavily charged with erotic energy, and not because it is driven by testosterone. Men must keep using it because they need to keep proving that they exist, that their 'humanity' is inextricably entwined with penis-possession; women must be constantly used by it to prove that men exist, that the sum total of a man is his penis. Because there is no humanity beyond the penis, what the penis can do it ought to do. Anything and everything must be subordinated to penile activity if men are to be what phallic ideology requires them to be. Although there are penalties and sanctions against the worst excesses of the penis, ranging from disapproval to imprisonment, the culture of male supremacy still gives permission for those excesses. There are prison sentences for rape, the murder of women, incest, for example, but there is also a plethora of excuses provided to demonstrate that nothing happened, or nothing of any importance.

Pornography is the ideology of male supremacist masculine desire writ large and shameless. It is the clearest, most unequivocal expression of male supremacist ideology in existence. As Sheila Jeffreys has said:

> Pornography made it clear that what constituted sex under male supremacy was precisely the eroticised subordination of women. Inequality was sexy and the sexiness of this inequality was the grease that oiled the machinery of male supremacy. The sexiness of male supremacy ... was the unacknowledged motor force of male supremacy. Through sexual fantasy men were able to reinforce the sense of their power and of women's inferiority daily and be rewarded for every thought and image of women subordinated with sexual pleasure; a pleasure acknowledged to be the most valuable form of pleasure in male-supremacist culture. (Jeffreys, 1990: 252–3)

Pornography is the ideology which reinforces the phallic desire of men who already want it because they seek it out and pay for it. It depicts the worst that men can do to women and encourages them to do it. It tells men they have a right to do whatever they want to do with their penises. It tells them that women are infinitely available to men, that they are endlessly compliant, that they are enamoured of the penis and enchanted with what it can do, that they will take anything, anything at all, and beg for more. It says that women are there for men to fuck, that that is the sole reason for female existence. It says that women are nothing but things, a collection of fetishized body parts, breasts, buttocks, hair, faces and legs arrayed for male delectation, orifices serving as receptacles for the penis. Because it portrays women as objects, it gives men permission to harm women. It tells them that women are not human, that they do not suffer, whatever is done to them. It tells men that they can hurt women because it is already being done and no one is complaining, including the women portrayed. Pornography is the theory; sexual violence, rape, prostitution and compulsory heterosexuality are the practices. This does not mean that pornography 'causes' male sexual violence, that it is separate from sexual violence and prior to it. Male sexual violence is not 'caused' by anything. To frame it in such a way is to be complicit with the ideological belief that male sexuality is 'natural'. Rather, male sexual violence is a moral evil for which the men who do it are responsible and about which they have choices. Pornography is an apologia for male sexual violence. It provides it with meaning, gives men permission for it, and deadens male ethical sensibilities.

The misogynist social implications of pornography, however, are largely hidden from women. Although some of its less blatant icons appear in public media, especially advertising which cynically evokes desires already in place, the worst productions of the pornographic imagination are still closeted in 'adult' bookstores, video shops and movie houses. Although men bring it home, they do so as individuals, and hence its systematic nature is disguised. It is for this reason that the struggle against pornography has come to occupy such a central position in the radical feminist critique of male supremacist relations of power. Radical feminist campaigns against pornography are intended to tell women how men are willingly being trained to view them. As Andrea Dworkin said:

> Women did not know. … I decided that I wanted women to see what I saw. This may be the most ruthless choice I have ever made. But … it was the only choice that enables me to triumph over my subject by showing it, remaking it, turning it into something that we define and use rather than letting it remain something that defines and uses us. (Dworkin, 1981: 304)

From the standpoint of male supremacist ideology, the meaning of pornography is that it is only fantasy, nothing but images and text used by individuals for their own personal private satisfaction, and the business of nobody but the isolated individual using it. In a backlash to the feminist challenge, it has also come to mean 'free speech', both of those who produce it and those who consume it. From a feminist standpoint, however, it is very real activity indeed. It is real for the women who are used in its production; it is real for the women who are used by the men it trains; it is real for the men it teaches; and it is real when they apply what they have learned to themselves and in their relations with others. From a feminist standpoint pornography means women's oppression. It obliterates women's humanity by portraying them as nothing but objects for the gratification of the penis. Those whose speech is 'free' are those who validate and reinforce relations of domination and subordination. Those who protest against domination, those who expose domination as domination, are not only not free to speak and be heard, they are permitted no right of reply and no redress for the harm caused.

What is purveyed by the ideology of pornography are the values of sado-masochism. These values are obvious, they cannot be hidden. They are presented as positive goods, as pleasures to be enjoyed, as the gratification of the needs of desiring individuals who have a 'right' to act on their desires, a 'right' to their own personal, private satisfactions, a 'right' to do anything and everything to avoid sexual frustration. That sadomasochism is the eroti-cization of domination and subordination is not denied by the ideology of pornography. But instead of being rejected as a moral evil, it is validated and glorified as delightful and beneficial, as innocent fun and pure enjoyment. Humiliation and degradation, violence, physical pain and mutilation, even death, the use on people of chains, whips, bonds, weapons, the torture of human bodies, are all valued as pleasure, only pleasure and nothing but pleasure.

The morality espoused by the pornographic imagination is explicitly to transgress the morality of human dignity. As such it requires fetishism, what feminism has called 'objectification'. Fetishism is the phallic desire which depends on an equation between human beings and things for its gratification. In the classic psychoanalytic case, an object – an article of clothing, a part of the body – is substituted for a person. The sexual urge is focused on the object, and sexual gratification is impossible without it. In Freud's account, the fetish symbolized the penis: 'we may say that the normal proto-type of fetishes is a man's penis' (Freud, 1977b: 357). The fetish was a penis-substitute for men who could not have sex with women without feeling threatened with castration. According to Freud, the sight of the female geni-tals aroused castration anxiety in these men because females lacked penises. The fetish stood in for the absent female penis, and allowed these men to engage in heterosexual sex without fear that they might lose their penises. The price they paid (although Freud did not mention this) was an inability to relate to women as human beings. Although a woman must *be* a human being if the lack of a penis is so threatening, and hence although male cast-ration anxiety is an acknowledgement that to be female is to be human too, the logic of male supremacy requires that the anxiety be managed by deny-ing that women are human. Fetishism is a way of managing the contradic-tion between women as human beings, and women's lack of the symbol of 'human' status, that is, the penis. It is both a recognition of women's human-ness and a denial of it. The fetish manages the contradiction between women as human beings and their non-humanity required by phallocratic conditions, by deflecting male sexual desire towards objects.

Freud's fetishist coped with women's humanness by avoiding it, by erecting the barrier of the fetish between himself and importunate female humanity. Pornography turns women themselves into objects. If women are nothing but objects, their lacking penises does not matter because they are 'not human beings' anyway. They can be used and re-used endlessly without arousing male castration anxiety, because there is no non-phallic humanity there to elicit it. Within the pornographic scenario, both sexes are fetishized. Men are nothing but their penises, women are nothing but objects to be used in its service. Because men are the penis-bearers, everything is permitted to them as long as it contributes to the gratification of the penis; because women are not penis-bearers, nothing is permitted to them unless it contributes to the gratification of the penis. Since women are only things, they can be used as a means towards the end of sexual gratification of the penis. That end has an absolute and essential priority to which everything must be subordinated. As things, the human beings used in the pornographic scenario have no rights. They exist simply as objects to be manipulated in the service of pornography's aim. The rights of human beings to be treated with respect, to be recognized as unique ends in themselves, to live free from coercion and harm, to engage in their own freely chosen projects, are all violated by the main motivating force of pornography: the gratification of the penis.

Within the terms of the pornographic imagination and under male supremacist conditions, sex is a male prerogative. Men want it, will fight for it, defend it at any cost, pay any price for it. This is not just a metaphor. Men do in fact pay money for sex. Prostitution exists. Male supremacist propaganda would have us believe that it has always existed. It is 'the world's oldest profession'. If it has always existed, it must serve an ineradicable male need. It must be a necessity, regrettable perhaps, but inevitable because male sexuality is a 'natural need' like hunger or thirst or sleep. Prostitution cannot be abolished because it is 'human' nature. But if the existence of prostitution is questioned from a feminist standpoint, it becomes a very bizarre thing indeed. From a feminist standpoint, prostitution exposes something very strange about male sexuality. Its sole reason for existence is so that men can pay money to have their penises stimulated to ejaculation by strangers whom they hold in contempt. These strangers are usually women, sometimes feminized males, and sometimes children of either sex. Prostitution involves human relationships which consist of nothing but penises stimulated to orgasm. It exists for men who need another human being to do the stimulating, but the other human being must then be fetishized into something less than human. Although the other human being is nothing but an object to stimulate the penis, not just any object will do. The object must be a human being because only a human being can recognize the paying customer as a penis-bearer, although the human being must be an object because she is there only to stimulate the penis. She has no desires, needs, feelings, thoughts or life of her own, or none that he is interested in or cares about.

Although the only reason for the existence of prostitution is to service male sexual desire, prostitution is, bizarrely, blamed on women. The persistent challenge which the humanity of the women poses to the continued existence of prostitution, is managed by holding women responsible for it. The dictionary definition of prostitution provides a telling example of how domination operates through the control of meaning. The *Shorter Oxford English Dictionary* defines 'prostitution' in the following terms: '1. Of women: The offering of the body to indiscriminate lewdness for hire (esp. as a practice or institution)'. In a figurative sense it means: '2. Devotion to an unworthy use; degradation, debasement, corruption'. The definition does not mention men at all, despite the glaringly obvious fact that serving male sexual 'needs' is the only reason the institution of prostitution exists. The 'lewdness' belongs with the men who require women offering their bodies for hire. It would not be possible for women to do the 'offering' in the first place unless men demanded it. And yet that crucial defining characteristic of prostitution is absent from the dictionary definition. Thus does the *OED* collude with the blaming of women for a corruption which actually belongs with men.

Concerned attempts to abolish prostitution are typically directed towards women. It is the women who are arrested, fined, gaoled, confined to certain areas and excluded from others. It is the women who are bashed, raped, murdered, who are held in contempt, who carry the burden of opprobrium and who are visited with the effects of the disgust felt by 'decent citizens'. The blame for the disreputableness of prostitution is laid on the women who solicit ('prostitutes'), rather than on the men who maintain prostitution through their patronage and their desire (and for whom there is no name). The moral disgrace of prostitution is located with women, rather than with the men who continue to use female human beings as things, whose obsession with their penises and what they can do overrides any ethical considerations whatsoever. If prostitution is to be abolished, it is men who will have to change because it is male desire which maintains it, not female desire. What women want is sufficient income to live in comfort and dignity. And yet the disrepute of 'prostitutes' is intrinsically connected to the penis. Women who are 'prostitutes' are women who are used by the penis. If it is being used by the penis which brings women in to disrepute, then the negative values of degradation, debasement and corruption belong with the penis. If it is the penis which disgraces women, then it is the penis which is the original disgrace. Thus does male supremacy expose itself for those with the will to see. The same connection between disgrace and the penis can be seen in the social construct of virginity. To the extent that loss of virginity brings shame upon a woman, it is the penis which has brought it. The disrepute which is culturally located with 'whores', 'loose women' (etc., endlessly) is actually a moral lack in men projected, in a strict psychoanalytic sense, on to women.

As the reverse of the morality of human dignity, the chief value espoused by prostitution and pornography is contempt. Used in this sense, the term 'contempt' does not refer only to a personal emotion belonging to individuals. It must be that too if populations are to consent to relations of domination. Social values operate as psychic mechanisms as long as people embrace them – by accepting them as their own motivations, by referring to them as their own reasons for acting, by defending them when they are threatened, by ignoring or not seeing alternatives – and to the extent that people refuse to comply, those mechanisms fail to operate. But contempt is more importantly a social value which ensures the making of meaningful, systematic distinctions between categories of individuals. As a hierarchically ordered social environment, where some people are structurally defined as less worthy than others of access to the means for ensuring even the most basic level of human dignity, male supremacy is a culture of contempt.

Within the parameters of male supremacy, under conditions where only men are 'human', social recognition of women as human subjects in their own right is lacking. Pornography and prostitution express and constitute that lack clearly and unequivocally. By defining women as nothing but things to be used in the service of the penis, they reinforce and maintain women's lack of social recognition. They function in accordance with the values of compulsory, that is, normal, heterosexuality to keep women 'in their place' in the minds of men.

Individualism

An ideology of desire is also an ideology of individualism. If the interests of the ruling class are to be presented as the interests of all, their systematic nature as domination must be disguised. Where better to hide the dominating nature of relations of ruling than in the depths of the individual psyche? If domination is desired, it cannot be challenged and opposed. If it constitutes the very roots of personal identity, it cannot be seen as systematic. If it operates by means of feelings and emotions, it belongs in the realm of private satisfaction, not public politics. If domination is fragmented and dispersed among individuals, it cannot provide the basis for common interests among the oppressed.

The ideology of individualism depicts 'humanity' as a set of isolated selves, floating freely in a space which is 'social' only to the extent that there are many selves. Each self is detached from every other, and contains within itself all that is necessary for identification as 'human'. Desires, needs, interests, beliefs, actions, feelings, attitudes and behaviours, are perceived as personal properties intrinsic to each individual, and as arising fully formed within each individual psyche. The desires, etc., of any one individual can come into conflict or competition with those of any other, or can provide a reason for co-operation. But social interaction happens only after those desires, etc., have been identified, after they have been located as the inherent property of an individual person.

In contrast, a feminist politics needs to be able to see that male domination is a social system of ideological meanings and values which certainly influence the hearts and minds of individuals, but which are not co-extensive with them. Although that influence is not monolithic and inevitable, it is intransigent to the extent that those meanings are perceived as essential attributes of individuals, rather than as ideological requirements of relations of ruling. If relations of domination and subordination are interpreted as nothing but properties of individuals, they cannot be seen as relations of ruling at all. They become simply a matter of preferences and choices engaged in by discrete individuals who have no responsibilities beyond their own immediate pleasures and satisfactions. In this libertarian discourse, politics vanishes. If only individuals exist, political critique can only be seen as personal insult or annihilation of the self, and disagreement becomes assertion of the self against threatening and hostile others. 'Freedom' is reduced to the absence of constraint, either on the part of the self or of others. The damage done to self and others by relations of ruling is either not addressed, or is purveyed as a positive good emanating from within desiring individuals.

The clearest examples of this kind of unthinking commitment to the ideology of the atomized individual can be found in the libertarian defence of 'sex radicals', 'sexual outlaws' or 'erotic dissidents'. In Gayle Rubin's paper, 'Thinking Sex' (Rubin, 1984), this defence is couched in terms of an account constructed around a set of unjustly treated individuals – 'paedophiles', 'fetishists', 'sadomasochists', etc. – who just happen to have a certain kind of intrinsic sexual desire which structures and informs their personal identity and makes them the kinds of individuals they are. As individuals with particular sexual needs, they have a 'right' to the expression of their sexual desire, a 'right' which they are unfairly prevented from exercising by moralistic prohibitions and sanctions which Rubin perceives as emanating both from the dominant heterosexual society and from feminism. Within the terms of Rubin's account, these sexual desires are self-evidently not socially constructed, because they are treated with social disapproval and moral outrage. Rubin assumes without question that these desiring individuals cannot possibly be socially constituted because they are despised and rejected. They are subjected to forms of social control only after they are recognized as the kinds of individuals they are. 'Society' only arrives on the scene once these individuals have been recognized for what they are, and the best thing 'society' can do is to leave them alone to exercise their individual rights and freedoms in peace and in private. It is no accident that Rubin's defence is couched in wholly individualistic terms, in terms of 'fetishists' rather than fetishism, 'sadomasochists' rather than sadomasochism, etc., in terms of 'people' rather than in terms of social practices with shared meanings and values. By keeping her focus firmly fixed on 'people', she can surreptitiously appeal to the whole range of assumptions embedded in the ideology of individualism – the 'public/private' distinction, the dichotomy between 'individual' and 'society', and the idea of 'freedom' as lack of constraint, of 'rights' as the untrammelled exercise of the will, and of 'desire' as the personal property of single individuals. By avoiding addressing 'desire' as social practice, Rubin can avoid addressing the origins of desire in the social conditions of male domination.

The ideology of individualism masquerades as collective interests via the notion of 'identity'. Within the terms of the ideology, people can organize collectively around a common 'identity', but the source of that 'identity' is located within each individual. It does not become social until it is recognized by other individuals, and either embraced as theirs too, or morally disapproved of and rejected. For example, in a book review, Mina Kumar says: 'In the strongest essays [in the book under review], rural lesbians reclaim their heritage from stereotypes about "rednecks", the last permissible target of ethnic jokes. [One of the authors] worries that privileged lesbian-feminists' "plan for getting rid of lesbian-bashing and women-hating and racism is to get rid of my kind of people"' (Kumar, 1994: 76). Here, the moral and political phenomena of misogyny and racism are seen as inherent qualities of 'people', and political critique is interpreted as attacking individuals. Opposition to misogyny and racism is viewed as attempting to 'get rid of people' because misogyny and racism are seen as what makes them the kind of people they are. So intrinsic to their identity is 'lesbian-bashing, women-hating and racism' that without it these 'people' would cease to exist as an identifiable group. But while it is certainly the case that the responsibility for harmful attitudes and behaviours lies with individuals, those attitudes and behaviours are not inalienable properties which people just happen to have; they are systematic meanings and values about which people have moral and political choices. Misogyny and racism are not of the same order as being a woman under conditions of male domination, or being black under conditions of white supremacy, or being deprived of a dignified standard of living under conditions of capitalism. One is not responsible for one's sex or one's ethnic origin, neither of which would be a problem were it not for the systems of domination which ensure that those so identified are deprived of human rights. Neither is one responsible for being poor. Characterizing poverty as an inherent property of poor individuals is a favourite ideological ploy of those who approve of economic policies which generate obscene accumulations of wealth in the hands of the few. In contrast to being a woman or a member of a minority ethnic group, misogyny and racism are questions of moral responsibility. To interpret them as something inherent in 'people' is to ignore the social and political milieu within which others are harmed by these attitudes and behaviours. To see them as an 'ethnic identity' is to obliterate their status as moral choices and to extract them from the social system of domination within which they arise in the first place.

There is a sense in which the above examples are instances of essentialism. Not only are they couched in terms of putative facts about individuals, those 'facts' are seen as inherent in individuals. They are thus placed beyond political contestation and moral debate. Sadomasochistic desire, or misogyny and racism, simply exist as a kind of bedrock beyond which no questions need to be asked, and about which no decisions need to be made. Racist and misogynist meanings and values are made into a form of 'ethnic' identity, and social values are interpreted as 'natural' properties of individuals, rather than as forms of social interaction involving moral responsibilities and political quiescence in the face of conditions of domination. 'Essentialism', however, has become a politically bankrupt term as a result of its use to vilify radical feminism. And what is at stake is more accurately identified as the ideology of individualism since its political function is to purvey certain beliefs about what it means to be 'a person'. The ideology of individualism conveys messages about what people 'can' do and what they 'cannot'. It 'enables' what does not threaten relations of ruling, for example, the 'choices' of super-market consumerism (one of the prime examples of which is that slipping and sliding concept of 'gender'); and it defines any challenge to current relations of power as impossible, meaningless or non-existent, as beyond the sphere of individual action and responsibility because it is not available for debate. Above all, the ideology of individualism must disguise the actual relations of ruling, and it does that by locating all agency within the domain of an atom-ized individual radically independent of others, and existing prior to any form of social interaction.

The 'individual' purveyed by the ideology of individualism is masculine. In the sense in which I am using the term here, 'masculinity' is not just a per-sonality characteristic of male persons. It is a social phenomenon, a system of meanings and values structured around relations of and with the penis, a system which women can embrace as well as men. It refers to ways of being a man under conditions of male supremacy although its maintenance does not depend only on men. Neither are men involuntarily implicated in ways outside their control. It is a moral and political phenomenon and hence resistible. It is none the less hegemonic in the sense that it constitutes the dominant reality for both women and men, for men as its bearers and for women whose exclusion from 'human' status is the unacknowledged pre-requisite for its continued existence. Women cannot *be* 'masculine' in any sense which implies that women can take on the rights, benefits and pre-rogatives of men (except in those rare cases where women have passed themselves off as men and been believed). But women can uphold the mean-ings and values of masculinity. This happens in the 'normal' case through the embracing of femininity and its function in shoring up the masculine ego. Masculinity and femininity are not complementary characteristics, attached, rigidly or otherwise, to their respective sexes. Rather, they constitute a value hierarchy whereby the male individual has the right to his own autonomous 'human' status and the benefits which flow from that, and the female has no rights other than to recognize, validate and maintain the 'human' status of the male. Femininity is not an 'other' to masculinity; it is a subset of it. Femininity exists to reinforce masculinity. It is the residual vestige of 'humanity' women are allowed, so that men can continue to define them-selves at women's expense. As Virginia Woolf expressed it: 'Women have served all these centuries as looking-glasses possessing the magic and deli-cious power of reflecting the figure of man at twice its natural size' (Woolf, 1946: 53).

Female support for masculinity can also take more 'transgressive' forms. For example, the sexual libertarianism which puts sex outside political critique, lesbian sadomasochism and 'lesbianandgay'[2] politics, involve women seeing the world and acting within it from a standpoint which, as Sheila Jeffreys points out, is palatable to men, a palatability which also involves a deliberate and active campaign of vilification of feminism. But whether 'normal' or 'transgressive', women's embracing of the ethos of masculinity involves a commitment to the ideology that only men are 'human'. Femininity is an acceptance of second-rate status for women; libertarian 'transgression' involves futile attempts at 'equality'. But neither questions the construct of the male as the 'human' norm.

The maintenance of masculinity requires suppression of the knowledge that men depend on women for maintaining the basic necessities of human existence. The basic form that suppression takes is denial of the maternal relation, the systematic forgetting of our infant origins in helpless dependence on a supremely powerful woman – mother.[3] That forgetting is engineered by interpreting the interdependence of the maternal relation as the mother's 'power-over' the infant, a perceived 'domination' which is fended off through contempt for the female who need not be considered 'human' because she lacks the penis. Without knowledge of that primary social relation, 'society' consists of no more than scattered adult individuals who came from nowhere because they have forgotten their origins. The ideology of individualism is entirely complicit with male supremacist conditions. The belief in the autonomous individual who can make and re-make himself at will depends on the obliteration of any awareness of the origin of all social relationships in our infant dependency on a woman. It also depends on obliterating knowledge of the social importance of women except to the extent that they provide selfless service to the male. With no memory of that primal helplessness, and with the systematic forgetting of the social contribution of women, social relationships are detached from their connecting links. From this standpoint, 'the social' appears as nothing but scattered entities, essentially antagonistic until they are brought together by fear or contract.[4]

Despite the above-mentioned connection between the belief in the male as the 'human' norm and the ideology of individualism, that ideology tends to exert a subterranean influence within feminist discourse itself, as is evidenced by the examples discussed above. But to criticize the ideology of individualism does not mean that feminism can dispense altogether with a concept of the individual. That our individual selves are unique and irreplaceable, that we have rights and dignities and are entitled to respect simply because we exist, that we are able to act and make a difference, and that we can take responsibility for our actions, are all vital ingredients of a feminist politics committed to creating a human status for women. Sarah Hoagland's concept of 'moral agency under oppression' postulates this kind of the human individual. Her account avoids both the determinism of a system of domination to which the individual is subjected and within which she is a passive victim of circumstances beyond her control, and the notion of a free will available to all without constraint. Hoagland argues against the idea that moral agency means control, of self, of others, or of situations. Given the reality of oppressive conditions, attempts at control are either futile since we are not in control, or complicit with the values of domination. Instead, she argues that

> moral agency simply is the ability to choose in limited situations, to pursue one possibility rather than another, to thereby create value through what we choose, and to conceive of ourselves as ones who are able to and do make choices – and thus as ones who are able to make a difference for ourselves and each other in this living. ... *It is not because we are free and moral agents that we are able to make moral choices. Rather, it is because we make choices, choose from among alternatives, act in the face of limits, that we declare ourselves to be moral beings.* (Hoagland, 1988: 231 – her emphasis)

For Hoagland the individual is the locus of moral choice, not absolutely, but within constraints. This means that, even under conditions of male domination, we do have alternatives and can make choices between them, and to the extent that this is possible we are responsible for our actions and hence free agents. At the same time, however, to the extent that we are subjected under conditions of domination, not only through outright coercion (violence, economic deprivation, etc.), but also through ideological manipulation of our hearts and minds, there will frequently be occasions when we are not responsible, either wholly or in part. In this account, the individual is she who makes decisions between accepting responsibility and refusing it, who acts when she can make a difference and refrains from acting, or withdraws, when she can't, and avoids de-moralization by struggling constantly against succumbing to the meanings and values of domination and holding fast to the values of a genuinely human status for all.

This work of Hoagland is in contrast to other attempts to open up a space of effective action within the domain of everyday life, which fail because they do not acknowledge the ideological structuring of everyday experience. Dorothy Smith, for example, interprets the 'lived actualities of people's lives' as a form of authenticity which she contrasts to the 'ideological apparatuses of the relations of ruling'. Her purpose is to give sociology a human face by extricating it from 'the objectivized forms of knowledge' of its present location in 'the textual realities of administration, management, professional discourse, and the like', and locating it in 'the lived actualities as people know them in their everyday/everynight lives' (Smith, 1990: 97 and *passim*). But despite her clear perceptions of particular manifestations of male domination, especially in her earlier book (Smith, 1987), Smith sees domination only in its bureaucratic forms, and not in its mundane aspects as manifested in everyday life. Instead, she appeals to everyday life, in the form of 'women's experience', as a corrective to the traditional masculine bias of sociology. She interprets domination as confined to objectified, bureaucratic forms of 'relations of ruling', and fails to see that the 'women's experience' to which she appeals is already structured within relations of male domination.

On the other hand, however, there is an element of truth in appeals to what Smith calls 'lived actualities', to the extent that they are attempts to open a space for resistance to domination in the domain within which people actually live. The problem with such accounts is that they say nothing about the ways in which domination already operates in this domain. As a consequence, they fail to recognize the vital role which the recognition of domination plays in the struggle against it. None the less, it remains true that, if domination operates in the sphere of 'everyday/everynight lives' (wherever else it operates as well), it can also be resisted there.

Within the terms of feminist theory, experience is 'agency within a life world'. It is the activity and receptivity for which the individual bears her own responsibility, in so far as she has access to the information which will allow her to decide whether or not she is responsible. For feminist purposes, experience is neither the passive reception of internal and external stimuli, nor the value-free perception of 'what is', nor the mute acceptance of authorized versions of the world-taken-for-granted. It is an active presence in the world, claiming the fullest possible responsibility for her place within it. That does not mean that we are responsible for everything that happens to us. To the extent that domination debars us from exercising the fullest possible control over our lives, obviously we are not. But we can still be responsible for how we act within oppressive conditions, and for deciding the extent and limitations of our freedom and constraint.

But if experience is no guarantee of the truth, accuracy, relevance or adequacy of theory, it is also the only guarantee there is. Without theory, experience is at best a blind groping in the dark, at worst a reinforcement of and collusion with the status quo; but without experience, theory becomes an esoteric mystery, a game for academic troglodytes. That game has traditionally been played best by those who can demand the services of others to take care of their mundane needs. The detached, disinterested nature of malestream theory is a function of the amount of distance the theorist can put between himself (or herself) and the messy, tiresome demands of everyday life. That distance depends on someone else doing the work of necessity, traditionally a woman or women. Distancing oneself from the everyday world, as feminist standpoint theorists have pointed out, threatens to divorce intellectual work from human concerns. Hence, theory must be visibly tied to experience. But neither provides any guarantee for the other. Theory can be impeccably 'ideologically sound', and still do grave damage to experiential reality; experience can be intense, pleasurable and deeply felt, and yet require theorizing which radically questions and undermines. Experience can be deceptive, and theory is only more or less adequate. None the less, there is a stopping point, which is also a starting point, which gives meaning, purpose and coherence to feminist theory and beyond which the questions and explanations must cease. That point is ethical. Feminist theory is, above and beyond anything else, a moral commitment to the kind of world we want to live in, and a moral resistance to the kind of world which, by and large, it actually is.

For not all meaning and value serve domination. For those not in the direst straits, for those who have access to the basic necessities of human existence – food, shelter, physical safety, freedom of movement and association, etc. – there is always the possibility of manoeuvre, negotiation and innovation, and meanings and values can be changed, although not easily. In that sense, anyone can be complicit and anyone can resist. But the two are not, of course, symmetrical. For the most part compliance requires no more than unthinking acceptance of what 'everyone knows to be the case', proceeding as usual without deliberation or reflection, knowing 'how to go on' without thinking about it, although even here there is room to move. Resistance, however, requires a greater degree of self-reflection and deliberate choice, questioning the 'world-taken-for-granted', espousing some values and rejecting others, seeing the world in one way and not in another. It involves recognizing both freedom and constraint, both the extent to which one is responsible and the extent to which one is not. And because these decisions cannot be made once and for all, it involves a constant readiness to reconsider.

What any particular individual might or might not do, ought or ought not to do, cannot be stated in general terms. Feminism does not lay down rules and regulations, prohibitions and prescriptions, for individuals to follow or avoid. What actions follow from any particular critique is for each of us to decide for herself (or himself). I would assert, as an ethical first principle, that human beings ought to be free to choose between alternatives, and that, as a matter of fact, we frequently are, at least those of us who are already provided with basic necessities. The individual is a free agent to the extent that she has access to alternatives, allows herself to recognize that alternatives exist, and acts with knowledge of the extent and limits of her responsibility. No one can do it completely alone. Non-compliance with dominant meanings and values involves risking social rejection, non-acceptance or irrelevance, and sometimes violence, or (because 'society' is not only 'out there' but also 'in here') madness. Effective refusal to comply requires an alternative body of mutual knowledge, of shared meanings and values, which provides a social context for resistance. This is what feminism supplies.

But just as male domination is not monolithic, rigid and static, neither is feminism an absolute alternative. Feminism's primary commitment is to the interests of women (and, not incidentally, also to the interests of men, to the extent that men can see that a human status achieved at no one's expense is in their interests too). Feminism is not concerned to criticize, or even theorize, current social arrangements as long as they do not operate against women's interests either by including women as men's subordinates, or by excluding women from humanly valuable forms of life. Neither is feminism critical of current arrangements which do not validate domination, which allow for mutual recognition, respect and caring between people. 'Male domination' is a theoretical construct devised for a certain purpose, to focus attention on those aspects of reality which must be denied if the social system that is male domination is to be maintained. The feminist focus on male domination provides a standpoint from which certain questions can be asked, and certain answers and actions can become conceivable. Because those answers and actions rebound on forms of life, they cannot be dictated. Everyone must decide for themselves. But the decisions cannot be made unless the questions are asked in the first place. The role of feminism is to provide the questions which allow the possibility of resistance and challenge to relations of domination.

In Part Two, I discuss a number of other ways in which feminism has been interpreted, other, that is, than defining the feminist political project in terms of the opposition to male supremacy. Many feminist texts have an ambivalent relationship to the concept of male domination. No feminist text can avoid acknowledging its existence, in however tangential, peripheral or covert a fashion. Feminism's evident concern for women means that even the most cursory examination of the situation of women is going to uncover the workings of male supremacy in women's lives. But in too many texts labelled 'feminist', the significance of that insight is missed, so that male domination either becomes just one problem among many; or it is reduced to a secondary phenomenon caused by something more basic, capitalism, perhaps, or pregnancy and childbirth, or women's mothering, or 'the public/ private distinction', 'binary oppositions' or 'dichotomies'; or it is confined to one particular social context – 'the family', or the work place, or the role of wife; or it is displaced entirely in favour of something else, usually 'women's oppression' or 'gender'; or it is given a neutral-sounding title like 'the sex/gender system'. Part Two is an extended discussion of some of these ways of evading what I have argued is feminism's central problematic, the existence of male domination.

Notes

1   This has been noted by a number of radical feminist theorists, among whom are Catharine MacKinnon, Andrea Dworkin and Sheila Jeffreys.

2   The term is Sheila Jeffreys'. She says: 'I use the term "lesbianandgay" to describe those theorists who apparently make no distinction between lesbians and gay men in their theory. They avoid feminist insights about the different sex class positions of women and men and homogenize experience to create a universal gay theory in which lesbian specificity disappears' (Jeffreys, 1993: 18 n. 2).

3   I am greatly indebted to Mia Campioni for countless conversations over many years on the male supremacist constitution of the maternal relation and the crucial part it plays in the management of male power (Campioni, 1987, 1991, 1997).

4   Hence the preoccupation throughout the history of malestream social thought, from Hobbes to Foucault, with 'the problem of social order', a preoccupation which establishes conflict and antagonism as the primal reality, as that which must be over-come in order for 'society' to exist. Malestream social thought has focused on the question: 'How is society possible given the original antagonism of the war of each against all?' Feminism, however, starts from the diametrically opposite question: 'How do antagonism and conflict come about, given that we all originate from within a social relationship?'

Part Two   Misunderstanding Feminism

4   Feminism undefined

The obvious place to look for definitions is, of course, a dictionary, and feminist dictionaries do exist. But they are no more useful for clarifying the meaning of feminism than any other text. Because their purpose is to provide as comprehensive an overview as possible, their main criterion for selection is anything called 'feminist'. As a consequence, they tend to reproduce the conflicts and contradictions without resolving them. The entries under 'feminism' are so disparate as to be little help in getting any coherent sense of what feminism is.

This is often a deliberate strategy on the part of the compilers since their aim is to include as wide a range as possible of what women have said about each topic designated by a word entry. But the word 'feminist' has a different status from all the other entries. When it appears in the title it provides the definitional focus for everything else. Hence, the place to look for this dictionary's definition of 'feminism' is the compilers' statement of their aims and intentions. Cheris Kramarae and Paula Treichler, for example, initially stated these largely in terms of 'women', for example 'to document words, definitions, and conceptualizations that illustrate women's linguistic contributions' (Kramarae and Treichler, 1985: 1). However, they were aware that for the purposes of a *feminist* dictionary, references to women alone were not sufficient. They said that they called the book a feminist dictionary rather than a women's dictionary because they were particularly interested in what has been said 'in opposition to male definition, defamation, and ignorance of women and their lives' (p. 12). In other words, they were aware that the need to focus on women arises out of male supremacist conditions, although in the interests of diversity that awareness does not appear clearly and unambiguously under the entry 'feminism' within the text itself.

Usually, though, this pluralist approach means that feminism comes to be defined only in terms of women. The editors of an overview of Australian feminism said that they 'did not even attempt to impose a singular definition of feminism ... because of the diversity in, and constant movement of, feminist terrain'. They did, however, offer a definition of feminism in terms of a concern with women's oppression and how to change that with reference to women's citizenship and participation in social life (Caine et al., 1998: x). Maggie Humm, too, defined feminism largely in terms of women – 'equal rights for women', 'in general, feminism is the ideology of women's liberation', 'the theory of the woman's point of view', etc. (Humm, 1989). Feminism is also characterized in terms of women in the Preface: 'feminist theory is fundamentally about women's experience' (p. xi). Under the heading 'Domination', she does acknowledge that 'A distinctive part of contemporary feminist theory is its analysis of male dominance and all feminist theory is designed to show how a male domination of women can be ended' (p. 55); and there is an entry for 'male dominance'. But that awareness is not included in the definition of feminism.

I know of only one text which explicitly addresses the issue of defining feminism. Karen Offen (1988) did present feminism in terms of male domination as the crucial issue for feminist politics. Feminism was 'a critical analysis of male privilege and women's subordination within any given society', and 'a political challenge to male authority and hierarchy in the most profound sense' (pp. 151, 152). But her chief concern was why the word 'feminism' so often evoked antagonism. She suggested that it was the individualist emphasis which alienated many women (and men), because it dismissed women's traditional experience and women's differences from men. She argued that the solution was to recognize the important role 'relational' feminism had played historically. 'Relational feminism', she said, 'emphasized women's rights *as women* (defined principally by their childbearing and/or nurturing capacities) in relation to men. It insisted on *women's* distinctive contributions in these roles to the broader society and made claims on the commonwealth on the basis of these contributions' (p. 136 – her emphases). She acknowledged that arguments for 'women's distinctiveness and complementarity of the sexes' had often been appropriated 'once again to endorse male privilege' (p. 154). But she believed that a feminism which valued women's traditional capacities for nurturance and relationship would appeal to more women than one which relied solely on abstract (and male-defined) concepts of individual rights and personal autonomy.

However, while she was right to argue that there is much that is valuable in women's traditional capacities, she misperceived the source of the antagonism towards feminism. Feminism antagonizes, not because it is too abstract and individualistic, but because it identifies male domination. The feminist problem with women's traditional roles is not that women in fact perform them, but that they ensure women's subservience to men. The problem is not that women are nurturant and caring (if they are), but that women are required to nurture men without reciprocity. It is the prospect of women withdrawing from servicing men that is so alienating, to men because they will lose women's unreciprocated recognition of their 'human' status, and to women because they will lose the only access to intimacy and 'human' status allowed them under male supremacist conditions. But Offen did not recognize that it is feminism's very opposition to male supremacy, an opposition which she herself found unproblematic, which is the source of the antagonism.

Too often feminist texts equivocate on the question of male domination, even, oddly enough, where it is explicitly named. Sandra Harding, for example, clearly recognizes the existence of male domination, since she defines 'sex/gender' as 'a system of male dominance made possible by men's control of women's productive and reproductive labor' (Harding, 1983: 311). 'Male domination' is synonymous with 'sex/gender system' throughout the paper. She tells us that it is probably unwise 'to assume that anything like the sex/gender system we know is a *universal* trait of human social life', and so confines the scope of her generalization to 'the vast majority of cultures to which we will ever have historical access' (p. 323 n. 10 – her emphasis). Hence any (hypothetical) cultures which were not male dominant would, it would seem, lack a 'sex/gender system'. But if male domination is the common and invariable characteristic of 'sex/gender systems', why is there any need to substitute 'sex/gender system' for 'male domination'? Given how prevalent is the evasion of naming male domination, the substitution is not innocent. It too often functions as a euphemistic denial of the relations of power challenged by feminism. Why it should appear in a text which otherwise identifies the power relations clearly, is puzzling.

While most self-identified feminist texts which fail to acknowledge male domination as feminism's prime antagonist do so implicitly and by omission, there are some texts which explicitly argue against it. For example, there is Judith Butler's argument against what she characterizes as 'the notion that the oppression of women has some singular form discernible in the universal or hegemonic structure of patriarchy or masculine domination'. She goes on to say:

> The notion of a universal patriarchy has been widely criticised in recent years for its failure to account for the workings of gender oppression in the concrete cultural contexts in which it exists. Where those various contexts have been consulted within such theories, it has been to find 'examples' or 'illustrations' of a universal principle that is assumed from the start. That form of feminist theorizing has come under criticism for its efforts to colonize and appropriate non-Western cultures to support highly Western notions of oppression, [and] because they tend as well to construct a 'Third World' or even an 'Orient' in which gender oppression is subtly explained as symptomatic of an essential, non-Western barbarism. The urgency of feminism to establish a universal status for patriarchy in order to strengthen the appearance of feminism's own claims to be representative has occasionally motivated the shortcut to a categorial or fictive universality of the structure of domination, held to produce women's common subjugated experience. (Butler, 1990: 3–4)

This single paragraph comprises the whole of Butler's critique within this text. The scantness of the argument indicates both Butler's belief in the self-evident nature of the critique, and her scorn for the 'form of feminist theorizing' she is rejecting. No evidence for or examples of 'fictive universality' are provided, so that the charge is impossible to evaluate in this particular instance. We are not told where 'the notion of a universal patriarchy' appears, nor where it has been criticized. We cannot therefore decide for ourselves whether or not there are any forms of feminist theorizing which 'colonize and appropriate non-Western cultures' and construct them as 'barbarous', nor which forms they might be.

Her argument is an instance of the 'false universalism' charge, and it functions in the same way all such charges against feminist theory function, that is, to deny male domination. She characterizes 'patriarchy' as a 'highly Western notion'. She insists that it is inappropriate when applied to 'the workings of gender oppression' and 'women's subjugated experience' in cultures other than 'Western' ones, thus denying that the concept of 'patriarchy' is relevant to cultures other than 'the West'. She does, however, acknowledge that 'gender oppression' and 'women's subjugation' exist in cultures other than 'the West'. But if women's subjugation is not the result of male domination, where does it come from? It would appear that 'universalism' is only false when what is being 'universalized' is male domination. There is no problem, it would seem, with seeing women's oppression as 'universal' in the sense that it exists in cultures other than 'the West'. What is forbidden by the accusation of 'false universalism' is the naming of the enemy.

To locate the cause of women's subordination in male domination is not to 'universalize' a peculiarly 'Western' notion and apply it to 'other cultures'. To identify the domination of women by men (and of some men by other men) is not to assert that there is only one singular form of male domination. Even in 'the West', it takes a multiplicity of different forms. Wherever men's interests prevail at women's expense, and the interests of some men override the interests of other men, male domination exists, whatever form it takes. While it is sometimes violent and blatantly dehumanizing, it is also as multifarious and all-pervasive as everyday life. While it takes different forms in different cultures and under different historical conditions, as long as 'human' existence continues to be defined in terms of the male, and the 'human' existence of some men is bought at the expense of other men, it remains male domination, in all its 'endless variety and monotonous similarity' (Fraser and Nicholson, 1990: 35).[1]

This reluctance among many who identify as feminists to name and identify male domination requires explanation. One frequently reiterated reason is a reluctance to characterize women as 'victims'. Focusing on male domination, so the argument goes, makes men out to be more powerful than they are, and can only make women feel trapped and helpless. To dwell at length on male power, to see it as all-pervasive, to find it everywhere encroaching on us, invading our lives, penetrating the deepest recesses of our psyches, entrenched in our most intimate acts, is to portray women as nothing but passive and helpless victims of men, or so it is argued.

This kind of argument is common in 'academic feminist' circles. Lois McNay, for example, says that the 'tendency to regard women as powerless and innocent victims of patriarchal social structures … hamper[s] many types of feminist analysis' (McNay, 1992: 63, 66). She says that it fails 'to account for the potential of women's creativity and agency within social constraints'. It is also oppressive to some women because it does not recognize 'that gender is not the only determining influence on women's lives', and because it 'takes white women's experiences as the norm and generalizes them'. She gives no examples of feminist work which supposedly exhibits this trait because, she says, it is 'well documented' (pp. 63–4). Yet she also says that there are 'undoubtedly … structures of domination, in particular constructions of gender, which ensure the overall subordinate position of women in society' (pp. 66–7). She does not perceive a contradiction between rejecting 'patriarchal social structures' with their attendant 'powerless and innocent victims' on the one hand, and accepting 'structures of gender domination' and women's 'overall subordination' on the other. It is not clear what kind of distinction is being drawn here.

Arguments like this make the same mistake they supposedly find elsewhere. They interpret references to male domination in terms of something monolithic and inevitable. But feminism's exposure of the victimization of women is intended to challenge it, not maintain it. If it cannot be named, it cannot be challenged. And the project of women creating for ourselves non-exclusionary and non-oppressive ways of being human is sufficient evidence that feminism does not define women only as victims. This kind of objection fails to take into account the sense of power, triumph and relief which comes with seeing the world clearly. It fails to take into account the pressing need we have to see just how bad things really are, and the sense of liberation which comes with knowledge. It ignores the political necessity of knowing what we are up against if we are to do anything about it. Those fearful of confining women to perpetual victimhood seem to have forgotten (or never to have known) the relief of hearing one's oppression named *as* oppression, rather than merely as a personal, idiosyncratic failing. It is a liberation all in itself to realize that the fault lies, not in one's flawed self, but in a reality to which one can say 'no'. This is a vital step in the process of extricating oneself from oppressive conditions. We probably all have a sticking point, a point at which we can take no more, a point at which enough is enough and the misery outweighs the relief. But the misery is not alleviated by refusing to see male domination when it is manifestly present, by calling it something less horrendous (like 'gender'), or by portraying women as powerful when we are not. Recognizing the constraints to which one is subjected is intrinsic to acknowledging one's own moral agency under oppression (Hoagland, 1988). Moral agency requires an ability to decide not only the scope but also the limits of one's own responsibility, the extent to which one is not responsible as well as the extent to which one is, when one cannot act, as well as when one can.

So naming male domination is not to portray women as nothing but victims. Women can also be collaborators, can embrace male supremacist meanings and values as their own and defend them vigorously. The system offers limited, but not thereby unimportant, benefits and advantages. It entices and seduces while it oppresses. Women can also be courageous and clear-sighted resisters. There is a sense in which feminism's challenge to male domination is not 'about' women at all. It refers to a social system which certainly operates to women's detriment, but with which anyone can be complicit and which anyone can resist. But it is important to be clear that women are its chief victims. To refrain from naming victimization is a failure to name oppression. By the same logic, we ought not to name any of the other great oppressions in history either. Should we also refrain from speaking about the Holocaust or colonialism? These great evils produced countless millions of innocent and powerless victims. Why can these victims be named as such, but not the women who are victims of male supremacy? How are we to know the extent of the harm done to women if we are forbidden to name the harm? To the extent that 'academic feminism' suppresses any reference to women as victims, it is in collusion with domination.

Note

1   These authors apply the phrase to 'women's oppression', not to 'patriarchy' or 'male domination'.

5 Other definitions

The central concern of feminist politics has been variously identified, usually implicitly, in a number of ways. Feminism has been seen to be concerned with: patriarchy (capitalist or otherwise); sexism; women; gender; race, class and gender; diversity; social construction. It has often been seen as a matter of self definition, that is, anything said or done by anyone who identifies as a feminist, even to the point where 'feminism' becomes little more than doing what you want to do and not doing what you don't want to do (as long as you're a woman). But interpreting something as 'feminist' simply because some women want it, is inadequate for a feminist politics because relations of domination can operate through the most intimate levels of desire. Although liberation partly involves being free to act on what we feel, what we feel can also be implicated in relations of power. Because feminism is a political analysis which identifies, challenges and resists how we are situated within relations of power, it also involves questioning our feelings and desires. To embrace without question our own desire to dominate or be dominated is not to challenge and eventually overcome it, but to remain fixedly embedded within the values of domination.

Most of the above issues are interrelated, and all of them have some bearing on feminist politics. But none of them clearly identifies the primary social problem exposed by feminism as male domination. Some of them come closer than others. 'Patriarchy' and 'sexism', for example, usually mean male domination of females, whereas the term 'gender' often seems to have been deliberately coined to avoid naming the enemy. But 'patriarchy' literally means 'the rule of the father', the domination, not only of women by men, but of sons by fathers, younger men by older men, powerless men by powerful men. And men do not acquire their dominant status because they are fathers, but because they are men. And although 'sexism' is sometimes used in an analogy to 'racism', that is, by identifying 'sex' as the basis of oppression in comparison with 'race' as the basis of oppression, it can be (and is) used by men to complain about their exclusion from affirmative action policies and women-only spaces.

Patriarchy

'Patriarchy' is the term most commonly used to designate the social problem identified by feminism (or it used to be – it would appear that it has been supplanted by 'gender'). But in its usual meaning of 'rule of the father', the term 'patriarchy' is a misnomer applied to the form of domination challenged by feminism. The paternal domination portrayed in western history, myth and literature is the rule of the father over the son. It involves the imposition of, or struggles against, the ascendancy of some men over other men. 'Patriarchy' in this sense is an affair between men, and is relevant to women only derivatively through our implication in power hierarchies among men.

But whatever the status of some males in relation to other males, the problem identified by feminism is the subjection of women to men. Or rather, because women have always resisted subjugation and asserted our own worth despite the male monopolization of the 'human' norm, as well as acquiesced, accommodated ourselves, manoeuvred for some space and freedom of movement, beat the oppressor at his own game, used his obsessions and weaknesses against him, etc., it is the male supremacist dream and reality of female subjection which is of concern to feminism, not struggles for ascendancy among men. To the extent that women aid the 'sons' in their battles with the 'fathers', no matter how worthy the cause, no matter how justified the sons' complaints, women are once again working in men's interests. These may indeed be women's interests as well, but that cannot be decided unless it is possible to see women's interests in the first place.

By identifying the enemy as 'patriarchy', feminism has somewhat misnamed it, although it has not always misrecognized it. To the extent that the problem of power-as-domination addressed by feminism is recognized as male domination, it is identified accurately, whatever it is called. Kate Millett, for example, named the problem 'patriarchy', but defined it primarily in terms of male supremacy: 'If one takes patriarchal government to be the institution whereby that half of the populace which is female is controlled by that half which is male, the principles of patriarchy appear to be twofold: male shall dominate female, elder male shall dominate younger' (Millett, 1970: 25). Ti-Grace Atkinson did not use the term 'patriarchy', but she did identify the problem addressed by feminism as the domination of women by men. Her preferred designation was 'the sex-class system':

> The ... radical feminist analysis of the persecution of women ... begins with the ... raison d'être that women are a class, that this class is political in nature, and that this political class is oppressed. ... If women are a political class and women are being oppressed, it must be that some other political class is oppressing the class of women. Since the very definition of women entails that only one other class could possibly be relevant to it, only one other class could possibly be oppressing women: the class of men. ... Women exist as the corollaries of men, and exist as human beings only insofar as they are those corollaries. (Atkinson, 1974: 41)

Socialist feminism's use of the term 'patriarchy' was usually equivocal. While socialist feminists were on the whole disinclined to use the term on the grounds that it was 'ahistorical' and 'universalistic', some were reluctantly prepared to accept it as a designator of the political problem addressed by feminism, although it tended to mean neither male supremacy nor the rule of the father. Although socialist feminism purported to resolve the question of which had political priority, capitalism or patriarchy, by asserting that capitalism was the latest historical form of patriarchy, and hence that capitalism was one form of patriarchy (Eisenstein, 1979), in fact within the socialist feminist context, 'patriarchy' was usually simply a form of capitalism. It was a capitalism expanded to include issues of concern to women – domestic labour, reproduction both social and biological, the family, the constitution of femininity, sex segmentation of the work force – but a capitalism none the less. Under this schema, 'patriarchy' was defined solely with reference to 'the oppression (or subordination) of women', with the source of that oppression either left unstated or reduced to just another aspect of capitalism. Hence, in this usage, 'patriarchy' had no referent as a form of domination.

Veronica Beechey considered whether or not the term should be abandoned. She argued, however, that it served a purpose for feminism by pointing to 'real political and theoretical problems', and that it should be retained, at least until 'we find some other more satisfactory way of conceptualizing male domination and female subordination, and, for Marxist feminism, of relating this to the organization of the mode of production as a whole' (Beechey, 1979: 68). She did not say why conceptualizing male domination as male domination was unsatisfactory.

Her criticism of previous conceptualizations of patriarchy is itself less than satisfactory. Her single example of a radical feminist text was Kate Millett's book.[1] Her criticism was that it provided us with 'a *description* of patriarchal relationships ... [but] is unable to provide a satisfactory *explanation* of their foundations' (p. 69 – her emphasis). True enough, and I am sure Millett would be among the first to agree. But Beechey herself gave us no pointers towards what might constitute an explanation as opposed to a description. Nor, in her concluding remarks, did she appear to regard explanatory power as a prerequisite for a more satisfactory account of patriarchy. Rather, her concern was that 'a satisfactory theory of patriarchy should be historically specific and should explore the forms of patriarchy which exist within particular modes of production ... [and] in particular social institutions' (p. 80). But she did not tell us how this would raise the theoretical enterprise from the level of mere description to that of explanation.

Neither did she tell us what a 'mode of production' might be, a not insignificant omission given the inconclusiveness of the debates within Marxism about that very concept (Coward, 1978). It would appear to relate to the question of historical specificity. Extrapolating from that single text by Millett to radical feminism as a whole, Beechey asserted that 'radical feminism ... leaves unexplained specific forms of male domination and female subordination' (1979: 69). But what she meant by this is unclear. Leaving aside the question of 'explanation' which Beechey herself never resolved, did she mean that radical feminism is not historically and culturally specific when it designates male domination and female subordination as the problem? If this is what she meant, then she is wrong. Given that feminist theory and practice is grounded in experience, it would seem obvious that it always takes culturally specific forms, namely the forms and variations which the feminist knows from her own experience. There may be problems with generalizing from one specific historical and cultural context to other historical periods and cultures. But those problems occur, not because the original account was not specific enough, but because it was inaccurately generalized to contexts where it did not apply (in which case its non-application needs to be argued for, not simply asserted as self-evident). On the other hand, if she meant that radical feminism is at fault because it 'leaves unexplained' every specific form of male domination and female sub-ordination, then she was demanding the impossible.

This appeal to historical (and cultural) specificity played an important role in socialist feminist attempts to amend what was regarded as the faults and naïveties of radical feminism. Michèle Barrett also objected to 'early radical feminist uses of the term' patriarchy, on the grounds that such uses 'invoke an apparently universal and trans-historical category of male dominance, leaving us with little hope of change' (Barrett, 1984: 12). But it is not clear what the charge amounts to. Why would 'invoking male dominance' leave us with 'little hope of change'? On the contrary, it is only by identifying the problem as male dominance that there is any hope of change at all.

Unlike Beechey, Barrett did not feel that the term 'patriarchy' was retrievable for present feminist purposes. She proposed to use it to refer only to societies 'where male domination is expressed through the power of the father'. Such societies, she said, are 'not capitalist ones' (pp. 250–1). However, this left her without a term to refer to those current relations of ruling challenged by feminism. Her preferred term for the problem addressed by feminism was 'women's oppression', and she did sometimes use the term 'male domination'. But she did not connect the two by attributing women's oppression to male domination, as of course she could not, because such an endeavour would be, in her own terms, 'universal' and 'trans-historical'. As a consequence she could only account for 'women's oppression' in terms of 'contemporary capitalism'. But while it is certainly the case that women are oppressed by capitalism, there are dimensions to that oppression – male sexual violence, to name just one – which even the most thorough investigation of capitalism would never uncover, and hence open the way to change. Barrett tried to resist arguing that women's oppression was a consequence of capitalism. She criticized attempts to account for women's oppression 'in terms of the supposed needs of capitalism itself' (p. 248), or as 'a functional pre-requisite of capitalism' (p. 249). But her own insistence on confining the account of 'women's oppression' to 'a material basis in the relations of production and reproduction of capitalism today' (p. 249) left her with no alternative.

I would suggest that the term 'patriarchy' has a limited usefulness for feminism, given its tendency to slide back into its original meaning of 'the rule of the father', and its socialist feminist history as a term emptied of meaning. At the very least, feminists need to be alert to traps laid for the unwary by ill-considered uses of the term. At the same time, it does have an honourable feminist history, and with a little feminist caution it can still provide good service.

Sexism

The problem with the term 'sexism' is that it does not contain domination as its immediate referent, and hence does not immediately identify the sex which dominates. It fits too easily into the individualist terminology of liberalism, of 'rights', 'discrimination', 'attitudes', and 'prejudices'. To the extent that 'sexism' means no more than distinctions based on sex, it assumes an original equality between sexed individuals, an equality which is transgressed by any action favouring one sex over another, including actions taken by women in defence of their own interests. As a consequence it can be used against actions taken to redress the wrongs done to women, as well as against attempts by women to establish (literal or metaphorical) space outside male intervention and control.

Although the term was widely used in the 1970s, it did not receive much theoretical discussion. There was some discussion in Australia which revealed the basic flaw in the idea, but instead of resolving it, the debate reproduced the confusion. 'Sexism' continued to be defined in the bland, neutral terminology of liberal pluralism, despite the discussants' awareness that such a definition depoliticized the term and rendered it useless for feminist politics (Refractory Girl, 1974a, 1974b; Summers, 1975: 22).

The Hobart Women's Action Group (HWAG) defined it in terms of 'organizing people according to sex and sexual behaviour, and attributing various behaviour, personality and status traits to people on the basis of sex' (Refractory Girl, 1974a: 30). The authors took some pains to argue that 'sexism' was not identical with 'a patriarchal society'. A society in which women ruled ('matriarchy'), or one in which the sexes had equal power and influence although in different spheres, would also be 'sexist', they argued, because it would still be structured along sex lines.

On another occasion, however, the HWAG did acknowledge a connection between 'sexism' and 'patriarchy'. They pointed out that, although it might be theoretically possible to have forms of sexism which were 'power-neutral' in that they were divisions of roles and personality without subordination, or even to have a 'matriarchal' form of sexism where women ruled men, in actual fact, they emphasized, *the only sexism that we know is sexism in its patriarchal manifestation*'. They criticized uses of the term which were purely theoretical in the sense that those uses did not locate sexism within current patriarchal society. At the same time, however, they themselves defined it solely in theoretical terms, by denying that it meant 'the "institutionalized subordination of women to men"' (Refractory Girl, 1974b: 2–3).

Despite the writers' own strictures against using 'sexism' in senses other than the patriarchal one, that was exactly what they themselves were doing. They did not give any reasons why the purely theoretical sense should be retained even though it referred to nothing in 'our society'. If those forms do not exist in the here and now, and never have existed, why retain the idea of them? Although the writers saw the neutral concept of 'sexism' as problematic, they also saw it as more basic than 'patriarchy/male domination'. Sexism was a precondition for patriarchy, since 'without sexism, patriarchy is deprived of its organizing principle'. But this makes no sense. It attributes something real – the 'patriarchal manifestation' of sexism – to something non-existent.

Confused though this argument is, it is permitted by the fact that the term 'sexism' does not explicitly identify the relations of power involved and name which sex is dominant and which subordinate. This neutrality also permits it to be used as a pejorative label tied to any action which 'discriminates' on the ground of sex, even those intended to challenge current relations of power. One example of this occurred in an editorial in the same journal discussing the reasons for producing an issue devoted specifically to lesbianism. One of the reasons given was the 'popularity' of the idea that 'lesbianism is the most radical position possible for a feminist to adopt' (Refractory Girl, 1974a: 2). The editors' comment on this was that it 'seems inherently sexist'. Because it excluded 'men and, perhaps, heterosexual women', they said, it was 'a form of sexual apartheid'. This is the sort of thing which is permitted by the HWAG's power-neutral definition of 'sexism'. It was not a genuine criticism of the idea of lesbianism as politically radical, because it made a nonsense of the actual relations of power. It ignored the political meaning of lesbianism as a challenge to the male 'right' of automatic sexual access to women. It also ignored the fact that women themselves were discovering a hitherto unrecognized lesbianism which included all forms of loving identification between women. In that feminist sense, lesbianism did not 'discriminate' against 'heterosexual' women – it was available to all women whether or not they availed themselves of it. By ignoring these implications, the editors colluded with the suppression of the lesbian possibility, even as they purported to challenge that suppression by producing a special issue focused on 'lesbianism'.

In acknowledging the problems entailed by the concept of 'sexism', however, I am not arguing for its complete rejection. It still has its uses, as long as the depoliticizing tendency is recognized and allowed for. It identifies 'sex' as the ground of oppression, as the term 'racism' identifies the oppression of 'race'. While neither term identifies which sex or race is dominant, both can still serve as handy short-hand descriptions of discriminatory behaviour.

Women

Feminism is necessarily concerned with women. It is the *women's* movement, and it is *women's* liberation which is at stake. It is women who are harmed, women who are oppressed and subordinated, women whose consciousness changed to see oppression for what it was, and to see, too, that it wasn't inescapable or natural and that it could be challenged. Feminism originated with women's experience, women's discontent, women's outrage at the confidence tricks perpetrated to keep us subservient, women's sense of betrayal at being excluded from all kinds of rights, benefits and privileges.

The dangers of failing to retain the focus on women are illustrated by Pierre Bourdieu's work on 'la domination masculine' (Bourdieu, 1990).[2] As Nicole-Claude Mathieu has pointed out, not only does Bourdieu tend to ignore most of the feminist work in the area, especially that produced in France (while making sweeping generalizations about feminism's supposed faults and failings), his emphasis sets up a symmetry between the sexes which does not exist (Mathieu, 1999). In Bourdieu's account, women are complicit with male domination, and men are also trapped. While this is true, it is also misleading. Men are not trapped in male supremacy any more than the slave-owner is trapped in the institution of slavery. They are primarily perpetrators and beneficiaries. And although women can be complicit with the system which oppresses them, the system also operates through actual violence, intimidation and deprivation. This is not, however, a distinction between 'the symbolic' and 'the real' (as Mathieu sometimes seems to be implying). Bourdieu is right to emphasize the important role of the symbolic (or of meaning as I would prefer to call it) in generating and maintaining the reality of domination. The problem is that Bourdieu's sociological perspective does not automatically translate into political awareness. It is still the case that the social positioning of privileged men engenders blindness to what is at stake for women, especially as women are still struggling to understand the ramifications and reach of male supremacist relations of power. Mathieu sees Bourdieu's work as a particularly telling example of male domination in its suppression or distortion of the experiences and analyses of women. She quotes Voltaire's famous advice to a young man: 'My friend, your work contains much that is good and new. Unfortunately, what is good is not new and what is new is not good.' Mathieu adds: 'what is bad is not new either' (Mathieu, 1999: 298).

None the less, it is not sufficient to define feminism only in terms of women. In the first place, a concern with women is not always a feminist enterprise. Gynaecology, for example, is concerned only with women, as is any misogynist discourse. The simple fact of being focused on women does not in and of itself make something feminist. What distinguishes feminism from other concerns with women is its explicit acknowledgement of and opposition to the social system which is male domination. Feminism's concern with women arises in the first place out of a concern with the harm done to women under the social conditions of male supremacy, with the aim of providing women with the means to take control of our lives into our own hands, insofar as that is possible and while recognizing the constraints and limitations placed on women by men's rule over the world. It is only acknowledging the social system of male supremacy as the main enemy that gives meaning to feminism's concern with women.

In the second place, confining the meaning of feminism solely to 'women' has unfortunate political consequences. Focusing political attention exclusively on women means that the only relations of power which can be seen are those which operate among women. 'Women's oppression' then becomes something that women do to other women. It is true that women are divided from each other in a myriad of ways, through their intimate relationships with individual men, through their domestic isolation with sole responsibility for children, through their identification with and membership of hierarchically arranged social collectivities such as race/culture/ ethnicity and class. But to define feminism only in terms of these 'differences' fragments the feminist project into a multiplicity of competing interest groups among women who have nothing in common because some are more (and some less) privileged than others. Feminism is reduced to nothing but a series of different and essentially antagonistic categories of women. That is not to say that differences of privilege and access to human rights and dignity among women are not feminist issues. They are. The problem is locating them only in differences among women. This is a political dead end. Without the acknowledgement of male supremacy, all that women have in common is that they are women as 'women' are currently constituted. All that women have in common are those traditional roles which tie them into their subordination to men, that is, nothing very much in common at all because the interests of men must take priority in women's lives. Unless it is possible to name the problem common to all women, and hence women's common interest in opposing the source of oppression, it is these hierarchical and oppressive differences between women which define feminism.

The solution to the problems of confining feminism to women is not to widen the focus to include men. That is to fall into the politically paralysing trap of the ideology of individualism. To pose the problem only in terms of 'women' and 'men' is to pose the problem in terms of types of individuals. This makes feminism vulnerable to attack on the grounds that some individuals do not possess the characteristics in question. But if feminism is not in the first place 'about women' in this individualist sense, there is no need to include men. Feminism's identification of and opposition to the ideological construct of the male as the 'human' norm already includes 'men' as the bearers and beneficiaries of the social relations of male supremacy. Demonstrating that some men refuse complicity with domination, or that some women acquiesce, is not an objection to feminism construed as the opposition to male domination, as long as male domination continues to exist despite the best will and intentions on the part of individuals. (For a further discussion of this in relation to heterosexuality, see Thompson, 1994, 1995.)

There is already some awareness within 'academic feminism' that there are problems with defining feminism solely in terms of 'women'. However, none of these arguments recognizes male domination as the central problematic of feminist politics. Rosalind Delmar, for example, identified a number of problems with defining feminism as a concern with 'women's issues'

(Delmar, 1986). She said that such a concern was not specific to 'feminists', that it threatened to marginalize women and maintain their exclusion from 'the general field of human endeavour', and that it implied a unity and homogeneity among women which did not exist. Although she kept returning to a definition of feminism as a concern with 'women's issues', she did not commit herself (or feminism) to any one definition, since she disagreed with the idea that there can be any ' "true" and authentic feminism' (p. 9). She provided what she regarded as a minimalist definition of 'a feminist' as 'at the very least … someone who holds that women suffer discrimination because of their sex, that they have specific needs which remain negated and unsatisfied, and that the satisfaction of these needs would require a radical change (some would say a revolution even) in the social, economic and political order' (p. 8). She found this definition unsatisfactory, not, however, because it failed to mention male domination, but because things were 'more complicated' than this.

She mentioned male domination, briefly and dismissively, only twice. She rejected any 'strong desire to pin feminism down' by means of a 'preoccupation with central concerns like sexual division and male domination', because of disagreements about the reasons for women's situation and about what should be done about it, and 'bitter, at times virulent disputes' (p. 9). The second mention occurred in the context of a discussion of 'sexual politics'. She regarded this as a new concept involving 'the idea of women as a social group dominated by men as a social group (male domination/female oppression)'. But she did not follow up this insight, concluding instead with the assertion that the feminist idea of sexual politics was primarily focused on 'the pursuit of questions about the female body and its sexual needs' (pp. 26–7). She did not discuss the possibility that feminism's concern with 'the female body' might be inspired by a need to challenge male proprietorship of female bodies. It is not therefore surprising that Delmar found feminism's concern with 'women' unsatisfactory, since she failed to acknowledge the reason why feminism might be so concerned, that is, women's exclusion from 'human' status.

Naomi Schor's definition of feminism, despite its inclusion within feminism of mutually exclusive positions, does implicitly characterize feminism as a concern with 'women':

I would propose a definition of feminism that makes of it a sum of contradictions, the nodal point where dissatisfactions with contemporary society and the place it assigns women, claims for equality, claims for singular or plural differences, assertions of an essential and transhistorical female nature, denunciations of a subaltern condition due to specifically historical and contingent factors clash and intertwine. In all feminism in the broadest sense of the term there would be equal parts of conservative and contestatory forces, of maternalism and anti-maternalism, of familialism and antifamilialism, of separatism and assimilationism. The apparently irreconcilable debate that currently opposes essentialists and constructionists is a false debate in that neither of the warring forces has an exclusive hold on the truth. Feminism is the debate itself. (Schor, 1992: 46)

As well as its concern with women – 'the place [society] assigns women', 'female nature', 'maternalism', 'familialism', etc. – this definition also displays a concern to challenge women's subordination – 'denunciations of a subaltern condition'. Hence it would presumably exclude from the ambit of feminism discourses which did not identify and oppose women's subordination. But it does not locate the reasons for women's subordination with male supremacy, and it is so inclusive as to be useless for feminist politics. The tolerant acceptance of contradictory positions closes down debate and precludes any possibility of clarifying, much less resolving, the contradictions. For example, the characterization of the 'essentialism' debate as a matter of 'warring forces' misrepresents it. There are not two symmetrical camps, one claiming an essentialist position and the other a constructionist one. No one deliberately embraces 'essentialism' as their own position. There is only one position here, and that involves the accusation that certain feminist writings, usually designated radical or 'cultural' feminism, are 'essentialist' (Eisenstein, 1984; Segal, 1984). Those so accused neither espouse 'essentialism' nor speak in their own defence, and hence cannot be seen to hold a position in the debate at all (Thompson, 1991). Schor's all-embracing characterization of feminism reduces it to nothing more than what is said by anyone who identifies as a feminist.

But women have varying degrees of awareness of and opposition to the realities of male domination. To define feminism only in terms of what women say, does not provide any criteria for distinguishing feminist statements from anti-feminist or misogynist pronouncements by women. To cite another example: to define feminism, as Carol Bacchi does (citing Linda Gordon), as 'a "sharing in an impulse to increase the power and autonomy of women in their families, communities and/or society"' (Bacchi, 1990: xix), allows no way of identifying as anti-feminist right-wing discourses on women. Right-wing women sometimes co-opt the feminist terminology for use in their anti-feminist crusade. For example, Babette Francis is a founder of the anti-feminist group 'Women Who Want To Be Women', a member of a number of 'pro-life' (that is, anti-abortion) groups, and a committee member of the right-wing 'Council for a Free Australia'. She considers herself, however, 'a feminist in the true sense of the word', that is, 'a believer in equal rights for women' (Rowland, 1984: 130–1). Francis speaks in terms of 'rights' rather than in terms of increasing women's power and autonomy. But she is certainly concerned with women's place 'in their families, communities and/or society'. Unless the limitations on women's power, autonomy and rights are located with male domination, there is too little to distinguish Francis' view of 'feminism' from a genuinely feminist one.

In fact, however, Bacchi does not confine herself to this definition of feminism, which she acknowledges is 'used loosely' in her text. Central to her own feminism is 'a social model which *includes* women in the human standard' (Bacchi, 1990: 266 – her emphasis). It is this model which provides the crux of her argument against the 'sameness/difference' model of relations between the sexes. In that sense, her account is not 'about women' at all, but about those conditions which cause us to 'lose sight of the fact that what is at issue are necessary social arrangements for humane living' (p. xv). In another sense, however, she is centrally concerned with women, but in a way which clearly distinguishes her account from right-wing discourses on women. By acknowledging the feminist project as working for the inclusion of women in the human standard, she is also acknowledging women's *exclusion* from that standard as the problem. In doing so, she is also acknowledging male domination as the problem, even though she does not use the terminology.

The chief problem with the category of 'women', or so it is said, is that it is 'essentialist'. While I argue that feminism is not in fact defined solely in terms of women, the 'anti-essentialist' argument is that feminism *is* defined in terms of women but that it ought not to be. Judith Butler's is one such argument (Butler, 1990). She disagrees with what she sees as the feminist assumption 'that there is some existing identity, understood through the category women, who not only initiates feminist interests and goals within discourse, but constitutes the subject for whom political representation is pursued' (p. 1). She says that, because identities are inescapably formed 'within a field of power', no appeals can be made on their behalf as a way out of relations of power. There is no subject 'outside' or 'before the law' which can provide a basis for challenging the law. 'The identity of the feminist subject', she says, 'ought not to be the foundation of feminist politics, if the formation of the subject takes place within a field of power regularly buried through the assertion of that foundation' (p. 6). In other words, feminism cannot appeal to women as the basis for its refusal of relations of power because 'women' are already constituted by those very relations.

But arguments like this depend on assuming that 'the foundation of feminist politics' *is* the category 'women', instead of male domination. Feminism needs to be able to refer to women if the harm done to women by the dehumanizing procedures of male supremacy is to be addressed. But the word does not refer to any asocial and monolithic 'essence'. It has perfectly serviceable uses. Sometimes the purposes for which it is used are male supremacist in meaning and value (although the prevalence of 'ladies' and 'girls' suggests some discomfort with the word 'women'). Sometimes the purposes are feminist. But it serves no feminist purpose to abandon the word simply because some of its uses are male supremacist.

Arguments like Butler's are politically stultifying. Such a move abolishes feminist politics, not only because it abandons the category 'women', but because it abolishes any possibility of ethical refusal of relations of domination. If the terms of the debate are so arranged that relations of domination constitute the whole of 'the social', because there is no way out of 'the social' (as everyone knows), there is also no way out of relations of domination, and hence no possibility of resistance and refusal. Putting it in these terms is to commit the same solecism the accusers of 'essentialism' supposedly find elsewhere. It is to reify 'the social' into a monolithic totality 'outside' the individuals who live and act within it. The fact remains that it *is* possible to refuse certain meanings, values and actions for certain purposes. People do it all the time. Whether something is an embracing of relations of domination, or whether it is a refusal, can only be decided by allowing that both possibilities exist. And such possibilities can only be seen to exist if male domination is not the whole of 'the social'.

The word 'women' is undoubtedly a social category. (What else could it be?) But that does not mean that it cannot be used for the feminist purpose of refusing complicity with male domination. Such refusals are not 'outside the social' in any absolute sense (if that makes any sense at all). They are a constant process of engagement with the social order which is male supremacy. If ever male supremacy ceases to exist, what will have gone is not 'the social' *per se*, but its nature as male supremacist. But short of such a utopian outcome, those occasions which are already refusals of complicity with male domination – and they must exist otherwise opposing male supremacy would not be thinkable – are not thereby 'outside the social'. To assume without question that they must be, is to fall into the very trap of 'essentialism' which is supposedly being avoided. It is also to argue for political passivity. If we cannot refuse domination because that would require being 'outside the social', there is nothing to be done and political activism is futile. Butler appears to be perfectly satisfied with this conclusion. I am not.

Neither is it necessary. The 'subject' of feminism is not 'women', either in the sense of theoretical subject matter, or in the sense of that 'identity' in whose name feminist politics proceeds. The subject matter of feminism is male supremacy. The theory and practice of feminism proceed in the interests of women because women are the chief victims of male supremacist relations of power, because women are more likely to be in a position to perceive the problems (although those perceptions are not automatic or inevitable), and because current relations of power benefit men at women's expense. The task of feminism is neither to improve the situation of women within conventional and subordinated statuses, nor to abolish them absolutely, but to recognize the importance, worth and human dignity of women, and to create (or maintain) possibilities for genuinely human choices for women however and wherever we are placed. More importantly, feminism is concerned with the whole of the human condition, and not just with that restricted sphere conventionally allocated to women (although still controlled by and for the benefit of men). Feminism is as much concerned with war as it is with nurturing, as much with planetary pollution as with housework, with capitalist accumulation as well as equal pay, with a revolution in meanings and values as well as childbirth, with reason as well as emotion, with the mind as well as the body. Nothing is outside feminist concern as long as male supremacy continues to exist.

Neither is feminism only, or primarily, about 'women's experience'. Feminism must remain grounded in experience, in some sense at least, if it is not to deteriorate into a set of academic exercises. But feminist theory cannot remain simply at the level of experience in the sense of incommensurable individual life histories, because experience is already theory-laden, context-dependent and collective. There is no 'experience' outside already constituted relations of power which provides experience with its meaning, purpose and value. There is no 'pure' experience which guarantees the truth of feminist theory. Neither experience nor any particular social location is a guarantee of feminist commitment. Since feminism is a politics and a morality, it requires more than a litany of appeals to 'experience'. It requires a change in consciousness and a deliberate political choice so that relations of domination and subordination, and our own positioning within those relations, can be perceived and challenged. It is feminist theory, and the ethical and political insights which inform it, which reinterpret the meaning and value of experience by challenging its male supremacist connotations.

To define feminism only in terms of 'women' is actively to discourage feminist politics. It does not distinguish feminism from other discourses which also address themselves to the question of 'women', including misogynist and anti-feminist discourses. It focuses on hierarchies of privilege between and among women, and interprets social oppressions only in terms of antagonisms between women. And it means that feminism can be too easily hijacked. Because it does not allow us to identify something as anti-feminist as long as it is said by women in the name of feminism, it can be put into service to defend anti-feminist positions simply because they are held by women. If feminism is only concerned with 'women', then how do we decide between conflicting views of 'what women want' as long as those conflicts emanate from the mouths of women? While feminism is certainly concerned with women's interests, and while each of us has to make her own decisions about where her priorities lie, unless feminism is defined first and foremost in terms of opposition to male domination, it becomes at best nothing more than a set of pallid opinions; at worst, outright conflict between women with no hope of resolution.

It seems to me, thinking back, that we used to know this once. The appeal of early feminist consciousness-raising to 'women's experience' was not a reassuring 'sharing', but a transforming of the meaning of those experiences, from a set of personal failings and deficiencies into a consequence of women's positioning within phallocratic reality. In this sense feminism was never an 'identity politics'. To define 'feminism' as an 'identity' as 'a feminist' is to remain caught up in the ideology of individualism. Since everyone is undoubtedly entitled to define her own 'identity', it stops debate before it even starts, and prevents any possibility of judging on feminist criteria anything said by anyone who identifies as 'a feminist'. This kind of relativism is ideological because it operates in male supremacist interests. By interpreting conflicting claims made in the name of 'feminism' as conflicts between 'feminists', it silences the feminist challenge. If 'feminism' is an 'identity', disagreement becomes personal offence because it is an attack on one's sense of self. In contrast, if feminism is clearly seen to be non-exclusionary, conflicts can hopefully be argued through without offending anyone because no one's identity is at stake. The question is not what women are or have been, but what women might become once we throw off the dead hand of phallocratic history and start seeing ourselves with our own eyes and living our lives in our own interests.

Gender

One way of describing the problem with much academic feminist writing is to characterize it as 'idealism' in the sense in which the term 'ideology' was used by Marx and Engels (1974). Transferring concepts from their original context to another context altogether, in this case from Marxist historical materialism to feminism, needs to be done with caution. None the less there does seem to be a similarity between the problem addressed by Marx and Engels in the middle of the nineteenth century, and a tendency in much academic feminist writing to avoid challenging male domination. Marx and Engels characterized a purportedly 'revolutionary' critique which failed to consider the real-life activity of human beings and their actual situation within capitalist relations of power, as a battle in 'the realm of pure thought'. In doing so, they were not suggesting that philosophers stop thinking and start acting. Rather, they were arguing that a philosophy which purported to give an account of the human condition without acknowledging the power relations in society was not just out of touch with reality, its obliviousness served a purpose. That purpose was to deny the existence of relations of power and disguise them as something neutral and universal. Hence, 'idealism' does not mean working with ideas rather than fomenting revolution on the factory floor or at the barricades. It means working with ideas which are detached from, and fail to acknowledge, social relations of domination. Since the relations of domination opposed by feminism are those of male supremacy, feminist accounts which fail to acknowledge this are idealist in this sense.

So the problem of idealism, in the sense in which I am using the term, is not just a problem of a split between ideas and reality, but of the kind of reality those ideas studiously ignore, that is, the reality of domination. My use of the term takes on its meaning in the context of a critique of ideology. Idealism is one form ideology takes. Although Marx and Engels did not make the distinction, it is a useful one because it makes the point that ideology is not just a matter of ideas, that it reaches into every sphere of human existence, including what is most intimate and commonplace. Idealism is that form of ideology to which academe is especially prone. It refers to the tendency for academic work to divorce ideas from the world of the mundane. That tendency is not inevitable. To the extent that ideas do not reinforce relations of ruling, they cannot be called 'idealist' in this sense, no matter how esoteric, abstract or removed from experience they may be. But because playing with ideas is endlessly fascinating in itself the disconnection can only be resisted through a conscious and deliberate commitment to a moral and political framework which maintains the link between ideas and what those ideas are for. Concepts like 'gender' fail to maintain that link.

In fact the term is meaningless, so much so that it is sometimes difficult to work out exactly what is being said. Linda J. Poole, for example, quotes the following sentence from a text on women and international relations: 'Ideologies can certainly wreak havoc on organizational performance, and gender ideology is no exception.' Poole's comment on this statement is: 'This from a woman who has been an active proponent on the issue of gender advocacies!' (Poole, 1993: 134). Poole seems to have read 'gender ideology' to mean 'feminism'. Her comment implies that the author of the sentence is reneging on her earlier feminism by asserting that the introduction of feminist aims and values could 'wreak havoc on organizational performance'. However, 'gender ideology' could also mean male supremacist ideology, and the sentence could mean that it was the ideologies which favoured men at women's expense and which were inefficient in terms of organizational performance. On the other hand, male supremacist ideology is unlikely to 'wreak havoc' since the organizations are already structured along those lines. So perhaps Poole is right after all, and 'gender ideology' in this context does mean 'feminism'. The point, though, is that it is simply not possible to decide.

The meaninglessness of the term 'gender' is a consequence both of the euphemistic role it plays within academic feminism (and the media, and wherever the word 'sex' would do instead), and of the incoherence of its origins. 'Gender' softens the harsh, uncompromising ring of 'male domination'. It provides the appearance of a subject-matter while at the same time enabling the real problems to be avoided. Originally it was set up in opposition to 'sex', to stress the point that the differences between the sexes are socially constructed, not natural. But the 'sex/gender' distinction does not challenge the 'society/nature' opposition – it remains wholly within it. If 'the social' is 'gender', and 'sex' is something other than 'gender', then sex is something other than social. If it is not social, then all that is left is the residual category of 'the natural', and 'sex' remains as 'natural' as it ever was. As a consequence the 'sex/gender' distinction does not disrupt and unsettle the 'society/nature' opposition, but reinforces it because it is the same kind of distinction.

I have argued elsewhere that it functions as a depoliticizing strategy by separating 'sex differences' out from the domain of the social and locating them in 'biology'. Since, as everyone knows, biology does not cause sex differences, this ploy allows the social construction of 'sex differences' to remain unexamined. The substitution of 'gender' for 'sex' places the debate at two removes from the actual relations of power challenged by feminism. It prevents the discussion of sex differences by extracting them from the realm of the social and allocating them to 'biology'; and by preventing discussion of sex 'differences', it prevents discussion of that crucial site for the investigation of male supremacist relations of power – the maintenance of sex 'differences' as they are currently constituted, and of compulsory heterosexuality as the mechanism for managing women's consent to their subordination to men (Thompson, 1991: 168–76; see also Gatens, 1983). But since feminism is a politics it is already concerned with the level of the social, the moral and the political. There is no need for 'gender' since the feminist concern with sex is already moral and political, and hence a social, not a 'biological', concern (whatever that might be outside the realm of the social).

Jane Flax says that 'The single most important advance in and result of feminist theories and practices is that the existence of gender has been problematized' (Flax, 1990: 21). Although she does not say what 'gender' is, it is clear that it is not male domination. She sees 'male dominance' as merely one form of 'gender relations', and as a hindrance to the adequate investigation of those relations. The nature of 'gender relations' has been 'obscured' by the existence of male dominance, she says (pp. 22–4). But this is idealist in the sense described above. (It also bears a striking similarity to the HWAG's account of 'sexism' discussed above.) It extracts 'gender relations' from the social conditions of male supremacy within which the relations between the sexes are currently structured, and posits a 'really real' of 'gender relations' outside the only terms within which they are knowable. If 'gender relations' are not those we are acquainted with at present, what are they and how can we know them? It may be that what Flax is trying to say is that relations between the sexes ought not to be structured in terms of male dominance, and that feminism needs to allow for that possibility. But unless male domination can be identified, it cannot be challenged and opposed. Far from 'obscuring' the nature of the relations between the sexes, identifying male domination clarifies what feminism is struggling against. It is *only* feminism's focus on the problematic of male domination which allows us to understand what is at stake.

On another occasion Flax appears to be defining 'gender' in terms of any social location at all. She tells us that there are 'at least three dimensions' to 'gender'. The first dimension is that 'gender' is 'a social relationship' and 'a form of power … [which] affects our theories and practices of justice'. But the only social categories she mentions in this context of justice are 'race and economic status'. Throughout her discussion of the other two dimensions of 'gender' – as 'a category of thought', and as 'a central constituting element in each person's sense of self and … of what it means to be a person' – there is no mention of the two sexes, women and men. It is not until the very end of the discussion, when she criticizes the idea of 'sex roles', that we are given any hint that 'gender' might be connected to the existence of two sexes (pp. 25–6). She makes no mention of the fact that feminism's concern with justice involves first and foremost justice for women, including women located within the dominating hierarchies of race and class, but primarily women as women assigned the subordinate role in the dominating hierarchy of sex. On this account, 'gender' means 'race' and 'class' *before* it means 'sex'.

This defining of 'gender' in terms of any social location at all is a consequence of detaching it from its original referent, 'sex'. But this seeming ability of 'gender' to be unhooked from 'sex' leaves 'sex' still immersed in biology as its only source of truth. As Ann Oakley once argued (Oakley, 1972), the cultural construction which is 'gender' is merely superficial, a matter of 'prejudice' (p. 16), of 'distortion' and '*apparent* differences' (p. 103 – emphasis added), 'simply ... the beliefs people hold' (p. 189), something that is 'learned' (p. 173) and hence can be unlearned. Biology, on the other hand, is 'fundamental' (p. 46). Oakley's account is replete with appeals to biology. To be entirely accurate, it must be said that she appeals to biology only when biology looks as though it substantiates her argument that there are no important differences between the sexes. She needs to argue against the existence of sex differences because she confounds 'difference' with inequality and inferiority. She wants to demonstrate that women are not 'really' unequal and inferior to men because they are not different. But wherever it is possible to do so, it is biology which is used to demonstrate the truth of that lack of difference.

The proponents of 'gender' deal with this ongoing subterranean connection between biology and truth by attempting to abandon any claims to truth. But the price of any such attempts is that same incoherence with which the 'sex/gender' distinction began. 'Gender is (a) representation',[3] says Teresa de Lauretis (1987: 3). 'The "real" and the "sexually factic" are phantasmatic constructions – illusions of substance', says Judith Butler (1990: 146). But words like 'representation', 'phantasmatic', 'illusion' only have meaning in terms of their opposites. To say that something is a representation is at the same time to say that there is something else it is a representation of; to say that something is a phantasm entails that there be something else which is real; and to say that something is illusion logically requires something else which is true. Otherwise, what is being implied – that everything is representation, phantasmatic or illusion? In that case it would make as much sense to say that everything is real, although it would not make any more sense, since the concept of the real also implies its opposite. The words only gain their meaning from the distinctions they make. If no distinctions are being made, why use these words rather than their opposites? But, of course, a distinction *is* being made. It is the same distinction which has bedevilled the detachment of 'sex' from 'gender' from the beginning, the separation of the 'biological' from the 'social', and the characterizing of the 'social' as in some way unreal. But if there is an unreal, there is also a real. Since it is biology which is society's other in this discourse of 'gender', it is biology which is real in the face of the unreality which is society. That this is so, is clearly, although inadvertently, stated by de Lauretis, when she says that 'gender is not sex, [which is] a state of nature' (de Lauretis, 1987: 5). So if 'gender' is a representation, then what 'gender' is not (namely sex, a state of nature) is also not a representation, but the original reality which 'gender' is a representation of.

Although de Lauretis appeared to be unaware of these implications, Judith Butler explicitly attempted to deal with them. She argued that gender is not to culture as sex is to nature; gender is also [*sic*] the discursive/ cultural means by which 'sexed nature' or 'a natural sex' is produced and established as 'prediscursive', prior to culture, a politically neutral surface *on which* culture acts. ... This production of sex *as* the prediscursive ought to be understood as the effect of the apparatus of cultural construction designated by *gender*. (Butler, 1990: 7 – her emphases)

In arguing that 'sex' is itself a social construct, and hence not natural or biological at all in so far as it is of concern to feminism, Butler is perfectly correct. But if that is the case, if sex is already social, what part is played by the term 'gender'? What does using 'gender' add, that is not already contained in 'sex' viewed from a feminist standpoint? According to Butler, 'gender' is an 'apparatus of cultural construction' which purveys 'sex' as 'natural'. But that can be said without recourse to 'gender', namely, 'sex is a social construction which presents itself as natural'. To say it like that is far more direct and challenging to conventional wisdom than interpolating 'gender' between sex and its social construction. It is after all *sex* which is the social construct, and not something other than sex. Using a different word, 'gender', for the social construct, implies that sex is something other than the social construct.

Butler herself is at least partly aware of this problem. She says: 'If the immutable character of sex is contested, perhaps this construct called "sex" is as culturally constructed as gender; indeed, perhaps it was always already gender, with the consequence that the distinction between sex and gender turns out to be no distinction at all' (p. 7). But she does not take the next step in the argument and dispense with the word 'gender', to focus instead on sex and its discontents. Retaining 'sex' and rejecting 'gender' would not fit in with her purpose, which is to open up a theoretical space within what she sees as feminism, for 'those "incoherent" or "discontinuous" gendered beings who appear to be persons but who fail to conform to the gendered norms of cultural intelligibility by which persons are defined ... [and whose] persistence and proliferation ... open up within the very terms of that matrix of intelligibility rival and subversive matrices of gender disorder' (p. 17). The examples she mentions in her text of such 'gender disorder' are lesbians, especially those who 'destabilize' and 'displace' the heterosexual norms of masculinity and femininity through 'butch/femme' role play (p. 123), Foucault's hermaphrodite Herculine Barbin, male homosexuality (pp. 131–2), and drag and cross-dressing (both male, although she does not say so) (p. 137). The term 'gender' is perfect for this purpose just because of its incoherence and idealism. Because it has no definite meaning, and because it is detached from the only referent that makes any sense, namely sex, it can take on any meaning at all. It is much more difficult to interpret 'sex' as 'a multiple interpretation', as 'a free-floating artifice', as 'a shifting phenomenon', as 'a complexity whose totality is permanently deferred, never fully what it is at any given juncture in time', as 'fictive', 'phantasmatic' and 'illusory'. 'Sex' remains too tied in with its ordinary meanings of male and female, and heterosexual desire and activity, and hence too close to those traditional sites of male supremacy.

Butler is not concerned to identify the ways in which sex is constructed under male supremacist conditions, with the aim of challenging, resisting, refusing and changing those conditions. On the contrary, she regards such an enterprise as impossible. 'There is no radical repudiation of a culturally constructed sexuality', she says. She agrees with what she refers to as 'the pro-sexuality movement within feminist theory and practice' that 'sexuality is always constructed within the terms of discourse and power'. The most we can expect to accomplish by way of 'subversion' is 'how to acknowledge and "do" the construction one is invariably in'. The only political option available involves 'possibilities of doing gender [which] repeat and displace through hyperbole, dissonance, internal confusion, and proliferation the very constructs by which they are mobilized' (pp. 30–1).

She herself does not believe in the 'invariability' of 'gender', since she is at some pains to argue that 'gender' is 'choice', and that it is possible to engage in 'the exercise of gender freedom' (Butler, 1987: 131, 132). But she never examines what is involved in this question of 'choice'. The goodness of 'choice' is self-evident, and the more the better because it allows more freedom. But she never asks what this freedom is for, and her account closes off any possibility of identifying some choices as bad. This libertarian stance enables her to avoid addressing the ethical issues raised by feminism's exposure of sex as socially constructed under male supremacist conditions. Although she herself would presumably not want to take a morally neutral stance in relation to the worst forms of male sexual behaviour, on her account such evils as male sexual abuse of children, rape, sexual harassment, prostitution, pornography, are nothing more than 'choices'. She does not, of course, say so. She simply avoids discussing these issues.

Martha Nussbaum concludes that Butler's argument 'collaborates with evil' because of the absence of an explicitly ethical stance on questions of social justice and human dignity, an absence which leaves 'a void at the heart of [her] notion of politics' (Nussbaum, 1999: 9), and because it can only recommend political quiescence in the face of obvious and pressing social wrongs (p. 12). While I would prefer to say that Butler's account is complicit with domination, I agree with Nussbaum that political defeatism is a consequence of Butler's theoretical schema. She insists that because we are socially constituted there is nothing very much we can do about oppressive social structures, except reenact them as parody while continuing to embrace them as our own sense of identity. In her later work, according to Nussbaum, Butler argues that the identities conferred on us by institutionalized oppression are not only inevitable and beyond the reach of any political resistance whatsoever, they are a positive good: '"because a certain narcissism takes hold of any term that confers existence, I am led to embrace the terms that injure me because they constitute me socially"' (quoted on p. 9). Although Nussbaum does not mention this, Butler is quite correct in saying that the injuries of social domination constitute the identities of those it holds in subjection. Where Butler is wrong is in her insistence that this is irreparable and must be eagerly accepted with pleasure and joy. To the extent that my sexual desire, for example, motivates me to harm myself or others, I am not doomed to endlessly repeat it. I can refuse to act on it, and if that means that I am thereby deprived of immediate sexual pleasure, then so be it. I may in fact find pleasure in divesting myself of complicity with something I find detestable, a pleasure which may lack the excitement of sexual degradation, but which provides compensations in my feeling that I am taking control of my own emotional life. Nussbaum locates Butler's work within the context of 'a new, disquieting trend' in feminist theory, a trend which demonstrates a marked obliviousness to 'the real situation of real women', in favour of 'academic publications of lofty obscurity and disdainful abstractness' (p. 2).[4] The term 'gender' is central to that disquieting trend.

There are some feminist theorists who use the word 'gender', and who explicitly reject the separation between 'biology' and 'society', and have no qualms about identifying male domination. But the term still generates confusion. Miriam M. Johnson uses 'gender' to refer to 'one's civil status as male or female', while reserving the word 'sex' to refer to 'genital erotic activity (sex in bed)' (Johnson, 1988: 202).[5] Johnson uses this distinction between 'sex' as sexual activity and 'gender' as social role, in order to avoid what she sees as the dominant tendency to define 'gender' in terms of 'sex'. She wants to avoid the assumption that the inequalities in the social situations of women and men are somehow caused by the male dominant/female submissive differences between male and female sexuality. She says: 'Using the word *sex* to describe sexual activity and the difference between males and females attests to the degree to which gender has been conflated with sex' (p. 220). The problem with this conflation, as Johnson sees it, is that women have been defined in terms of femininity, passivity and submission, and men in terms of masculinity, dominance and aggression, because that is the way it happens in bed. 'Separating gender from sex', she says, 'helps to break up this assumption.' She argues that the influence is the other way around, that male and female sexuality are different because the social roles of women and men are different and unequal. It is not the case that sexual activity, defined in this way, is definitive of what she calls 'gender'. On the contrary, it is 'gender', defined as male dominance and female submission, which has been reflected in the differences between female and male sexuality.

But although she is correct in this, separating 'sex' from 'gender' merely confuses the issue. Once again, if 'gender' refers to the social, then 'sex' must refer to something else. But heterosexual sex is also social. It is part of the social definition of female and male, not something other than it. The distinction remains an idealist solution, that is, it is a distinction in thought, not in the actual social relations of male power. Merely saying something is not so will not make it go away. And there is the danger that making the verbal distinction will mask the feminist perception of the ongoing social reality.

'Gender' ought to be expunged from the feminist vocabulary, unless it is confined to its original grammatical and linguistic context. *Words* have gender, *people* have sex in both senses of the word, in the sense that there are two sexes, and in the sense of sexual desire and activity. That they are usually confused, as Johnson pointed out, is a consequence of the heterosexual hegemony – sexuality happens because there are two sexes, that is, sex is always heterosexual. Substituting 'gender' for sex compounds the confusion because it evades the necessity for disentangling it. More importantly, because in most of its usages 'gender' is meaningless, it can take on any meaning at all, including anti-feminist ones. By being detached from its ordinary language referent 'sex', it floats freely in a discursive space far removed from the actual social relations of male supremacy. It is politically unlocatable. The frequency with which this happens gives rise to the suspicion that that is what has been intended all along.

Dichotomies

Another way of designating the problem addressed by feminism is through a critique of 'dichotomies' (or 'binary oppositions' or 'dualisms'). Such criticisms do recognize a hierarchical relation between the two terms whereby one term is always valued over the other, as well as locating the valued term with the male and the devalued one with the female. But they tend towards idealism to the extent that they see the oppositional logic as the basic problem generating the differential valuations of men and women, rather than seeing that logic as itself a consequence of the social relations of male supremacy.

Moira Gatens, for example, summarizes her overview of some of the ways philosophy has conceived of women as follows:

> In the introduction, it was suggested that the mind/body, reason/passion and nature/culture dichotomies interact with the male/female dichotomy in extremely complex ways, often prejudicial to women. What has been shown in the ensuing chapters is the way that these dichotomies function in the work of particular philosophers and the consequences of this functioning for their views on sexual difference. It has become apparent in the course of this analysis that in contemporary thought it is the private/public distinction which organizes these dualisms and gives them their distinctively sexually specific character. (Gatens, 1991: 122)

Despite her frequent insights into the ways in which the 'human' norm is purveyed as only male, by substituting 'dichotomies' organized around the 'private/public distinction' for the explicit acknowledgement of male supremacist relations of ruling, she reduces men's rule to an effect of something more basic. In this account, the feminist political task is not to mount a direct challenge to male domination. Rather, it becomes a matter of working towards 'the "break[ing] down" of the coherence of Western culture' in order that it may be 'reassembl[ed] in a more viable and polyvalent form' (p. 121 – first interpolation in the original). The problem to be addressed is the 'coherence of Western culture', and the solution is to break this down in the interests of 'polyvalence'. Whatever this might mean, it involves no reference to the actual relations of power within which women are subjected, nor to the possibility of a new world for women free of male definition and control.

Seyla Benhabib and Drucilla Cornell also interpret feminist politics in terms of 'binary oppositions' (and 'gender'). They ask:

> where do we go beyond the politics of gender? To a radical transcendence of the logic of binary oppositions altogether or to a utopian realization of forms of otherness, immanent in present psychosexual arrangements, but currently frozen within the confines of rigid genderized thinking? (Benhabib and Cornell, 1987: 15)

The problem here is the 'opposition' itself and its 'rigidity', not the fact that that 'opposition' (between the sexes) constructs the male as the norm, as the only 'human' subject, at the expense of any interests females might have in our own human status. But it is not the fact that the differences between the sexes are 'rigid' or even 'opposed' that is the main problem for feminism, but the fact that the 'differences' encode and enforce male supremacy (MacKinnon, 1990). The feminist task, then, is not to shatter and fragment the grand dichotomy of male and female into a multiplicity of fluid and shifting 'genders', 'sexualities', 'identities' or 'forms of otherness' (other than whom?), but to continue to oppose male domination, however and wherever it manifests itself, in the interests of a female human status which is not defined at the expense of anyone at all.

Notes

1 Before she discussed socialist feminist writings, Beechey expressed some disquiet at the possibility that she might be being 'unfair to particular writers' by confining her discussion to an 'incomplete survey', instead of providing 'a comprehensive review of the Marxist feminist literature' (1979: 72). She did not express any such disquiet at the incompleteness of her review of radical feminist literature.

2 Bourdieu later expanded this paper into a book (Bourdieu, 1998).

3 The parenthetical 'a' is not meant to imply the first of a series, to be followed by 'b', 'c', 'd', etc. It signals that the sentence is actually two sentences compressed into one – 'Gender is representation' and 'Gender is a representation.'

4 Nussbaum's review evoked a number of protests (*The New Republic*, 1999). But even those sympathetic to Butler's work have been known to express many of the same concerns as Nussbaum. Seyla Benhabib, who was one of those who protested at Nussbaum's review, has said: 'in *Gender Trouble* at least, Butler subscribes to an overly constructivist view of selfhood and agency that leaves little room for explaining the possibilities of creativity and resistance' (Benhabib, 1999: p. 2 of 17).

5 Catharine MacKinnon makes the same kind of distinction (MacKinnon, 1987, 1991: xiii). She says that she tends to use the words 'sex' and 'gender' interchangeably, since she does not agree with the distinction between 'biology' and 'society' entailed in the 'sex / gender' distinction. I prefer not to use the word 'gender' at all because of its apolitical connotations.

6 'Difference'

As Hester Eisenstein has pointed out, the feminist concept of 'difference' has two aspects to it: differences between the sexes, and differences between and among women. Both aspects have been consistent preoccupations of 'second-wave' feminism. That does not mean, however, that 'the theme of "difference" has been integral to modern feminist thought', as Eisenstein goes on to assert (Eisenstein, 1985: xv; see also Eisenstein, 1984: *passim*). On the contrary, far from being 'integral' to feminism, the concept of 'difference' has too often functioned as a diversionary tactic. Whether the focus is on differences between the sexes, or on differences between and among women, male domination tends to be accorded a subsidiary status or ignored altogether.

In the case of differences between the sexes, male domination (when it is acknowledged) is usually presented as a secondary formation, or euphemistically designated 'sexual' or 'gender inequality' or 'women's inequality'. Given that feminist debates about sex differences have tended to confound difference with inequality,[1] an initial feminist response was to argue those differences away (Oakley, 1972). A more recent response was to grant a limited and strategic value to women's differences from men, because failure to acknowledge female specificity, biological or social, sometimes works against women's interests (Rhode, 1990).

In the case of differences between and among women, acknowledgement of male domination tends to be displaced in favour of race and/or class and to drop out of the analysis altogether. Invidious distinctions between women are attributed to feminism or to the attitudes and behaviour of (usually unidentified) 'white middle-class feminists', and the origin of those distinctions in hierarchies established among men is ignored. In the most general sense, 'difference' functions, like 'gender', as a euphemism to avoid naming the main enemy, male domination.

Differences between the Sexes

The problem with focusing feminist attention on differences between the sexes has already been adequately criticized in the literature (Jaggar, 1990; MacKinnon, 1987, 1990). As Catharine MacKinnon in particular has pointed out, whether women are asserted to be 'the same as' or 'different from' men, the male remains the norm against which women are measured. Keeping the debate at the level of 'sex differences' serves the purpose of avoiding the question of the systematic subordination of women to men. Once this is recognized, the question of whether women are 'the same as' or 'different from' men becomes irrelevant. Women can be 'the same as' men, and still be subordinated. 'Exceptional' women can be isolated from other women to supply a token female representation in hierarchical positions normally reserved for men, while those positions continue to function in the interests of men and against the interests of women. And although women's 'difference from' men is usually justification for women's subordination, it can also be a source of women-only power and identification.

I have identified three contexts within which the question of differences between the sexes has been discussed within 'second-wave' feminism, the first two of which I mention only briefly here. The first of these debates originated in psychology, with token excursions into sociology, anthropology, primatology, ethology, endocrinology and the medical model in general. There is a fairly extensive literature on the subject, but it has limited use for feminist theorizing because it tends to be empiricist and positivist. It assumes unquestioningly that sex differences are objective matters of fact discoverable through the purportedly value-free methods of psychological testing, some of which involve only animals and not human beings at all (e.g. Maccoby and Jacklin, 1974). In its commitment to 'objectivity', it fails to address the values which are an inherent part of relations between the sexes, a failure which drains its investigations of meaning. Refusing to address value questions directly within the inherently moral arena of human interactions does not abolish moral judgements. It merely ensures that those moral judgements which do structure and inform the research will be those of the status quo, of the world-taken-for-granted which feminism is challenging. Painstaking and detailed though much of this work was, it was ultimately pointless because it failed to ask recognizably human questions about sex differences.

The second context in which discussion of sex 'differences' is supposedly to be found is what has been called 'French feminism'. But this designation covers such a large and disparate group of theorists that it is impossible to discuss them under a single heading. Since any attempt to do so must fail, given the intricacies and sheer volume of these works, I mention them only in passing.[2]

Feminist Object Relations Theory

The third context is feminist object relations theory (Benjamin, 1989; Chodorow, 1978, 1989; Dinnerstein, 1976; Keller, 1985). Although there are a number of problems with the theory so far, it is more fruitful for feminist theorizing than the positivistic approach which treats sex differences as empirical data. The kinds of 'sex differences' feminist object relations theory exposes – the relational, caring, nurturing female, and the detached, contemptuous, masculine individual – are the kinds of differences which might be expected given current conditions of male domination. Its emphasis on infancy and early childhood makes it one of the few social theories which does not assume that we enter social relationships as fully formed adults. And it does at least attempt to challenge the male supremacist demand that only women mother, even if it does not take that challenge far enough.

It is already a partial acknowledgement of male domination, in that it is an account of social inequalities that are sexed (even if it does call them 'gender'). Although its critique of masculinity does not go deeply enough, it does have one. Nancy Chodorow tells us that men's 'nurturant capacities and needs have been systematically curtailed and repressed', that men 'have tended to repress their affective relational needs' (Chodorow, 1978: 7, 199). Men are incapable of relating to women, she says, because of men's intense ambivalence towards women: 'men defend themselves against the threat posed by love ... demanding of women what men are at the same time afraid of receiving' (pp. 196, 199). She describes men's feelings towards women in terms of contempt, disparagement and devaluation on the one hand, and resentment, fear and dread on the other. She also says that men are incapable of relating to other men, because their 'training for masculinity and repression of affective relational needs, and their primary non-emotional and impersonal relationships in the public world make deep primary relationships with other men hard to come by' (p. 196), and because they tend 'to develop ties based more on categorical and abstract role expectations' (p. 199). Moreover, they are incapable of relating to children because 'the relational basis for mothering is ... inhibited in men, who experience themselves as more separate and distinct from others' (p. 207).

Not only did Chodorow not draw out the implications of her own descriptions of masculinity, she held that current arrangements of mothering by women were responsible for reproducing it. But she did not tell us how mothering by women reproduced masculinity, apart from references to the need for boys to separate from their mothers. Neither did she tell us why misogyny and contempt for women are so integral a part of the masculine psyche. On the one occasion where she attempted to do so, she omitted the crux of the matter. She said, quoting Freud, that 'A boy's struggle to free himself from his mother and become masculine generates "the contempt felt by men for a sex which is the lesser"'[3] (Chodorow, 1978: 182). But it is not the boy's struggle which generates the contempt, but rather the contempt which provides the motivating force for the struggle. Or rather, because children of both sexes grow out of the helplessness and dependency of infancy, it is contempt which provides the extra impetus for the male under male supremacist conditions. Chodorow got it the wrong way round because she left out the key step in the process, the 'threat of castration'. It is this threat which Freud said 'leads to two reactions, which ... permanently determine the boy's relations to women: horror of the mutilated creature or triumphant contempt for her' (Freud, 1977a: 336). On Freud's account, the devaluation of women is a direct consequence of the female lack of the penis. Freud was wrong in the way he characterized the meaning and value of the penis. 'Penis-envy' and the devaluing of those who lack penises are 'secondary formations' (to use his own terminology), the result of the male supremacist culture's glorification of the phallus – penis-possession as the symbol of 'human' status – which Freud himself never questioned. None the less, his account does supply us with the reason for misogyny and contempt for women. Within those male supremacist terms so clearly exposed by Freud, women are contemptible because we lack penises. Masculinity is reproduced through the over-valuation of penis-possession. It depends on contempt for and hatred of the female, because to acknowledge the humanity of women would be to render the penis meaningless as the symbol of 'human' status. Male castration anxiety is a dread of the loss of meaning of penis-possession, a loss which the very existence of women constantly threatens. The masculine psyche develops at the expense of a human status for women, and must guard itself against the 'horror' of human beings who lack the necessary symbol.

The extent to which men are incapable of human relationships is exactly the extent to which the penis-as-phallus comes between the male self and others, and blocks the possibility of recognizing others as fully human individuals lacking nothing. Masculinity renders men incapable of the mutual recognition necessary for reaching out to others when penis-possession stands as a barrier between the male self and others. Men are unable to relate to women when men are complicit with the phallocratic requirement that women be treated as non-human. They are unable to relate to each other if their 'humanity' is already impaired by that same phallocratic requirement. By acquiring their 'human' status by denying it to women, men render themselves unfit for any genuine human interaction. In treating women as things, they fetishize themselves and each other into objects whose worth is measured by positions on hierarchies of extraneous criteria, of which the two most obvious are race and class. By the same token, women are more able to involve themselves in human relationships because they are more capable of recognizing the humanity of others. It is not because women are inherently more nurturant, caring or loving than men, but because women do not have any masculinity to defend at others' expense. Women, not having penises, have less at stake in defending the meanings and values of penis-possession,[4] and hence lack the chief barrier to relating to others as unique and irreplaceable ends in themselves. By deliberately abandoning the original Freudian insight into the hypervaluation of penis-possession, feminist object relations theory has rejected the key insight into the meaning of masculinity.

Feminist object relations theory gives an inadequate account of sex 'differences' because it fails to ask the right questions in the first place. It is agreed that there is a 'difference' between mother and male infant. It is in fact the crux of the argument. In Nancy Chodorow's account, males are incapable of mothering because they are so 'different' from mother, and mothering is reproduced in females because they are 'the same' as mother. In Jessica Benjamin's account, women lack subjectivity because they are mothered by women who lack subjectivity and girls are 'the same' as their mothers, while men are subjects in their own right because as boys they are 'different' from their mothers and can identify with their fathers (Benjamin, 1989). But the theory never asks how the distinction is noted. What counts as male and female? What *is* the 'difference' which establishes and maintains the acculturation process which makes infants into sexed individuals? In their understandable haste to disassociate themselves from 'penis envy', feminist object relations theorists move too far away from Freud, and abandon his important insights (misnamed though they were) into the meaning of penis-possession. To assert, as Benjamin does, that 'it is not anatomy ... that explains women's "lack"' (p. 86), is to extract 'anatomy' from the social order within which it acquires meaning and value. The lack of female subjectivity which Benjamin calls 'a "fault line" in female development' (p. 78) does not originate with women, although it manifests itself in women's lives, but with a male supremacist culture which refuses to allow women a fully human status because they do not possess the prized anatomical organ. To locate the 'fault line' with women is to fail to see that the penis is already glorified as the sign of sexual difference, as the marker of a valued presence and a contemptible absence, as that which sets the process in train and which structures the cultural context into which each individual is born. Unless the phallus is situated at the centre of sexual domination, its role as the justification for male domination cannot be exposed.

Feminist object relations theory is also flawed by its tendency to reverse the logic of the social 'causation' involved. By locating the 'causes' of male domination in the activities and developmental processes of individuals in familial environments, rather than interpreting those familial environments as structured and made meaningful by the social system which is male domination, the theory gets it the wrong way round. Unless familial arrangements are identified as generated by the requirements of present historical conditions of male supremacy, they tend to assume an unwarranted explanatory importance, as the 'cause',[5] rather than as a consequence, of the social arrangements of male supremacy. One aspect of current social arrangements – usually mothering by women – is made responsible for the whole of the 'society' which is male supremacy. While mothering by women is a necessary prerequisite for the maintenance of the social relationships of male supremacy, that is not because it causes those social relationships, but because mothering by women is what is required if men are to continue to feel justified in demanding of women selfless devotion to male interests, needs, projects and desires, and if women are to continue to acquiesce in those requirements.

Jessica Benjamin's task was to elucidate the failure of mutual recognition between the sexes within 'our culture' under conditions of 'gender' domination. Her purpose was to show how and why the balance between assertion of the self and recognition of the other breaks down into relationships of domination and subordination. Like Chodorow's, her account, too, attempted to explain society ('our culture') in terms of one of its parts. Her focus on familial relationships reads as an argument to the effect that 'domination' originates within families, and is then taken out into the wider society, where it persists because individuals are already structured that way. As she herself says, she aims to 'show how the structure of domination can be traced from the relationship between mother and infant into adult eroticism, from the earliest awareness of the difference between mother and father to the global images of male and female in the culture' (Benjamin, 1989: 8). On another occasion she says that she 'will offer some observations on how the split that constitutes gender polarity is replicated in intellectual and social life, and how it eliminates the possibilities of mutual recognition in society as a whole' (p. 184). On Benjamin's account, the 'family' is not only the 'basic unit' of society, it structures the whole of it. Her failure to characterize as male supremacist the 'culture' within which dominant and submissive individuals are constituted, means that that 'culture' is reduced to an epiphenomenon of the family. Society is the family writ large.

This is a consequence of her refusal to locate the phallus at the centre of the meanings and values of male supremacy. She tells us that it is 'the father – not the phallus – [which] is the locus of power' (Benjamin, 1989: 96). The father represents access to the wonderful, exciting world outside the mother–infant relationship, for both sexes. But whereas he accepts his son's identification with him, and encourages the boy's striving for independence and activity, he rejects his daughter's and withdraws from her. As a consequence, daughters are pushed back to their mothers, where they have no possibility of developing a sense of self because the only avenue to individuation is blocked. Benjamin does not ask how it is that fathers (and mothers and others) distinguish between sons and daughters. Yet this is surely the crucial question. In infancy there is only one discernible difference between females and males – sex. And the distinguishing mark of sex is the presence or absence of the penis, a sign which has been recognized and whose significance has been operative since birth. The father recognizes his son as a penis-bearer with the potential for autonomous subjecthood like himself, and refuses to recognize his daughter because she lacks that symbol of identity, in the sense both of likeness to him and of selfhood. But it is not the father's fatherhood with which the boy identifies, and the girl tries to, but his maleness. Because of this insistence on the centrality of the father rather than the phallus in the establishment of psychic patterns of domination, the only adult males who appear in Benjamin's account are fathers (and sometimes husbands, who are, however, also called 'fathers' because of the significance for the children of their dominant position in relation to the mother). Fathers, in terms of Benjamin's analysis, are not men. Or rather, by avoiding the question of phallic supremacy, her analysis provides us with no account of fathers as men.

None the less, Benjamin's account of what is already involved in mother–infant relationships despite male supremacy, is a welcome antidote to certain currently popular theories which portray the mother–infant couple as an undifferentiated, 'symbiotic' unity into which the phallus must intervene in order to wrench the child into the symbolic order. As Benjamin puts it in her critical comment on this aspect of the work of the child analyst, Margaret Mahler:

> The problem with this formulation [of an initial unity] is the idea of a separation from oneness; it contains the implicit assumption that we grow *out of* relationships rather than becoming more active and sovereign *within* them, that we start in a state of dual oneness and wind up in a state of singular oneness ... the issue is not only how we separate from oneness, but also how we connect to and recognise others; the issue is not how we become free of the other, but how we actively engage and make ourselves known in relationship to the other. (Benjamin, 1989: 18 – her emphasis)

Benjamin argues that the infant is active in relation to the mother from birth. The baby can respond to soothing and holding or resist, co-operate or turn away, focus on the mother's face, react to the mother's voice, and (although Benjamin does not mention this) smile, during the first few weeks of life. The possibility of mutual recognition, of 'emotional attunement, mutual influence, affective mutuality, sharing states of mind' (p. 16) between mother and infant is there from the beginning. The mother–infant relationship is one already capable of mutual recognition. Infants are 'active participants who help shape the responses of their environment, and "create" their own objects ... the infant's capacity to relate to the world is incipiently present at birth and develops all along' (pp. 16, 17); and 'real mothers in our culture, for better or worse, devote most of their energy to fostering independence' (p. 152).

The implication of Benjamin's argument concerning 'the first bond' (between mother and child) is that it is *only* the relationship between mother and child which holds the potential for generating mutual recognition, and that the father's intervention irrevocably destroys the possibility of mutuality between the sexes, at least under present conditions and to the extent that adult individuals do not resist the dominant trend. The father's intrusion ruptures, not a solipsistic 'oneness', not an undifferentiated unity, but a mutuality, a flexible balance of separation and connection responsive to the needs and desires of both mother and infant, a reciprocity of give and take which is already present. Mothers and infants, it would seem, do very well all by themselves. As Benjamin herself says: 'if ... we believe that infants take pleasure in interpersonal connection and are motivated by curiosity and responsiveness to the outside world, we need not agree to the idea that human beings must be pulled by their fathers away from maternal bliss into a reality they resent' (p. 174).

What Benjamin's account suggests (although she herself does not draw out the implication) is that women cannot be left alone to get on with it if male supremacy is to be maintained. Women are not to be trusted to be whole-hearted in the male cause. They must not be left to raise children, especially male children, without intervention. Once the child starts reaching out to the world, the disruptive intrusion of the father becomes necessary. Not, however, as a father, either literally or symbolically, nor merely as 'the first outsider ... represent[ing] the principle of freedom as denial of dependency' (p. 221), as Benjamin puts it, but as the nearest significant adult male. Single mothers of sons are gravely cautioned about the dire consequences for their sons' masculinity of the absence of 'male role models'. The small male must be provided with a model of what he can aspire to, one who is personally present and who actively intervenes to show the boy the kind of place waiting for him once he has repudiated the world of the feminine. He has his own little symbol of all that he is heir to, but it *is* little and mother is still powerful, loving, nurturant and needed. The small female must start her lessons in heterosexuality. She must learn that full human status is not her birthright, and that her only access to it is second-rate and via subordination to those who bear its anatomical symbol. Ideally, she should learn to love it. But given the prevalence of father–daughter incest, and its social condonation by way of silence and denial, love is obviously not a prerequisite for the female's training in heterosexual desire. Indeed, if the female is to be trained in sexual subservience, then sexual violence from an early age would seem to be entirely functional for that training process.

In light of this analysis, the solution to whatever problems might be connected with women's mothering is not shared 'parenting', as feminist object relations theory recommends, at least not in the foreseeable future. Given that the theory itself points out the unlikelihood of fathers 'mothering' to the same extent that women do, it is not clear how it might be brought about. If current arrangements of mothering render males more or less incapable of human relationships, and if that incapability is not just an unwillingness, but is an intrinsic aspect of the masculine sense of self, deeply embedded in unconscious processes of fear and desire, hatred and contempt, then male 'mothering' will not become a social norm simply through conscious decision and rational choice on the part of men. The very meaning of masculinity itself must change. It must be divested of its contempt for and dread of the female (and of the reverence and adoration which serve as a superficial gloss masking the actual relations of power), of its competitiveness, aggression, violence and addiction to hierarchy, and of its eroticized obsession with penis-possession, in favour of a genuine humanity which excludes no one from human rights and dignities.

Until and unless that happens, it is dangerous to suggest that men take on the care of infants and small children. Even if they were to do so in any numbers, a large 'if' given the great hurdle of male reluctance, at the very least they would simply dominate 'mothering' at the expense of women, just as they dominate everything else. But there is an even greater danger involved as long as the penis continues to function as the symbol of the only 'human' status allowed, and that is male sexual abuse of children. It is foolhardy to recommend that men have greater access to children, unless the glorification of penis-possession has first been acknowledged and overcome.[6] What must also be overcome is the demand for self-abnegation placed on women by the kind of mothering required under conditions of male supremacy. Instead of focusing yet again on men, what is needed is support for the women who already mother, especially those women who are mothering without men, since this is already a challenge to male control of mothering. If those mothering arrangements are to be changed in the interests of everyone, social resources, both material (such as adequate income and child-care) and intangible (such as respect), need to be provided in abundance for the women who already mother.

As should be obvious by now, it is not feminist object relations theory as it currently stands that I find fruitful for feminist theory, but the role it serves as an accessible way into certain issues of vital importance to feminism. Although it refuses to acknowledge the phallus, explicitly in Benjamin's case, the gap that refusal leaves is marked by its failure to account for male supremacist relations of ruling. It does set up a logic of causes, and then proceed to get the determinants the wrong way round by arguing that the structure of the family determines 'our culture', rather than regarding a particular family formation as a requirement of more systemic relations of power. But it also brings out into the open the fact that it is women who mother, and challenges the denial and suppression to which that surely unremarkable fact is subjected under male supremacist conditions. And it insists that sex 'differences' are neither deliberately imposed nor consciously adopted, but result from processes originally beyond the control and awareness of the immature psyche of the helpless and dependent little individuals we all are to begin with. As Chodorow put it: 'The capacities and orientations I describe must be built into personality; they are not behavioral acquisitions' (1978: 39); and as Jessica Benjamin said: 'submission [is] the *desire* of the dominated as well as their helpless fate' (1989: 52 – her emphasis).[7] It is an attempt to explain why current social relations are so intransigent, and has implications for explaining the strength of the resistance to the feminist challenge to those relations. It is important for a feminist politics to be able to give an account of the ways in which relationships of domination and subordination are embraced by individuals out of what is experientially felt to be intrinsic desire, rather than portraying those relationships only as impositions. Feminist object relations theory is not yet that account, but it gives suggestive hints for how to go about providing one.

In discussing a number of the ways in which feminism has come to be defined implicitly, I have argued that these definitions pay insufficient attention to male supremacy. As a consequence, these ways of seeing feminism are more or less inadequate as programmes for feminist political change. The term 'patriarchy' is arguably the least inadequate, since it is usually used in a feminist context to mean male supremacy. But its conventional meaning of 'rule of the father' has led some feminist theorists to locate male ruling with fathers rather than with men (Benjamin, 1989; Mitchell, 1974a, 1974b). This has adverse consequences for feminist politics. It largely ignores the present dangers for women and children of the male supremacist structuring of intimate relations, and diverts attention away from the need to validate women's mothering and rearrange the social conditions within which women mother. By according familial relations a causal role in determining social relations in general, it confines feminist attention to the family. The term 'sexism' can be used as a short-hand reference to male supremacy. But its neutrality on the question of which sex is dominant means that it can be too easily co-opted to serve men's interests at the expense of women. Couching the feminist critique in terms of such phenomena as 'dichotomies', 'binary oppositions' and 'dualisms' does acknowledge the hierarchical valuing of one term over the other, and usually allows that the 'male/female' distinction is the basic principle underlying all the others. But it is difficult to see what follows from that in practical political terms. Should feminism refrain from 'dichotomies' altogether? In that case, it is a recommendation that feminism refrain from alluding to those meanings and values to which it is utterly opposed, that is, those which serve the interests of male supremacy. Or is it a recommendation to refrain only from those 'dichotomies' listed? But if feminism cannot allude to the distinction between male and female, once again it cannot address the social order of male supremacy which creates the antagonisms between women and men in the first place. As for the term 'gender', in most of its usages it serves anti-feminist purposes by appearing to supply feminism with a subject-matter, while actually obliterating the central concern of feminist politics. All it can recommend by way of 'feminist' practice is a limitless plurality of personal 'choices', unrestrained by any ethical considerations whatsoever (or none that are mentioned). With its covert appeal to something other than the social as 'the truth' of human existence, 'gender' transforms 'society' into nothing but unfair and (implicitly) unnatural constraint, and interprets 'the social' as a superficial and dispensable gloss on the essential reality of the desiring individual.

Defining feminism in terms of 'women' would seem to be the most plausible way of characterizing it, since feminism is clearly concerned with the struggle of women by women and for women. It becomes inadequate as politics, however, when the focus is only on women, and feminism as the struggle against male domination is omitted, denied or ignored. Without the centralizing focus of opposition to male supremacy, feminism is reduced to antagonisms between and among women. In what follows, I look at some of the ways in which those antagonisms have been played out in the context of that crucial category of 'race'.

Notes

1 Alison Jaggar recognizes the confounding as a problem but does not resolve it (Jaggar, 1990).

2 'French feminism' in the Anglophone academic context has been criticized as an Anglo-American construct which misrepresents the actual history of feminism in France (Delphy, 1996; Moses, 1998; Winter, 1997).

3   Interestingly, this quote appears in Freud's text in the context of a discussion of the consequences for *girls* of 'envy for the penis'. Freud said: 'After a woman has become aware of the wound to her narcissism, she develops, like a scar, a sense of inferiority. ... she begins to share the contempt felt by men for a sex which is the lesser in so important a respect' (Freud, 1977: 337).

4   That is not to say that women have nothing at all at stake in those meanings and values. To the extent that women, too, can see no alternative to the male as the 'human' norm, and no alternative for themselves but a secondary status as men's auxiliaries, women too have a stake in maintaining penis-possession as the symbol of 'human' value.

5   Or *a* cause. Chodorow was later to acknowledge that she was mistaken in her earlier writings in implying that 'women's mothering was *the* cause or prime mover of male dominance' (1989: 6 – her emphasis). She felt that 'women's inequality may be multiply caused and situated'. But this is still seeing the problem the wrong way round. The problem lies in seeing women's mothering as having any causal role at all in generating the social system which is male supremacy, rather than seeing it as a consequence and a requirement.

There is, of course, another problem with characterizing social phenomena in terms of 'causes', and that is the implication of determinism. To talk about 'causes' in social life is to imply that people have no choice, that they are nothing but bearers of social relations and/or the inert outcomes of what happened to them in infancy and early childhood. But to the extent that human beings are moral creatures, we do have choices, as long as we have knowledge of alternatives. The maintenance of relations of domination requires the suppression of that knowledge, a suppression that manifests as repression and the unconscious at the level of the individual psyche.

6   There are, of course, men who do not define their humanity solely in terms of penis-possession, who are not obsessively driven to use their penises with complete disregard for the rights and feelings of others, and who are deeply horrified by child sexual abuse and rape. But they remain individual exceptions to the general rule of male dominance which still prevails, as long as there is no general recognition of the problem of over-valuation of penis-possession.

7   Once again, the postulation of unconscious processes and desires for subordination originating in infancy gives rise to questions about determinism. But the shape of desire is not fixed for all time in childhood. It is possible to change one's desire, although not easily, and not at all if there is no access to alternative readings of the way the world is. Psychoanalysis itself holds out the promise that desire can be reconstructed (although that promise is weakened by psychoanalysis' individualism and continuing complicity with male supremacy).

7 Differences among women

The question of 'differences' between and among women revolves chiefly around the contentious issues of race and class. What is being said in these debates is that some women are in a dominant position in relation to other women, that some women oppress other women because they are more privileged than other women – white women in comparison with black or third-world women or women of other ethnic minorities, middle-class women in comparison with working-class women or women of poverty. To the extent that this focus on differences between women allows no room for locating the invidious and hierarchical differences within a culture of male domination, it fragments the feminist project into a myriad of oppressive distinctions among women with no common meeting ground. To the extent that it appeals only to a hierarchy of oppressions among women, it reinforces that hierarchy. It displaces the source of domination from the male power system to women themselves, and by ignoring the nature, manifestations, scope and influence of male domination, it misrepresents the feminist project. And because these invidious and hierarchical distinctions undoubtedly exist among feminists, those accused react with guilt, self-recrimination or shamed silence. This problem of 'differences' among women has at times reached such a pitch that it occupied a large part of the feminist terrain, paralysing debate, and too often diverting feminist energy away from the main enemy.

Feminism cannot afford to give priority to the politics of race or class while ignoring male supremacy. As I have been arguing throughout, to ignore male supremacy is to empty feminist politics of its central meaning. With that central meaning in place, the political challenge to pernicious distinctions based on race and class takes on a different appearance. The categories of 'race' and 'class' also contain men, and any category which includes men tends to be dominated by the interests of men. Because men are more secure in their human status, they tend to have a clearer apprehension of their exclusion from human rights than women do. Men tend to know what they are entitled to and what they are being deprived of. Racism or class exploitation are more readily perceivable than the oppression of women, because they involve the dehumanization of men. Moreover, the allocation of people in terms of racial categories tends to reproduce the ideology of the male as the 'human' norm, so that the categories are automatically male unless women are specifically mentioned. Because women are still struggling for a human status, we frequently cannot even express what we want, much less get access to the necessary resources, especially if women's needs come into conflict with what men perceive as their justified claims against other men. Too often, women become the terrain over which battles for supremacy among men are waged, unless the feminist insight into the male supremacist defining of the 'human' as only male is kept constantly in mind.

That is not to say that *feminists* cannot give political priority to race and/or class. There are times when politically committed women must challenge the oppressions of class and/or race directly because the urgency of the situation demands it. Andrea Dworkin argued this in terms of 'states of primary emergency'. What she meant by this was that, in certain contexts, certain identities brought with them more pressing, immediate and dangerous problems than others. She gave the examples of the Jew in Nazi Germany, and the Native American during the colonization of the US. 'That first identity', she said, 'the one which brings with it as part of its definition death, is the identity of primary emergency' (Dworkin, 1974: 23). Even short of death, the economic deprivation which capitalism visits upon a large proportion of the world's population, and the dehumanizing effects of racism, require their own specific politics. But unless feminism is a constant presence in those politics, women will continue to be excluded from agendas devised by men in their own interests. As long as feminism is conceived as a commitment to the human dignity of all, it is already a commitment to opposing race and class oppression. But feminist involvement in these politics focuses on the effects on women of the hierarchies of class and race, both the ways in which those hierarchies specifically disadvantage women, and the ways in which women reproduce those hierarchies among ourselves. Once male domination is identified as the main problem addressed by a feminist politics, it can be acknowledged that women experience male domination differently, depending on where they are situated in relation to race, class, or any other social location.

I am not going to discuss class in this present work, despite the lack of resolution of many of the questions involved in discussions of women and class – the difficulty of allocating women to class positions (not to mention the difficulty of allocating men); the derivative nature of 'class' for women and its dependence on their relationships to men;[1] confusions about what 'class' means, whether it can be accounted for in terms of status, prestige, privilege and access to resources, or whether it is confined to the Marxist concept of ownership and non-ownership of the means of production (in which case it is irrelevant to women); and, most importantly, the absence of any acknowledgement of the existence of a ruling class. Although there are some discussions in the feminist literature which deal explicitly with class (for example, Lesbian Ethics, 1991; Phillips, 1987), within the category of 'differences between and among women' it is the question of race which has received the most attention. 'Class' has tended to play a subsidiary role, mentioned only briefly and tangentially in discussions primarily concerned with 'race'. Moreover, the main problem with the feminist 'race' debate – the ignoring or denial of male domination and the concomitant focus on hierarchies among women – is also to be found in discussions of 'class'. Hence, much of what is said about 'race' is also relevant to 'class'.

Feminism and 'Race'

In raising questions about the 'race' debate within feminism, I am not intending to cast doubt on the occurrence of racism among feminists, much less its existence more generally. There can be no doubt about its existence. A feminist stance does not mean that women cannot behave in racist ways; nor does it mean that anything and everything said in the name of feminism is automatically excluded from criticism on the grounds of racism. Racism is not always violent, blatant and overt. It can be subtle, devious and sometimes ambiguous, and hence difficult to identify and describe. But it is not helpful to refer to such instances as 'feminism'. Rather, they are *failures* of feminist insight. Seeing them as examples of feminism is one example of the consequences of not defining feminism. Feminism becomes anything said or done by anyone identified as 'a feminist'. Feminists are no more immune from errors of judgement than anyone else, but without a clear idea of what counts as feminism, it is not possible to decide what counts as an error.

Racism is undoubtedly an important issue. But attempts to theorize it in a feminist context have not so far met with much success. Feelings of being excluded may be real enough, but it is not helpful to define feminism as some kind of private property of 'white, middle-class' women, and of no relevance to women variously identified as women of colour, black women, third-world women, indigenous women, or women from ethnic minorities. The construct of 'false universalism' which is meant to warn against feminist complicity with Western imperialism is too confused to be useful. The three categories of 'gender, race and class' fail as an account of domination because the categories remain both too distinct and separated, and focus on categories of the oppressed rather than on the social structures which oppress. Most importantly, the 'race' debate lacks an account of the male supremacist aspects of race and class and largely ignores the problematic of male domination. But it is only the focusing of feminist attention on the social construct of male monopolization of the 'human' which promises to address that sense so many women have of feeling excluded from much of what is labelled 'feminism'. It is only that political focus which can make sense of feminism for women everywhere subjected in a multitude of different ways to the dehumanization inherent in the social order of male supremacy.

If the debate has been, at the very least, unhelpful for feminist politics, it has also been inadequate as an anti-racist politics for the same reason that it is inadequate as a feminist politics, that is, its deletion of the question of male domination.[2] There is too little discussion of the male-dominated nature of the human categories on whose behalf the anti-racist struggle is waged, categories which contain only men unless women are explicitly mentioned. The exclusion of black women or women of colour is blamed on a 'white women's movement', when the original exclusion is a male supremacist one, that is, the exclusion of women from every 'human' category because they are not men. In contrast, starting from the standpoint of opposition to male domination allows the problem of women's exclusion from all 'human' categories to be addressed directly, in a way that focusing exclusively on 'race' does not. Texts authored in the name of 'feminism' can be complicit with this exclusion of women from categories defined in terms of 'race', but it does not originate there. Rather, it originates with the male supremacist ideology that only men count as 'human'. Starting with that same ideological construct in mind also promises to throw light on the male supremacist aspects of racism and imperialism, connections between racism and masculinity which are hinted at in some of the malestream anti-racist and post-colonialist literature, but which remain at the level of suggestive insights for lack of a feminist analysis. Ignoring the ideological constitution of the male as the 'human' norm means failing to identify the ways in which racism and imperialism have mirrored the domination of women by men, and the male supremacist nature of the anti-racist and post-colonialist struggle itself.

Although raising these issues goes against the grain of most of what has been said in the name of an anti-racist feminism, there is no benefit to be gained, either for feminism or for the anti-racist struggle, in refusing to address the problems because they are too hard, too confusing, or too threatening. Ignoring the problems will not make them go away. Silence, whether well-intentioned or guilt-stricken, leads nowhere except to political paralysis. As it stands at the moment, the debate provides no ground from which to start righting the wrongs which are supposedly at issue. A feminist anti-racist politics must involve more than the simple acceptance and meek reiteration of anything and everything said by or on behalf of women of colour without challenge, argument or debate. Otherwise it does a grave injustice both to feminism's own insights and political priorities, and to those of the anti-racist struggle.

Exclusion

One of the chief complaints levelled against feminism is that it has excluded women of colour. Roxana Ng, for example, said, 'Working in the women's movement ... women of colour ... feel silenced from time to time. Our unique experiences as women of colour are frequently overlooked in discussions about women's oppression' (Ng, 1993: 197). Ng does not identify any agents of this silencing and overlooking. She does not say what it might be that leads to women of colour to feel this way, but given the prevalence of the problem I have called 'academic feminism', women of colour are not alone in feelings of alienation and irrelevance in relation to much of what is published as 'feminism'.

Alice Walker (1982) also gives some examples of this kind of exclusion. The first involved Patricia Meyer Spacks' book, *The Female Imagination* (1976). Spacks herself acknowledged that her research was confined to writings by 'white, middle-class' women, because, she said, she was reluctant to theorize about experiences she hadn't had (1976: 5). But, as Walker pointed out, this was an inadequate excuse for excluding writings by US black women, since Spacks included the Brontës although she had no experience of nineteenth-century Yorkshire either. But the problem with Spacks' book went further than this. Not only did she fail to include writings by black women, she did so in the face of a golden opportunity to expand her own 'female imagination'. At the time she was writing the book, she was sharing an office with Alice Walker who was teaching a course on 'Black women writers', and who was prepared to share the fruits of her own research with Spacks. Walker's second example involved Judy Chicago's exhibition, 'The Dinner Party', which included only one plate referring to black women, the one devoted to Sojourner Truth. Walker's objection was not just to the tokenism of including only a single example. It was also directed to the kind of example it was. Although all the other plates depicted stylized vaginas, the Sojourner Truth plate did not. Instead, it depicted three faces, one weeping, one screaming and one smiling. Walker commented that, although there is something to be said for depicting women in terms of faces rather than vaginas, that was not what the exhibition was about, and the faces were nothing but tired old clichés about black women. Walker's third example involved a brief exchange at an exhibition of women painters at the Brooklyn museum. In response to one woman's question about whether there were any black women painters represented, another woman replied: 'It's a *women's* exhibit!'

These are the kinds of things for which a feminist politics needs to be alert, and to resist. But it is not clear that couching the problem in terms of exclusion is an adequate way of addressing it. It implies that the solution is inclusion, and any attempt to include solely on the grounds of race threatens to become tokenistic. This may be motivated by the best of intentions, to rectify the structural inequality of exclusion and as a form of positive discrimination in favour of those who are automatically discriminated against unless deliberate action is taken to include them. But because it involves sorting women into racial categories, it threatens to relapse into the very racism it is designed to combat. To the extent that it is only race which matters, at the expense of any other criteria of judgement, it reinforces racial divisions among women, and reaffirms 'white' in the dominant position of being able to afford magnanimity. I do not think there is any general solution to this dilemma. The problem could be partly redressed, however, if those who have the power to make decisions about inclusion and exclusion – for example, organizers of conferences, editors of anthologies, publishers – kept feminism in the forefront of the decision-making process, and refrained from making race the sole criterion of judgement. But that involves being clear about what feminism is in the first place.

Couching the problem in terms of exclusion (and the solution in terms of inclusion) does tend to have the unfortunate consequence of dividing feminists into 'them' and 'us' if decisions are to be made about who is to be included on the grounds of race. The consequence is that 'they' are once again 'other' than 'us', even to the extent that feminism becomes identified as 'ours' (although its errors and omissions are deplored). Marilyn Lake, for example, tells us that there is currently a 'fifth and final phase of feminism' which she calls 'post-colonial feminism'. She says that 'indigenous women and women of non-Anglo backgrounds' have 'powerfully challenged' what she sees as 'the basic assumption that has traditionally informed feminism, the assumption that the category "women" is a meaningful one for theoretical and political purposes'. As a consequence, she says, 'feminists have had to fundamentally reconceptualize their relationships with these "other" women' and 'to reformulate feminism' (Lake, 1998: 135). This implies both that 'these "other" women' are not feminists, and that only those who are feminists have the power to reconceptualize and reformulate it (or not).

Even when the speaking position is reversed, when 'the other' (in Lake's terms) is 'us', the dichotomy still constructs a category of women who define and monopolize what counts as feminism. Barbara Omolade, for example, held women she designated as 'white, middle- and upper-class' responsible for preventing US black women from speaking:

> The question of ... why [US] black women have not joined the women's movement in large numbers and have been generally hostile to feminism ... has been raised ... by white feminists in order to develop better ways to recruit black women into their movement. ... In discussing this issue, there is a need to put aside the narrow and limited confines of feminism as defined and dominated by mainly middle- and upper-class white women to reach a broader analysis that could include the experiences of all women under white male domination. ... white feminists ... have objectively excluded [women of color] from equal participation in the women's movement. ... the racism of white women will not allow them to give us the right to speak on our own behalf. (Omolade, 1985: 247, 256)

Omolade herself admitted that 'white feminists' had at least attempted 'to recruit' black women. Perhaps those attempts at 'recruitment' were attempts 'to reach a broader analysis' and include women of colour within feminism. In the absence of any account of what those methods of 'recruitment' were, we cannot know how or why they failed. But putting it in terms of 'recruitment' attributes an unrealistic level of power to those 'middle- and upper-class white women'. It implies that these women have the power to monopolize feminism as their own private property, to invite other women in or refuse them admission. It says that feminism belongs to one particular category of women to the exclusion of women who do not belong to that category. It also implies that feminism is some kind of scarce resource or commodity which can be monopolized by particular groups of women at the expense of other women. It characterizes those who are not 'white' as supplicants who can only demand concessions, and who have no power to create feminism themselves because feminism belongs to someone else and hence is something other than their own conviction. But that cannot be so. Perhaps what she was talking about was access to resources like academic credibility, respectability and employment, publishing, invitations to speak, etc. And it is true that not all feminists, not even all feminists who want to write, speak and publish, have access to these resources. But if this was her point, it was not entirely accurate. Even at the time she was writing (1980), US black women (the 'we' of her text) had been writing and publishing within feminism for at least ten years (for example, Beal, 1970; Black Women's Liberation Group, 1970; Kennedy, 1970; Norton, 1970; Ware, 1970) and presumably they were doing so out of their own feminist insights.

Without the unifying practice of struggling against male domination, 'feminism' becomes simply a question of 'women' who have nothing in common to the extent that not all women share all forms of oppression. bell hooks, for example, defines feminism as 'the struggle to end sexist oppression' (hooks, 1984). The term 'sexist oppression' does not refer to the social system of male domination and hence focus attention on the sex whose interests are maintained by 'sexist oppression', the sex which benefits from permission to oppress women. Rather, the 'sex' referred to by hooks' concept of 'sexist oppression' is the female sex. The concept refers to any oppression suffered by women:

> By repudiating the popular notion that the focus of feminist movement should be social equality of the sexes and emphasizing eradicating the cultural basis of group oppression, our own analysis would require an exploration of all aspects of women's political reality. This would mean that race and class oppression would be recognized as feminist issues with as much relevance as sexism.
>
> When feminism is defined in such a way that it calls attention to the diversity of women's social and political reality, it centralizes the experiences of all women, especially the women whose social conditions have been least written about, studied, or changed by political movements. (hooks, 1984: 25)

But this involves an unacknowledged contradiction. It abolishes the distinctions between sex, race and class which hooks herself wants to maintain. She defines sex, race and class only in terms of oppression suffered by women, and yet she wants to maintain that they are distinct forms of oppression because not all women are subjected to all three. She frequently refers to 'white bourgeois women' who not only do not suffer race and class oppression, but who oppress other women on those very grounds. While 'white bourgeois women' are subjected to 'sexism', in the case of race and class oppression they are themselves the oppressors, according to hooks. But not only does the concept of 'sexist oppression' as hooks defines it have unfortunate consequences for feminist politics because it locates hierarchies of oppression and domination only among women, its contradictory nature makes it inadequate for any other form of politics as well. It cannot be used to designate the form of oppression peculiar to women because it refers to different forms of oppression among women; and it cannot be used to designate those different forms, such as race, because it does not name them. Naming feminism's chief antagonist as 'sexist oppression' would be a move in the right direction, if the referent of this form of oppression were confined to sex, and if the sex which is dominant were clearly identified. But it merely confuses the issue to include race and class under the heading of 'sexism'.

By confining her analysis of domination to race and class hierarchies among women, hooks argues that the primary, if not the only, problem faced by US black feminists and by feminists belonging to minority cultures is the racism of 'white, middle-class' feminists, and that male domination is not a problem in US minority cultures. She does recognize some manifestations of male domination within what she refers to as 'lower class and poor groups, particularly those who are non-white'. She refers to the relative privilege of the men of those groups in comparison with the women, and to 'exaggerated expressions of male chauvinism' on the part of black men. But she attributes those 'exaggerated expressions' to 'the male's sense of himself as powerless and ineffectual in relation to ruling male groups, rather than an expression of an overall privileged social status' (hooks, 1984: 18). While this is certainly true, it also raises questions about black men's complicity with the meanings and values of masculinity. She does not ask why these men should take out their rage and frustration (if that is the import of the phrase 'exaggerated expressions') on women who are even more powerless than the men themselves, and who are certainly not responsible for the men's powerlessness.

In hooks' view, identifying the oppressor as either men or male domination is simplistic and individualistic. It might indeed be simplistic to assert no more than that 'men are the enemy', since women too can despise women, treat women with contempt, and uphold the male as the 'human' norm. But challenging 'male supremacy and the ideology of sexism' is no more 'individualistic' (hooks, 1984: 25) than challenging racism or capitalism. This refusal to name male domination rules out the possibility of asking questions about the complicity of black men with the meanings and values of male supremacy, a complicity which works to the disadvantage of women, including black women. And it confines 'feminism' to struggles between women, struggles which are irresolvable to the extent that they are identified in terms of a personal characteristic, namely 'white', which is not moral and political because no one can do anything to change it. This does not mean that racism is irrelevant to the feminist struggle. On the contrary, pursuing the feminist aim of a human status for women at no one's expense requires a constant readiness on the part of all feminists to refuse to be implicated in racist meanings and values. But that cannot happen unless it is possible to identify what counts as racism and what does not.

The dichotomous dividing of women into 'white' and 'other' fails to throw any light on this question. Gloria Joseph and Jill Lewis, for example, designate something they call 'the White women's movement' which, they say, 'has had its own explicit form of racism in the way it has given high priority to certain aspects of struggles and neglected others, and it has often been blind and ignorant about the conditions of [US] Black women's lives' (Joseph and Lewis, 1981: 4). They do not identify this 'White women's movement' any further. They do not tell us which struggles have been given priority in which feminist writings or practices, nor which aspects have been neglected. Instead, they go on to tell us that the movement was 'bound' to emphasize some things and ignore others, because it was started by women who experienced 'specific White realities'. But this is by no means self-evident. If we look at the issues raised by feminism – rape and other forms of male violence, for example, or women's access to a living wage, or control over our own reproductive capacities, or freedom from male imposition and constraint – it is not at all obvious that these are only 'White realities'. Neither do we know whether feminism was 'started' by 'white women', or even if the idea of feminism being 'started' by anyone makes any sense, given the long and varied history of women's resistance to male power, a history which has not always been written down, but which must have existed because male domination is nowhere absolute.

But the authors do not address any of these questions. Once they have labelled feminism, even in part, as the 'white women's movement', its 'racism' appears as a kind of logical necessity. On this account, the 'white women's movement' was inevitably and inescapably racist because it was 'white'. The authors do acknowledge that 'women's liberation did and does touch on questions which in different ways affect *all* women's lives – and men's lives too' (emphasis in the original), that is, that women's liberation is not only 'white'. But if it is not only 'white', then its supposed racism cannot be the result of being concerned only with 'white' women. There must be other reasons why feminism, or the 'white' aspects of it, is 'racist'. But the authors do not give us any other reasons, or at least, no other reason which makes any sense. They do give us one other reason, and that is that 'the movement did not begin with women who had some all-encompassing political and historical knowledge' (p. 4). But in that case, they are blaming feminism, or that aspect of it they designate 'the White women's movement', for not doing the impossible, for not having 'some all-encompassing political and historical knowledge'.

It cannot be the case that racism is nothing but an aspect of being 'white'.[3] In the first place, racism is a moral issue. It involves attitudes and behaviours about which people have choices. It is possible to refuse to be implicated in racism, and those who are complicit with racism can be held responsible. And in the second place, racism is a manifestation of the social system of racial supremacy which purveys 'white' as the criterion of 'human' status. As such, its meanings and values insidiously influence the choices, decisions and world views, not only of those who qualify for the benefits and privileges of being white, but also of those it most oppresses. As a consequence, it cannot be assumed that the social system of white supremacy has no influence on those who are not white. That is not to say that negative attitudes towards whites on the part of, say, Aboriginal people are 'racist', even when those attitudes explicitly refer to race. Because the system of domination is white supremacy, blacks cannot be racist towards whites. In white supremacist terms, 'white' is always the reference point of highest value against which other racial groups are measured and found wanting, and it occupies that supreme position by virtue of being not a 'race' at all, but a signifier of the 'universal human'. But because white supremacy is a social system of meanings and values, complicity can be found even among those most oppressed by the system. Like any system of domination, it operates through the inculcation of self-hatred and self-depreciation among the oppressed, as well as through blatant imposition.

For example, in her study of the writings of a number of US Afro-American women, Mary Helen Washington discussed what she had found was 'a persistent and revealing theme in the lives and literature of Black women'. She called this theme 'the intimidation of color'. By this she meant the harsh judgements made, sometimes by black women about themselves, sometimes by both women and men about other black women, judgements which made invidious comparisons between black skin and Afro hair on the one hand, and white standards of beauty on the other. She quoted from the Introduction to a volume of short stories by Afro-American women in which the author wrote: 'In almost every novel or autobiography written by a black woman, there is at least one incident in which the dark-skinned girl wishes to be either white or light-skinned with "good" hair' (Washington, 1982: 210). Michele Wallace provides another example. She tells us what happened when, at the age of 13, she went to school one day with her hair openly displayed in an Afro, instead of being hidden in braids disguised in a long flowing scarf. She said that black men on street corners 'began to whoop and holler' at her. When she asked someone why, she was told: ' "They think you're a whore, sugar" ' (Wallace, 1982: 5–6). This experience of Wallace illustrates the intertwining of white supremacy with male supremacy. The black men, debarred from fully human status themselves by the system of white supremacy, could still embrace the values of that system by judging black women according to male supremacist criteria. Such attitudes are not strictly speaking 'racist', since racism involves attitudes and behaviours on the part of members of the dominant group imposed on those judged 'inferior'. The point at issue here is that they are not separate from racism, they too are part of the social system of white supremacy which needs to be challenged by a feminism committed to women's interests, as indeed they have been, particularly in the writings of US Afro-American women.

The solution to the problem of a self-styled 'feminism' which is either incomprehensible or actively hostile to what many of us know as feminism, lies in feminists taking responsibility for feminism, for its significance for and relevance to our own lives, for what we will accept as feminism and what we will not, for contesting and debating its meaning, for continuing to struggle for access to resources. Feminism is never located somewhere else apart from the speaker's own position. It is not something other than the speaker's own political engagement. It is not the prerogative of any particular category of women with the power to invite or exclude other women. It is a political and moral struggle available to anyone. If a woman of colour engages in that struggle, then that is where feminism is, wherever else it may be as well. As Alice Walker put it:

> There was never a time when Our Mother [i.e., herself] thought, when someone spoke of 'the women's movement', that this referred only to the women's movement in America. When she thought of women moving, she automatically thought of women all over the world. She recognized that to contemplate the women's movement in isolation from the rest of the world would be – given the racism, sexism, elitism, and ignorance of so many American feminists – extremely defeating to solidarity among women as well as depressing to the most optimistic spirit. Our Mother had travelled and had every reason to understand that women's freedom was an idea whose time had come, and that it was an idea sweeping the world. (Walker, 1982: 41)

Irrelevance

Another objection which has been raised against feminism in the context of the 'race' debate is that it is irrelevant to the lives of women subjected to racial oppression. At the beginning of this 'second wave' of feminism in Australia, there were many Aboriginal women who expressed this view.[4] The Aboriginal women at the Women and Politics conference in Canberra in 1975 did not see themselves as feminists, but located their political priorities with the struggles of Aboriginal people. They regarded the oppression of Aboriginal people by white society as the most urgent problem, and the Aboriginal struggle as far more important than what they perceived to be the comparatively trivial concerns of women they saw as more privileged than themselves. They also saw themselves as less in need of feminism than white women, because Aboriginal culture allowed women more equality than white culture did, because Aboriginal women were already in the forefront of the movement for Aboriginal self-determination, and because Aboriginal women had always had supportive networks among themselves (Aboriginal and Islander Women, 1975a, 1975b).

This stance on the part of Aboriginal women is not surprising, based as it was on a well-founded suspicion on the part of Aboriginal women of anything seen to emanate from white Australia. But the seeming antagonisms between Aboriginal politics and feminist politics were due to a number of misinterpretations. Feminism was often trivialized by Aboriginal women activists, as 'mak[ing] men do the washing up' (Grimshaw, 1981: 88), as 'chatter ... about sexual oppression and the competitive orgasm' (Sykes, 1975: 318), as a struggle for 'a more equal distribution of power between the white sexes' (Sykes, 1984: 66), as the opposition to 'male chauvinism' and as 'an extremely anti-male ideology' (Venceremos Brigade, 1975). Another common misinterpretation concerned the perception of feminism in terms of a 'white women's movement' consisting of organized groups. Since Aboriginal women refused to join these groups, they interpreted this as a refusal to join feminism. But the refusal of Aboriginal women activists to join groups organized by white women did not mean that feminism was irrelevant to Aboriginal women (although that was the way some of them saw it). Given that feminism is a struggle on the part of women for their own rights, self-respect and human dignity, the struggles of Aboriginal women on their own behalf is itself a feminist struggle.

Another misinterpretation was to see feminism as responsible for antagonisms between women and men. Hilary Saunders said: 'we can only hope to achieve [self-determination] as one people not a race of men, nor a race of women but of black People United' (Saunders, 1975). Vi Stanton said: 'I can't get interested in women's liberation. To me, as an Aboriginal, it's not relevant, for the simple reason that our whole people have to be liberated. I don't consider that we split forces here, between women and men' (quoted in Grimshaw, 1981: 87). Eve Fesl commented: 'One aspect that sets our women's groups apart from most non-Aboriginal women's groups is that we work along with, and stand as partners beside, our men – we do not as a whole oppose men *per se*. (It seems to some of us that in Euro-Australian women's groups there is often an element of man-hatred)' (Fesl, 1984: 114; see also Huggins, 1994). This argument was reiterated by a group of Aboriginal women more recently. 'We continually find', they said, 'we are being jockeyed into the position of fighting and separating from our men and we will not. We are women and men together who have suffered grave injustices by the white invaders. We have all suffered' (Huggins et al., 1991: 506). This objection has also been raised by other women engaged in anti-racist and anti-imperialist struggles, who have rejected feminism on the grounds that they need to work alongside their men in struggling to liberate all their people.

But it is not feminism which is responsible for antagonisms between the sexes. Rather, those antagonisms are the result of the male violence against and contempt for women which feminism is struggling *against*. That this is so even within Aboriginal communities, has become increasingly apparent (Atkinson, 1990a, 1990b, 1990c; Bell, 1991a, 1991b; Bell and Nelson, 1989; Bligh, 1983; Langton, 1989; Mosey, 1994; Queensland Domestic Violence Task Force, 1988; Sculthorpe, 1990). To the extent that there are antagonisms between Aboriginal women and men, those antagonisms are not a consequence of feminism, but of the behaviour of men. Aboriginal men do not refrain from violence towards women and children just because they are Aboriginal. While it is true that Aboriginal people as a whole have been subjected to genocidal policies, and it is also true that Aboriginal women and men work together in their struggle against a common oppression, yet Aboriginal women, like women everywhere, suffer at the hands of men, and not only men of the dominant classes. Within Aboriginal communities, as elsewhere, the interests of women and men can come into conflict. For example, Aboriginal women have been denied legal representation by the Aboriginal Legal Service (ALS) in cases of domestic violence where their partners are also Aboriginal. Because of its policy of not acting in any case against an Aboriginal person, the ALS will not represent Aboriginal women who charge Aboriginal men with violence (Hole, 1994).

Struggling against male domination is antagonistic to men only to the extent that men are committed to male domination. The feminist practice of excluding men from women-only groups, events and activities was sometimes perceived by Aboriginal women as 'man-hating' (for example, Fesl, 1984: 110). But it is no more than a strategic decision to provide for women some space, always temporary and sometimes contested, which men cannot dominate because they are not present. Provision of women-only occasions, spaces and support networks was part of many traditional Aboriginal societies, and continues among Aboriginal people today (Bell, 1983, 1987; Hamilton, 1981).

The political struggles of Aboriginal women for their own identity and dignity as women in solidarity with each other, bring Aboriginal women into conflict with Aboriginal men only if Aboriginal men are committed to the meanings and values of male domination, only if Aboriginal men, too, are violent towards women, and collude with male contempt for the female. In opposing the racism of white Australia, Aboriginal women are also opposing male supremacy, because the colonization of Australia, and what was done to Aboriginal people by the European settlers, was male supremacist as well as white supremacist. Aboriginal women were not raped by white women. Neither were the massacres of Aboriginal people perpetrated by women. That does not mean that European women were innocent of racism. They may have been complicit with the actions of the male colonizers. Many white women exploited the labour of Aboriginal women and girls as unpaid domestic servants (Tucker, 1977; Ward, 1987), although it is as well to remember that the chief beneficiaries of the domestic labour of Aboriginal women were white men, and that the households were managed for the ease and comfort of the husbands, sons, fathers and brothers of the white mistresses. European women may have blamed Aboriginal women for the sexual misbehaviour of white men; they may have condoned, excused or justified the massacres. But whether they protested or not, women have never had the social power necessary to colonize and subdue people. The European women involved in the colonization of Australia were mostly wives, prostitutes and servants, that is, under male control.

The male supremacist nature of the colonization of Australia appears not to have been recognized by some of the participants in the debate. For example, Bobbi Sykes' all too brief history of 'black women in Australia' (1975), is a history of the rape of Aboriginal women by white men. This issue of rape, which is so clearly of concern to all women, was used by Sykes to argue for the irrelevance of feminism to Aboriginal women. She was able to do this, firstly by ignoring the inherently male supremacist nature of rape, and defining it instead as an aspect of racism, and secondly by characterizing feminism as white women's groups which Aboriginal women refused to join. But the feminism of Aboriginal women is not dependent on their membership of groups organized by white women, whether or not Aboriginal women choose to characterize their political commitment as feminist (and some do, at least for some purposes).

Another example of the male supremacist nature of the European colonization of Australia concerns the differential effect of colonization on the lives of Aboriginal women and men. Both sexes suffered under European colonization. But Aboriginal women, like the women of all invaded or colonized peoples, were subjected to the extra burden of sexual exploitation and violence (Grimshaw, 1981: 90). Moreover, to the extent that the European colonizers dealt with Aboriginal people as human beings, they dealt only with Aboriginal men, defining only men as breadwinners, paid workers, informants, cultural experts and 'owners' of the land. This European commitment to the ideology of the male as the 'human' norm undermined the economic arrangements of traditional Aboriginal societies whereby the survival of everyone depended on the food-providing activities of Aboriginal women. It also obliterated women's cultural knowledge, spiritual expertise and relationship to the land. To the extent that the domination of European culture was successful (and it has not always been), Aboriginal women lost a great deal of the independence they had within traditional societies (Hamilton, 1975, 1981).

And yet, looked at in another way, the disruptive effect of colonization on Aboriginal culture has been more demoralizing for men than for women. The Queensland Domestic Violence Task Force report partly located the causes of the high level of domestic violence in Aboriginal and Islander communities in the 'breakdown of traditional culture'. The report pointed out that 'Aboriginal men's roles have been seriously undermined' as a result of European settlement. The 'attempts by various authorities to manage the so-called "Aboriginal problem"', and 'the murder and maltreatment of Aboriginal persons', the report commented, has meant that Aboriginal men's 'opportunities for mastery and positive achievement in the new culture have not been effectively realized'. The report went on to say that 'Aboriginal women do not appear to have suffered such dramatic changes in their roles', and attributed this to 'their ongoing role as child bearers and rearers. They have had to cope for the sake of their children.' The report quoted from a submission to the task force, arguing that 'the traditional role of men in Aboriginal society has been eroded with the result ... [that] in a lot of cases the men [use] violence on the women folk to re-assert their authority' (Queensland Domestic Violence Task Force, 1988: 258–9). Patricia Grimshaw also suggested that men of a colonized culture experience greater shock and disruption than women do, because the men have more to lose. She said that, because men are the religious and political leaders, male identity is more closely tied up with their culture than is female identity, and hence men suffer greater dislocation when their culture is threatened. Women at least have some continuity in their responsibilities for children and in their female support networks (Grimshaw, 1981: 90).

But there are problems with this kind of account. There are indications from the work of female anthropologists that this supposed cultural 'leadership' of men is a construct of the male supremacist nature of colonization. Given the important part played by women in the cultural life of the people in traditional Aboriginal societies, it is not at all clear that men were the spiritual 'leaders' in traditional societies (leaving aside the question of what might count as a 'leader' in those societies). Both sexes had spiritual responsibilities. Sometimes these were joint responsibilities, but sometimes they were so separate and distinct that men were not permitted knowledge of women's rites, and vice versa. As men, whether as anthropologists, government officials or curious individuals, the colonizers would not be informed of 'women's business', and hence it would appear that the spiritual life of the people was largely 'men's business'. Although I would agree that there is a sense in which men are more demoralized by the destructive effects of colonization than women, I would suggest that that is yet another consequence of the male supremacist values of the dominant culture, which promises colonized men a 'human' status and deprives them of it at one and the same time. They are 'human' because they are men, but they are also 'less than human' because they are not members of the dominant race. It is in this sense that Aboriginal men have more to lose than Aboriginal women, not in the sense that they are deprived of something they once had, but in the sense of a savage double-bind which women escape because they are not given the promise of 'human' status in the first place. The colonizer is unlikely to grant to the women of what he sees as an 'inferior race' what he does not allow to the women of his own race.

Sometimes the relevance of feminism has been acknowledged by Aboriginal women. For example, Hilary Saunders said: 'Women's Liberation has played a part in bringing about a certain form of awareness in Black women.' She went on to qualify that statement by saying that Aboriginal women could not afford to let that awareness go too far because of the injustices suffered by Aboriginal people as a whole. But she did point out that Aboriginal women needed to struggle against attempts by Aboriginal men to 'protect' them, thereby placing Aboriginal women in a subservient role and denying them the right to speak and to take up positions of leadership (Saunders, 1975). But often Aboriginal women activists spoke as though there were no common meeting ground between Aboriginal women and white women, as though the only men who ever caused women any trouble were white men, as though Aboriginal men were only comrades, kin and fellow sufferers in oppression, and never raped, bashed or molested women and children. The motive behind the silence about Aboriginal male violence against women and children (and each other and themselves) is understandable. No one committed to the interests of Aboriginal people wants to provide ammunition for racists. But the silence has been lethal for Aboriginal women (Queensland Domestic Violence Task Force, 1988). As Diane Bell put it:

by framing violence as a racial problem (i.e., it is Whites oppressing Blacks), women are rendered mute. ... It is helpful to ask the question feminists asked when scrutinising the violence hidden in the home: In whose interests is silence maintained? Under what conditions may women be able to put their safety and that of their children above the needs of the men who beat and rape them? ... the need to work from within the race construct has constrained findings that might empower women. (Bell, 1991a: 389)

It has been argued with some justification that manifestations of male dominance, including the level of male violence, within present-day Aboriginal communities is a consequence of European colonization, that traditional Aboriginal societies allowed women far more autonomy, independence and influence, and that that female autonomy has been eroded by the cultural imperialism of white Australia. There is a great deal of evidence to support that argument (Bell, 1983, 1987; Grimshaw, 1981; Hamilton, 1975, 1981). But traditional Aboriginal society no longer exists uninfluenced by European imperialism. Many Aboriginal people are generations away from traditional society. Even among the desert people who have retained their languages, spiritual life and connections to the land despite the depredations of European settlement, government, policies and practices, those very depredations have irrevocably changed Aboriginal society. The worst evils of male dominance may indeed have been imposed on Aboriginal people by European imperialism. But that makes feminism, and its championing of the cause of women, more relevant to Aboriginal women, not less. As Aboriginal activist Marcia Langton has pointed out:

without the concerted effort of feminists to raise the issue of domestic violence over the past two or more decades, Aboriginal women would face a grim future. ... In my view, the determining character of the imbalance in gender relationships is the ability of men to use force, in the last analysis, to preserve male dominance in ideology, in structures and in relationships. (Langton, 1989)

Hence, feminism is relevant to Aboriginal women, because Aboriginal women, like women everywhere, suffer under the regime which is male domination.

Denying Male Domination

The chief problem with much of the 'race' debate within feminism is the denial of the existence of male supremacy. Sometimes this denial is explicit. Hazel V. Carby, for example, uses the racist oppression of black men as an argument against feminism. She argues that the concept of 'patriarchy' should be abandoned by feminism because black men are subordinated to white men. This point is reiterated a number of times throughout the paper, for example, 'Racism ensures that black men do not have the same relations to patriarchal/capitalist hierarchies as white men' (Carby, 1982: 213). But this is not an argument against feminism. That some men are oppressed by other men is a consequence of the male supremacist regime of power challenged by feminism, and not a construct of feminism itself. Carby's objections rest on her assumption that the feminist concept of 'patriarchy' means that all men are equal, and that, since all men are not equal, the term should be dropped from the feminist repertoire because it makes false, and racist, assumptions about black men. But feminism has never argued that all men are equal.

Chandra Mohanty also objects to any use of the term 'patriarchy'. 'There is', she says, 'no universal patriarchal framework ... unless one posits an international male conspiracy or a monolithic, ahistorical power hierarchy' (Mohanty, 1988: 63). She goes on to acknowledge the existence of 'a particular world balance of power', which she characterizes (quoting Anouar Abdel-Malek) as including: '"the military-industrial complex and the hegemonic cultural centers of the West ... monopoly and finance capital ... the scientific and technological revolution and the second industrial revolution itself"' (p. 63). That this 'world balance of power' may itself be an international 'patriarchal framework', consisting of the concentration of the world's wealth in the hands of a few men, in the interests of their own power and prestige and at the expense of the majority of people, is not a connection Mohanty makes.

Denying the existence of male domination is central to her task of exposing the ways in which some examples of 'Western feminist writing on women in the third world' are, as she sees it, complicit with this 'world balance of power'. These writings, she argues, demonstrate their complicity with the colonization of women in the third world through 'the production of the "Third World Woman" as a singular monolithic subject', a discursive construct which results in the 'suppression ... of the heterogeneity of the subject(s) in question' (p. 61). There is certainly something like this involved in the defining of women only in terms of race along a 'white'/'non-white' axis. But Mohanty is not talking about this. Instead, what she dismisses as 'appropriating' and 'colonizing' are writings which explicitly identify male domination.

One of the strategies she uses to finesse questions about male domination involves exaggerated terminology like 'universal', 'conspiracy', 'monolithic' and 'ahistorical'. Such language functions to stop any discussion before it starts. It supposedly shows the absurdity of the concept of male domination without actually providing any argument or evidence against it. The naming of male domination is characterized as a 'process of homogenization and systematization of the oppression of women in the third world', and as an exercise of power over third-world women on the part of 'much recent Western feminist discourse' (p. 63). But she writes as though third-world women were not in fact oppressed by male violence, colonialism, economic development, etc., as though they were not powerless in the face of 'particular socio-economic systems', as though the only problem is that 'Western feminist discourse' says they are: 'in these texts ... women are defined consistently as the *victims* of male control' (p. 67 – her emphasis). She clearly means this as a criticism of these texts, the implication being that third-world women are not victims of male control, but are merely portrayed as such by 'Western feminism'.

This strategy draws distinctions which are terminological rather than substantive, since they are distinctions between something described in neutral language and something described pejoratively. For example, in her criticism of Fran Hosken's work on genital mutilation, she acknowledges that 'it is true that the potential of male violence against women circumscribes and elucidates their social position to a certain extent'. But, she goes on to say, 'defining women as archetypal victims freezes them into "objects-who-defend-themselves", men into "subjects-who-perpetrate-violence", and (every) society into powerless (read: women) and powerful (read: men) groups of people' (p. 67). The difference in emotional tone between these two statements points to another difference between them. In the second statement, men are named as the perpetrators of violence against women, whereas in the first they are not. 'Male violence against women' is only 'potential'; it not only 'circumscribes', it also 'elucidates' (whatever that might mean in this context); and it does not even circumscribe women, but only their 'social position', and only that 'to a certain extent'. The implication is that, if the responsibility of men for their violence against women is to be named, it must at the same time be rendered non-existent by being exaggerated to the point of absurdity. Hence, Mohanty's denial of male domination also involves denying men's responsibility in the maintenance of women's subordination.

Mohanty insists that writings on third-world women must confine themselves to 'empirical studies of gender differences' (p. 77), which she contrasts with 'universalistic, ahistorical categories' (p. 78). She says that she is not arguing against 'generalization', but against those generalizations which are not 'careful, historically specific' and 'complex' (p. 77). The difference appears to be whether or not men are identified as the beneficiaries or perpetrators of women's subordination. The single 'Western feminist' text which she views favourably does not mention men, or at least not in the quoted excerpt. The women lace-makers discussed in this text are exploited by a 'hegemonic ... world market', a 'production system', a 'culturally specific mode of patriarchal organization', a 'housewife ideology', etc., but not by men it would seem (p. 74).[5] In contrast, in a criticism of a book on women in Africa, Mohanty says that she does not object to 'the use of universal groupings for descriptive purposes', such as the phrase 'all the women of Africa'. The problem, she says, is that 'descriptive gender differences are transformed into the division between men and women'. She clarifies the nature of this 'division' in the next sentence: 'Women are constituted as a group via dependency relationships *vis-a-vis* men, who are implicitly held responsible for these relationships' (p. 68). The generalization she objects to here is 'holding men responsible'. (And once again it appears that such 'divisions' are solely a construct of 'Western feminist discourses' and that none exist in reality.) The distinction Mohanty herself supposedly draws between those generalizations of which she approves, and those of which she disapproves, is one between generalizations confined to a single cultural context, such as the lace-makers of Narsapur, India, and generalizations across cultures, for example, 'all the women of Africa', or 'third-world women'. But it is only some cross-cultural generalizations she disagrees with, that is, those involving men and male domination. Although she couches the generalizations she disagrees with in terms of women – 'all the women of Africa', etc. – in fact, she does not disagree with this generalization until it is 'transformed into the division between men and women'. She is also quite happy with cross-cultural generalizations which are sufficiently abstract, 'a hegemonic, exploitative world market', for example. It is indeed unhelpful to couch the problem solely in the individualistic terminology of 'men and women', rather than in terms of social systems of male domination. But to recommend silence on the question of male agency in defending their benefits and privileges at women's expense, often violently, is to recommend political quiescence.

What Mohanty is criticizing in the texts she discusses, what she is interpreting as a form of Western domination, is any attempt to bring feminist insights to bear on the situations of third-world women. In doing so, however, she abolishes the possibility of acknowledging, and hence struggling against, any form of domination at all. It is not possible to give an account of domination, however it is characterized, *without* identifying both its victims and its beneficiaries. To disqualify talk of victims is also to disqualify talking about oppression. But there is also a sense in which to talk about domination is not at all to talk about victims. Rather, it allows people the opportunity to make decisions they would not otherwise have been able to make, because seeing domination and the forms it takes provides people with alternatives they would not otherwise have had. To prohibit discussion of domination is to place a ban on alternative ways of seeing the world and one's place in it. As well, to disqualify explanation and analysis is to disqualify theory and politics, because both theory and politics are ways of understanding systematic regularities. Forms of domination cannot be challenged unless those regularities are made explicit by a theory and a politics which reaches beyond mere 'description'. To demand that feminist accounts restrict themselves to 'description' is to demand that they abandon theory and politics. It is a demand that they leave the status quo intact, and refrain from challenging those regularities which already structure conditions as oppressive. It is a demand which ensures a retreat from political engagement. If male domination cannot even be acknowledged, wherever it is to be found, however varied its subtle or brutal manifestations may be, it cannot be challenged and opposed, and feminism ceases to exist.

Notes

1   As Virginia Woolf so elegantly put it, struggling with the same issue in the British context: 'Our ideology is still so inveterately anthropocentric that it has been necessary to coin this clumsy term – educated man's daughter – to describe the class

whose fathers have been educated at public schools and universities. Obviously, if the term "bourgeois" fits her brother, it is grossly incorrect to use it of one who differs so profoundly in the two prime characteristics of the bourgeoisie – capital and environment' (Woolf, 1952: 265 n. 2).

2   There are exceptions (Lorde, 1978, 1979a; Wallace, 1990).

3   Racism does not always take the form of white supremacy, although it always involves domination and subordination. The racism of Japanese society, for example, is not directed against Koreans or the indigenous people, the Ainu, because they are not white, but because they are not Japanese. Even in the West there are forms of racism, such as anti-semitism, which are not white supremacist.

4   There were also Aboriginal women who were feminists, who had had harsh personal experience of male violence and who were committed to feminism as the struggle against it (Janne Ellen (Reid), personal communication, March 1995). Their presence has been expunged from the record.

5   In fact, Maria Mies makes it quite clear that it is men who exploit the women and benefit from their labour: '[The] men may belong to different classes, but they have in common that their own productive activity is based on the exploitation of female labour, both of their own women as well as that of other women' (Mies, 1982: 109).

8 What does it mean to call feminism 'white and middle-class'?

There do exist feminist texts which seem to obliterate the existence of women of racial, ethnic and cultural minorities. This obliteration, at least as it relates to US black women, is succinctly expressed in the title of an anthology of writings on Black Women's Studies: 'All the Women Are White, All the Blacks Are Men' (Hull et al., 1982). Two papers by Catharine Stimpson, dating from 1970 and 1971, and reprinted in 1988, exemplify the problem. The first paper is an account of the political contradictions faced by a white teacher teaching black literature. With the benefit of hindsight gained since the paper was first published, Stimpson herself recognizes that this text excludes black women writers. It 'makes grievous, ironic errors. Using the generic he, I write as if all black writers are male. This pronominal reductiveness erases black women writers and their daunting, renewing texts' (Stimpson, 1988: xv). The paper was reprinted without amendment, however, and she did not comment on the second paper although it, too, tended to erase the existence of black women. For example, towards the end of the paper, Stimpson says: 'women [sic] use blacks to describe themselves'. She goes on to quote at some length from a women's liberation pamphlet which draws the analogy between 'women' and 'blacks' no less than eleven times: '1. Women, like black slaves, belong to a master. ... 2. Women, like black slaves, have a personal relationship to the men who are their masters. 3. Women, like blacks, get their identity and status from white men.' Stimpson admits to liking this pamphlet, although she eventually disagrees with it – not, however, because of its erasure of black women, but because it is parasitic on black politics. That women have been excluded from the category 'black', she does not appear to notice.

The argument sets up two separate and symmetrical categories, 'women and blacks', which leave no place for those who live in both categories. This is a consequence of ignoring the feminist insight that all 'human' categories are automatically male unless care is taken to focus attention on women. The crucial error, for feminist purposes, of such arguments is their failure to apply the feminist insight into the male supremacist constitution of the male as the 'human' norm. All 'human' categories under male supremacist conditions are male, unless specifically stated otherwise, or 'marked', to use a linguistic term (Spender, 1980: 19–24). The category 'blacks', too, is male; here also, 'male' is the default option, the 'neutral' referent which switches in automatically, and which can be displaced only by adding extra qualifiers. It may be that it is this kind of exclusion that black feminists are referring to when they accuse feminism of being 'white, middle-class'. But the error in Stimpson's paper, as with all such arguments, is due to a failure of *feminist* commitment, a failure to recognize the male supremacist implications of using any term referring to a category of human individuals without explicitly rectifying the exclusion of the female.

Elizabeth Spelman places a great deal of emphasis on this 'women and other oppressed groups' usage as evidence for the 'white, middle-class' nature of feminism (Spelman, 1988). She quite rightly points out that equating the social position of women with the social positions of 'other oppressed groups', such as 'blacks', 'slaves', 'proletariat', ignores the existence of the women of the other oppressed groups, women who are blacks or slaves or exploited workers. If 'women' are contrasted with 'other oppressed groups', then the only women being referred to are privileged women who are not members of other (than women) oppressed groups. But her argument depends on how important the 'women and other oppressed groups' analogy is to feminism. She obviously regards this analogy as at least important, if not central, to 'dominant Western feminist thought', since she gives it a great deal of attention.

It is true that the early radical feminists sometimes referred to oppressed groups 'other than' women as though those groups contained no women. For example, Ti-Grace Atkinson said: 'Women have been *murdered* by their so-called *function* of childbearing exactly as the black people were murdered by their *function* of *color*' (and black women by both, although Atkinson did not say so) (Atkinson, 1974: 5 – her emphasis). But the analogy has rarely been used by feminists, simply *because* it excludes categories of women. As Robin Morgan put it at the beginning of this 'second wave' of feminism: 'It ... seems obvious that half of all oppressed peoples, black, brown, and otherwise, are *women*, and that I, as a not-starving white American woman living in the very belly of the beast, must fight for those sisters to *survive* before we can even talk together as oppressed women' (Morgan, 1970: xxxix – her emphasis).

Far from being a vital component of feminist theory, as Spelman seems to think, the parallel between 'women and other oppressed groups' has never been anything but an aside, an extra bit of special pleading. In the early 1970s it was a reference to the political movements feminists had been active in and were leaving behind because of those movements' male dominance – the anti-Vietnam war protests, and anti-racist and civil rights movements. It was an attempt to argue the case for women's oppression by pointing out the similarities between the oppression of women and other forms of oppression. It was also (and still is) a product of frustration. It is usually used in the context of a stubborn refusal to see women's oppression. Drawing a parallel between oppression on the grounds of sex and oppression on the grounds of race is an attempt to make women's oppression more visible. But the analogy is problematic for feminist purposes, because it tends to undermine the feminist challenge to the male monopolization of 'human' status. Not only does it exclude women, that female exclusion is a consequence of the male supremacist belief that all 'human' categories are only male. The analogy does seem to confine the referent of 'women' to women of the privileged race and class, that is, to women who are not among the oppressed, as Spelman points out. But it also portrays 'oppressed groups' as only male, and in doing so colludes with the male supremacist belief that only males matter.

bell hooks also criticized the analogy between 'women' and 'blacks' on the grounds that it obliterates the existence of black women (hooks, 1981: 138–44). As indeed it does. She attributed this to the racism of white women who refused to find common cause with black women. But she failed to see that the 'women and blacks' usage obliterates black women, not because they are not white, but because they are not men. All women have a common interest in combating the automatic belief that only the male is 'human'. This common interest may or may not translate into practical politics. But failing to recognize manifestations of male domination will not advance the cause of feminism.

Exactly what is involved in the charge that feminism is 'white and middle-class' is by no means clear. Audre Lorde, for example, criticized Mary Daly's *Gyn/Ecology* on the grounds that it 'dismissed my heritage and the heritage of all other noneuropean women' and depicted those women only 'as victims and preyers-upon each other' (Lorde, 1979b: 67–8). Daly's book, said Lorde, portrayed only 'white, western-european, judeo-christian … goddess-images' while ignoring images of powerful and divine women from Africa. But this objection is beside the point because it rests on a misinterpretation of what Daly's book was about. Daly's purpose was not to present a feminist mythology within which women could find images of female strength and divinity, but rather to criticize and expose the ways in which Western European patriarchal religion and mythology had co-opted and distorted the goddess-worship which preceded it. On that interpretation, Daly's confining of the discussion to Europe was intrinsic to her purpose.[1] As well, Daly's discussion of goddesses did not portray them as figures of female strength and divinity, since she saw them as already containing elements of male supremacist distortion. For Daly they hardly provided unambiguous role models for women to emulate or look up to, since they were already characterizations of male supremacist purposes and values.

Daly did not, it is true, portray any 'black foremothers', 'black women's heritage' or images of 'noneuropean female strength and power'. But neither did she portray any images of *European* female strength and power. It has never been her purpose to provide historical examples of female strength and power because, for her, history is invariably patriarchal. For Daly, women's strength starts now, with radical feminism, and with women's complete separation from patriarchal institutions, meanings and values. Whatever objections might be raised against the possibility of that project, it is in principle available to all women without exception.

Lorde's second objection to Daly's text – that it depicted women of 'other cultures' only as victims – is one that can (and has been) levelled against feminism's depiction of women in general. But how is it possible to speak about the atrocities committed against women without talking about the victimization of women? All women are victims of patriarchal practices (if that is the way it must be interpreted). Besides, Daly did not confine her depiction of women's victimization to other cultures – most of the second part of her book is devoted to Western Europe, to the witchcrazes and modern Western medical practices. Moreover, Daly's critique was not primarily a depiction of women at all, but an exposure of the workings of male supremacy. Women are its chief (although not the only) victims because male supremacy thrives at women's expense. But to demand that women not be portrayed as victims is to demand that the critique of male supremacy cease.

Gyn/Ecology has, however, been subjected to other criticisms. Elly Bulkin criticized Daly's selective quotation from two of the texts she used in her research (Bulkin, 1991). Bulkin argued that Daly discussed the first of these books, Katherine Mayo's *Mother India*, published in 1927, only in favourable terms, while ignoring its racism. Bulkin illustrated this racism with excerpts from Mayo's book. Mayo depicted 'the Indian' in terms of 'inertia, helplessness, lack of initiative and originality, lack of staying power and of sustained loyalties, sterility of enthusiasm, weakness of life-vigor itself'. She also described Indian men as 'broken-nerved, low-spirited, petulant ancients', in comparison with 'the Anglo-Saxon' of the same age, who 'is just coming into the full glory of manhood'. She also said that Indians would never be free of British rule because 'their hands are too weak, too fluttering, to seize or hold the reins of government' (Bulkin, 1991: 125–6).

These descriptions are undoubtedly racist, and it is true that Daly did not mention them in her discussion of Mayo's text. But Daly's omission can be defended, at least in part, in light of the reason why Mayo was so scathingly contemptuous of Indian men. That reason was the entrenched practice within the Indian higher castes of marrying off very young girls. Mayo's argument was that men who had been mothered by these children would never be fit to rule. Her intemperate racist language was a consequence of her horror at the cruelties which marital rape visited on girl children. She was also outraged that widows were forced to throw themselves, or were forcibly thrown, on to their husbands' funeral pyres. The racism of her text was directed towards men who treated women and girl children abominably. While that does not excuse it – her outrage could have been expressed in other ways, and racism is also abominable – it does make it more understandable. Her argument can also be criticized on other grounds, for example, her implicit belief that men mothered by adult women *are* fit to rule; her lack of awareness that high-caste male children were unlikely to have been cared for by their child mothers, but by adult female servants;[2] and her lack of awareness that the rape of female children is not confined to the

Indian subcontinent. None the less, what must not be forgotten in any criticism of Mayo's work is her exposure of what are atrocities by any criterion. It must also not be forgotten that she was fighting in the interests of women, for a world where such things as the mutilation and casual murder of girl children and the enforced immolation of women would not exist. The racism in Mayo's text was directed towards the very men who were responsible for the suffering. Challenging the racism would mean defending the men who systematically raped and murdered women and children. It is not uncommon in the feminist 'race' debate, to find that challenging racism means defending the men of the subordinated race (for example, Spelman, 1988), rather than black or third-world or indigenous women whose interests are once again elided in favour of men. That Daly refused or neglected to do this is not altogether to her discredit.

Bulkin does, however, make a more cogent point in relation to her discussion of another text cited by Daly.[3] Daly used this text as a source of information about the career of J. Marion Simms, known in the US at the time of his death in 1883 as 'the father of gynecology'. Daly quite rightly points out that Simms was a brutal butcher who perpetrated the most appalling tortures on women in the guise of 'science', and who was honoured by the male medical establishment for doing so. But as Bulkin points out, although Daly does acknowledge that Simms originally learned his vile trade on the bodies of black female slaves, that acknowledgement is cursory. And yet Barker-Benfield's text describes Simms' experiments on black women in some detail, along with Simms' own admission that he used black women, some of whom he bought for the purpose, because as slaves they had no power to refuse and no right of redress. If Daly's purpose was to expose the worst excesses of male brutality towards women, her failure to present her readers with an account of what Simms did to black women can be seen as complicity with the racist belief that what happens to black women is unimportant. The same suspicion arises in relation to Daly's discussion of the experimental use on women of contraceptive technology. She allows that 'low-income and nonwhite' women are 'victimized in a special way', but she says no more about this, and immediately proceeds to discuss 'well-educated (miseducated) upper-middle-class women'. While her discussion is apt and to the point, in failing to discuss what was done to black and third-world women she once again passed up an opportunity to expose some of the most chilling aspects of gynocide (Bulkin, 1991: 126–7; Daly, 1978: 225–7, 259). Perhaps it is this kind of thing that Audre Lorde was alluding to in her criticisms of *Gyn/Ecology*, but she did not say so.

False Universalism

One of the chief ways in which feminism is held to be 'white and middle-class' (and 'Western' and imperialist) is through the charge of 'false universalism'. Linda Nicholson says, for example: 'From the late 1960s to the mid-1980s, feminist theory exhibited a recurrent pattern: Its analyses tended to reflect the viewpoints of white, middle-class women of North America and Western Europe' (Nicholson, 1990: 1). Along with Nancy Fraser, she asserted that some 'modes of theorizing', which the authors identified as 'philosophy' and some forms of feminist theory, 'are insufficiently attentive to historical and cultural diversity, and they falsely universalize features of the theorist's own era, society, culture, class, sexual orientation, and ethnic, or racial group' (Fraser and Nicholson, 1990: 27). Arguments like those of Shulamith Firestone were 'essentialist' because 'they project onto all women and men qualities which develop under historically specific conditions' (p. 28). Firestone's 'appeal to biological differences between women and men' did not allow for the way these differences varied across cultures and throughout history (Nicholson, 1990: 5), and hence 'falsely universalized' Western cultural values.

But although Nicholson is quite right to point out that Firestone's argument is wrong, she does so for the wrong reasons. It is true that, as Nicholson says, childbirth is not the cause of women's oppression, as Firestone argued it was. But what is wrong with Firestone's argument is not that she 'falsely universalizes' childbirth as a biological difference between the sexes – it is, after all, universal. What is wrong about Firestone's argument is wrong for *any* cultural context, including her own. She perceived pregnancy and childbirth as inherently oppressive of women, and hence could only recommend that they be abolished by technological means.[4] She did not see that their oppressiveness to women was a consequence of their happening under conditions of male domination, and that they could be a source of joy and excitement if women had control over the conditions under which they got pregnant and gave birth. Hence, the problem with Firestone's argument was not that she made inappropriate generalizations from her own culture to other cultures; the problem was that it was false for her own culture as well. Childbirth is not inherently oppressive, even in the West. And neither is women's lack of control over the conditions under which they get pregnant and give birth peculiar to the West. Nor does the issue of women's taking control over their own bodies and reproductive capacities have relevance only for 'white, middle-class' women.

Other examples Nicholson gives of 'theory that generalizes from the experiences of Western, white, middle-class women' involved 'attempts by many feminist theorists to locate "the cause" of women's oppression', by

> the postulation by many influential feminist anthropologists in the 1970s of a cross-cultural domestic/public separation, ... later appeals in the late 1970s and early 1980s to women's labor, to women's sexuality, and to women's primary responsibility for childbearing [*sic* – does she mean child*rearing*? How can women not have responsibility for child*bearing*?]. In all of these cases, aspects of modern Western culture were postulated as present in all or most of human history. (Nicholson, 1990: 5–6)

Nicholson does not tell us which aspects or forms of 'women's labor' and 'women's sexuality' are 'Western', etc., and which are not. In the case of women's labour, if she is referring to the 'domestic labour debate', it failed to give an account of women's oppression, not because it was extrapolated to 'other' cultures, but because the Marxist concepts within which it was couched could not be stretched to fit feminist concerns. Like Firestone's argument, it was false for its own cultural context, let alone any other. In the case of women's sexuality, if she is referring to lesbianism, it is not in fact confined to 'the West', even as a simple sexual preference. As a feminist practice, it has relevance for women wherever they are subjected to male sexual imposition, and that is not confined to 'the West' either. As for the 'domestic/public separation', even women who are not 'white' or 'middle-class' have to struggle with the conflicting demands of paid work in the public sphere and unpaid work in the domestic sphere, of dependence on a male wage, or lack of access to one. And given the world-wide domination of Western economic and cultural imperialism, criticism of Western values, institutions and practices is not entirely irrelevant to the 'other' cultures. Once again, the problem with these postulations is not that they are peculiar to 'modern Western culture', but that they are inadequate as explanations for women's oppression even in 'the West' unless they are situated within the context of an exposure of male supremacy.

The lack of clarity starts with the term 'false universalism' itself. It is unclear whether it is an instance of redundancy – if 'universalizing' *per se* is false, then it does not need to be named as such – or whether it means exactly what it says – the qualifier 'false' implies that there are some universals which are true. Given the feminist principle that feminism must be relevant to all women, it might be assumed that it is the latter meaning which is intended, that is, that there are some true universals at least as far as women are concerned, although the particular universals under discussion are not among them. But those who level the charge of 'false universalism' do not provide any instances of true ones, and they are dismissive of those they do encounter (or believe they do). So it is more likely to mean that universalizing in itself is false, that is, that it cannot be done, that no statement in a universal form can possibly be true. In that case, the charge both accuses (some forms of) feminism of 'universalizing' and at the same time asserts its impossibility. But if it is not possible to 'universalize', how can anyone be doing it? If it is something which *cannot* be done, the question of whether it *ought* not to be done does not arise. There is no point in disapproving of something which does not happen because it cannot. If 'universalism' does not exist, it is pointless to judge it as ethically wrong.

Empirical universals are indeed not possible, in the sense that no one can ever be in a position to know every instance of anything (although it is reasonable to allow that there are some human empirical universals – that everyone is born of woman, for example, and that everyone dies). But theory and politics require empirical *generalizations*. And if no generalization can be universally inclusive, neither can its limits be specified, because to do so would require that very universal vision which is impossible. To the extent that excluding something involves saying what it is that is being excluded, it is *in*cluded.

The confusions contained within the term 'false universalism' carry over into the feminist attempts to avoid it. Those attempts involve the require-ment that what the feminist theorist says be confined to her own cultural and historical context. At best, the requirement is nothing but a 'tick the boxes' exercise, delineating a set of social characteristics which say nothing at all about the moral and political, and hence the feminist, stance of the speaker. At worst, it involves a logical impossibility – I cannot know what is only mine unless I also know that it is not yours; but to do that I would have to know what is yours, and that is just what I cannot know, according to the requirement that I remain confined to what is mine. In order to draw the boundaries, I need to know what is outside as well as what is inside; but if I know what is outside, then it is already inside. It is true that I (or anyone else) can speak only from within my own culture and experience. But to say as much is to say nothing substantive, since it is unavoidable. No one can do otherwise. It is not possible to speak from 'outside' the only form of life one knows. But in that case, it makes no sense to insist on remaining 'inside', because without an 'outside' there is no 'inside' either.

There *is* a boundary between comprehension and incomprehension, although it is not one that can be drawn in language. Across that boundary, I could not hear what was said since I could not understand it. But once I have understood it, there is no longer any boundary. That does not mean that there are no longer any problems. There is the possibility of misunder-standing (which is still a kind of understanding, a false one – it is not the same as incomprehension). It is still possible to disagree, to dispute or reject. To understand is not necessarily to forgive, to tolerate or to accept. Neither does understanding automatically bring equality, since it might arise out of a framework which bolsters my own superiority at someone else's expense. None the less, when I listen to what others say from their own different locations (Lugones, 1987), it is incorporated into my own world. When I engage with it, it becomes part of the way I situate myself in the world. Whether that understanding reinforces relations of domination, or whether it challenges them, is a separate issue which must be addressed with refer-ence to the particular instance in question. It is not resolved by reciting a list of social indicators.

For Fraser and Nicholson, philosophy is the primary site of 'false univer-salism'. Feminist writings are implicated only to the extent that those writ-ings continue to cling to the canons of traditional Western philosophy. Fraser and Nicholson argue that this complicity remains despite feminist criticism exposing 'the contingent, partial, and historically situated charac-ter of what has passed in the mainstream for necessary, universal, and ahis-torical truths' (Fraser and Nicholson, 1990: 26). But although the feminist critique may have these implications, that is not primarily what it is about. The problem with Western philosophy from a feminist standpoint is not primarily that consists of particular and partial viewpoints masquerading as timeless truth, but that it operates in male supremacist interests while defining itself as in the interests of all. Constructs of the 'universal human' are false, not because they are factually inaccurate or partial, but to the extent that they are ideological, that is, to the extent that they purvey the interests of domination as the interests of all, by constructing reality in such a way that relations of ruling vanish from sight because they are the only reality given meaning and value. The feminist task, then, is not to provide an alternative (women's) framework to set alongside, or replace, the existent 'contingent, partial and historically situated' (male) one. Feminism's task in relation to the Western intellectual tradition is to evaluate whether or not, and if so to what extent, frameworks owe allegiance to male supremacist interests, meanings and values, and to challenge and oppose those frameworks in the interests of a human status for all.

This is not the way Fraser and Nicholson characterize feminism, however. Rather, because they pose the problem in terms of 'false universalism', all they can recommend as a solution is attentiveness to a plethora of particular oppressions. They see this as already exemplified in 'postmodern-feminist theory'. This framework, they assert, 'would replace unitary notions of woman and feminine gender identity with plural and complexly constructed conceptions of social identity, treating gender as one relevant strand among others, attending also to class, race, ethnicity, age, and sexual orientation' (Fraser and Nicholson, 1990: 34–5). But this limitless multiplication of separate tasks is unnecessary if feminism is construed as the struggle against male domination. If feminism's concern with women is a consequence of that struggle, the question of 'feminine gender identity', whether 'unitary' or 'multiplicitous', does not arise. Or rather, it does not arise as a general theoretical problem for feminism, although it certainly arises for each individual feminist grappling with the problem of how to locate herself in relation to male supremacist relations of ruling. But that process cannot even begin unless male supremacy is recognized in the first place.

As it currently stands, the 'false universalism' problematic focuses on the differences between women, instead of on women's common interest in opposing male domination whatever its particular manifestations, and it locates relations of domination primarily among women. It sets up a dichotomy between those women who have the power to hear, those labelled 'white and middle-class' or 'Western', and those who have no obligation to listen because they do not have the power to be heard, those identified as black women, third-world women, women of colour, indigenous women. The dichotomy depicts two antagonistic categories of women, with all the duties and obligations on one side, and all the rights and entitlements on the other. All it can recommend is magnanimity on the part of the former towards the latter, while from the latter nothing is expected. It creates a fantasized category of 'white and middle-class' or 'Western' women who are portrayed as more powerful than women have ever been. It is an attribution of power to women who, in the grand scheme of things, have relatively little. Women do not have the power to 'universalize' because women are not even human in our own right, a state of affairs which feminism is centrally concerned to address. Women can, and frequently do, support men in their projects, embrace men's interests as their own, set aside, ignore, deny or actively seek to undermine their own needs, and by so doing, acquire some modicum of recognition and some small participation in the 'universal human' that man has made to suit his own interests. But no women anywhere have the power to 'universalize' in their own name. The most women can do is reproduce male supremacist 'universals'. If that is what is being done in the name of feminism, then it certainly needs to be addressed. It is not, however, addressed by the construct of 'false universalism', the nonsense of which arises from construing 'universal' as meaning all-inclusive as a matter of fact. Since no content can be given to any claims about 'all the facts' of human existence, this is meaningless. Feminism does not need to try and confine itself to one particular cultural context in order to avoid (empirical) 'universalism'. If 'universalism' is not possible, nothing need be done to avoid it.

There has recently been some tentative re-thinking of 'universalism' on the part of those who had previously been opposed to accepting any such notion (Benhabib, 1999). Seyla Benhabib says that there 'is a renewed respect for the universal', largely because of the atrocities committed in the name of particular ethnic, cultural and religious identities. Quoting Naomi Schor, she instances the fact that Nazism was opposed to '"the Enlightenment ideal of universalism"', implying that there must be something positive in an ideal which was so antithetical to Nazi and fascist ideology. Schor is also quoted as saying that '"the ongoing ethnic cleansing in Bosnia-Herzegovina, has if not revived universalism then called into question the celebration of particularisms, at least in their regressive ethnic form"' (Benhabib, 1999: pp. 10–11). So a link is starting to be made between the absence of any ideal of a common human condition and the worst forms of inhumanity.

Benhabib distorts feminist history, however, when she attributes 'suspicion' of generalizations to 'the feminist movement of the 1980s' across the board. In a masterpiece of agent deletion, she asserts:

> Every claim to generalization was suspected of hiding a claim to power on the part of a specific group; every attempt to speak in the name of 'women' was countered by myriad differences of race, class, culture, and sexual orientation that were said to divide women. The category 'woman' itself became suspect; feminist theorizing about woman or the female of the species was dubbed the hegemonic discourse of white, middle-class, professional, heterosexual women. We are still reeling from the many divisions and splinterings, the amoeba-like splittings, of the women's movements. (Benhabib, 1999: p. 10 of 17)

Benhabib is quite right in her account of what happened, and in pointing out that this has had deleterious consequences for feminist politics. But she is wrong in her belief that these kinds of accusations emanated from the women's movement as a whole. On the contrary, it is not the case that feminists in general are only now starting to realize that an ethical insistence on a common humanity is a basic feminist requirement. Some of us have known it all along. The accusations were usually levelled by one or another variety of academic feminism against radical feminism's insistence that women had a common interest in combating male supremacy (Bell and Klein, 1996). Benhabib may indeed have been led to rethink her rejection of concepts of the universal human by her recognition that appeals to cultural particularity can lead to gross abuses of human rights and dignity. But she remains unaware of what was at stake for feminist politics in the ban on 'universalism', that is, a denial of women's common interest in challenging male supremacy and claiming a human status of our own.

The sense in which feminist theory is universal does not entail that feminism is as a matter of fact all-inclusive, either of women or the human race, but that it is open-ended and non-exclusionary. Feminism has a universal relevance because it addresses itself to the human condition. It is an ethical insistence on the human rights and dignity of women (and of men too to the extent that they can divest themselves of their phallocratic interests). As such, it is precisely *non*-empirical, since if women were already in fact recognized as full members of the human race, there would be no need for feminism. As Marx and Engels once pointed out, each new revolutionary class speaks in the name of the universal human (Marx and Engels, 1974). Unfortunately, with the exception of feminism, all revolutionary classes have fought only for the 'humanity' of men. None the less, if it is the case that the oppressed, those deprived of human dignity and status under conditions of domination, must appeal to a universal human in making claims for their own humanity, then to demand that feminism dispense with universal claims is to demand that feminism refrain from claiming a human status for women.

The construct of 'false universalism' purports to demonstrate the falsity of feminism's claims to universal relevance. It says that feminism, too, is limited in its ethical claims, that it confines itself to the interests of comparatively privileged women, and by so doing is complicit with domination. But, as Marx and Engels pointed out, the claim by the revolutionary class to represent the interests of all the non-ruling classes is true 'in the beginning', that is, it is true as long as the revolutionary class does not become the new ruling class. The claim to universal relevance only becomes an illusion when the revolutionary class acquires a vested interest in domination, and defends *that* interest as the interests of all (Marx and Engels, 1974: 65–6). It is unlikely that feminism's ethical claim to universal relevance has yet developed into this kind of illusion, given that nowhere are women the new ruling class (although they can be complicit with the old male supremacist one), and given that feminism has consistently demonstrated a readiness to oppose any and every form of domination. That opposition is a consequence of the fact that all forms of domination harm women, including that form which no other revolutionary class has ever recognized: male domination.

To sum up: the charge of 'false universalism' is misleading. It is incoherent in asserting an impossibility, that forms of theorizing are 'universalizing' when they cannot be; and it misses the point, both about what is wrong with some of the theories propounded in a feminist context, and about the nature of domination. To the extent that the theories criticized under the banner of 'false universalism' are wrong, they are wrong simply because they are wrong and not because they are culturally specific or because they purport to be cross-cultural when they are not. And the form of domination feminism is centrally concerned with, male domination, is not confined to any particular cultural context but can be found wherever men monopolize 'human' status and women are confined to roles and statuses in subordination to men, that is, potentially anywhere. There is no 'false universalism'. Instead, there are various feminist attempts to come to grips with the phenomenon of male supremacy. To the extent that we cannot specify any limits to male domination, neither can we specify any limits to feminism.

Imperialism

Whatever is happening to elicit the charge of 'false universalism', and the correlative demand that the theorist confine what she says to her own culture, it is not 'universalizing' but something else altogether. It is an attempt to warn against feminist complicity with Western imperialism. While this is an important issue, it needs to be carefully and cogently argued, and it needs to keep the feminist exposure of male domination at the centre of the critique. Too often, the charge of feminist complicity with 'Western imperialism' is neither apposite nor accurate, and functions to deny the existence of male domination in 'other' cultures (Mohanty, 1988).

Hazel Carby does make one point which appears to support her claim to find a Western imperialist bias within feminism. She says that some feminist writings portray the third world as 'backward' and the West as 'more "enlightened" or "progressive"'. She provides two quotations from a paper by Maxine Molyneux, the second one of which does indeed appear to support Carby's contention. That quotation reads:

> There can be little doubt that on balance the position of women within imperialist, i.e., advanced capitalist societies is, for all its limitations, more advanced than in less developed capitalist and non-capitalist societies. In this sense the changes brought by imperialism to Third World societies may, in some circumstances, have been historically progressive. (Molyneux, 1981: 4 cited in Carby, 1982: 217)

Carby interprets this to mean that 'since "Third World" women are outside of capitalist relations of production, entering capitalist relations is, necessarily, an emancipating move' (Carby, 1982: 217).

But Carby misses the point of Molyneux's argument, which was that if colonialism led to the abolition of such traditional practices as 'polygyny, the brideprice, child marriages, seclusion, and forms of mutilation such as footbinding or female "circumcision"' (Molyneux, 1981: 3), that could only advance the cause of women's emancipation. Molyneux acknowledged that 'of course imperialism has also had negative consequences for women'. She said that capitalist employment conditions for women in the third world 'are often extremely oppressive – whether in urban sweat-shops, free-zone economies or rural plantations'. She said that 'development programmes' have often worsened women's situations by eroding the respected statuses women had before colonization, and by making use of existing forms of women's subordination. And she deplored the growth of large-scale prostitution and sex tourism as consequences of Western imperialism (pp. 4–5).

Molyneux did not believe, as Carby said she did, 'that it is only through the development of a Western-style industrial capitalism and the resultant entry of women into waged labour that the potential for the liberation of women can increase' (Carby, 1982: 222). On the contrary, she referred to the 'economism and reductionism' of such a view. She pointed out that it involved a failure 'either to problematize relations between the sexes or to acknowledge the differential effect of class relations on men and women' (Molyneux, 1981: 9). Her task anyway was not to compare third world countries with 'advanced' capitalist ones, but to evaluate the record of *socialist* countries in the light of their official stated policies on women's emancipation. In the case of the third world, far from arguing for the 'progressiveness' of capitalist relations, Molyneux argued the exact opposite. 'Whatever the failures of socialist society', she said, 'it is evident that in the Third World its record is none the less impressive when matched against capitalist societies of comparable levels of development and religio-cultural background' (p. 5).

She did not argue that third world countries were 'backward' in comparison with the 'progressive' West, as Carby said she did: 'Maxine Molyneux falls straight into this trap of "Third Worldism" as "backwardness" ... footbinding, clitoridectomy, female "circumcision" and other forms of mutilation of the female body have been described as "feudal residues" ... linked in reductionist ways to a lack of technological development' (Carby, 1982: 216, 222). Although Molyneux used the term 'feudal residues', she was not presenting this as her own opinion. She was pointing out that this was the way traditional practices were viewed in the 'official literature' of 'Third World post-revolutionary states' when those practices were seen by the ruling parties in those states as 'an obstacle to economic and social development' (Molyneux, 1981: 4). Her point of comparison was the historical past of those countries themselves, not the West. She was concerned with the degree to which women had been emancipated within nation states which claimed to be working towards that goal. On the feminist criterion of women's liberation, the abolition of cruelty and injustice towards women *is* progress, and it is unlikely to be only 'Western feminists' who are saying so.

This seems to be a difficult message to get across. It invariably arouses hostility, even though there is also a large measure of agreement, including within the United Nations (United Nations, 1995, 1996). Some of the reactions to a recent argument of Susan Moller Okin are a case in point.

Okin argued that multiculturalism is antagonistic to feminist aims to the extent that it is insufficiently critical of the ways in which 'culture' too often depends on the subordination of women. In the course of her argument, Okin provided a number of examples of 'cultural' practices which deprived some of the members of minority communities, notably the women, of even the most basic liberal democratic rights, including the ways in which those practices are justified by appeal to religious tradition. She argued that the role of liberal democratic states should be to support the rights of women against group rights when they come into conflict (Cohen et al., 1999).

Many of those who responded to her arguments agreed wholeheartedly. Others, however, disagreed more or less vehemently. The disagreement which is most relevant for present purposes is the accusation that Okin was speaking *for* or *about* the women of oppressed cultural minorities and not allowing them to speak on their own behalf. In other words, her argument was complicit with Western imperialism. Azizah Y. Al-Hibri, for example, asserted that Okin was 'speaking in her dominant voice about the *inessential Other*'. She went on to say: 'So inessential is this Other that, even when included in the discussion, it is rendered remarkably indistinguishable and voiceless. It is allowed into the discussion only through the voice and perceptions of the dominant "I"' (Cohen et al., 1999: 42). As Okin herself pointed out, however, it was not she who was silencing women, but 'the male-dominated religions with which they live', together with 'those feminists who downplay the patriarchy of many variants of their religions, but who enjoy every moment of their own lives' freedoms which are unthinkable to those "Others" whose voices they think I am drowning out' (p. 123). Okin's response is to the point, since even Al-Hibri herself acknowledged that 'this Other' was 'included in the discussion'.

Those who raise objections about the 'imperialism' of 'Western feminism' are not saying that 'Western feminists' should ignore the wrongs done to women in 'other' cultures, that they should focus on their own wrongs and leave 'other' women to worry about theirs. They are saying that the cultures in question are not as male dominated as 'Western feminists' say they are. But if the women whose cultures they are say so (even if not all of them do), and if women's control over their own lives is demonstrably curtailed by their subordination to men, then this argument is patently false. It may indeed be the case, as Al-Hibri argues, that Islam is not in principle male-dominated. (Martha Nussbaum argues the same case for reform Judaism – Cohen et al., 1999: 105–14.) But if women's subordination is constantly justified on religious grounds, this needs to be said, rather than, as Okin says (p. 123), being denied or played down.

Whatever the objections raised to Okin's argument, it was clear that defending the interests of women meant coming into conflict with 'culture' in some form or another. Okin herself tried to maintain a balance between the interests of women and the interests of cultural difference, but the subsequent debate emphasized once again the antagonistic nature of the relation between 'women' and 'culture'. As Katha Pollitt put it:

In its demand for equality for women, feminism sets itself in opposition to virtually every culture on earth. You could say that multiculturalism demands respect for all cultural traditions, while feminism interrogates and challenges all cultural traditions. ... fundamentally, the ethical claims of feminism run counter to the cultural relativism of 'group rights' multiculturalism. (Cohen et al., 1999: 27)

Race, Class and Gender

The expectation that feminism should address all forms of oppression because all forms of oppression harm women is an important enterprise, but it is not clear from the debate so far how it should be done. The usual form the debate takes involves attempts to combine different forms of oppression under the headings 'race, class and gender'. But this is unsatisfactory. Such attempts misrepresent the feminist project by excluding the problem of male domination from the outset. Calling the central concern of feminist politics 'gender' ensures that male domination will not even be seen, much less challenged and addressed. But the categories are also unsatisfactory in their own terms. If 'race, class and gender' need to be combined, then they must have been separated out in the first place. The categories have their own separate objects of knowledge – 'race, class, gender'; their own separate forms of oppression – 'racism, classism, sexism'; their own separate constituencies of the oppressed – 'blacks (etc.), workers, women'; and their own forms of politics – 'anti-racism, socialism,' feminism'. Once they have been separated in this symmetrical way, the categories have nothing in common.

This problem is a consequence of the politically neutral language within which the debate has been couched. The terms 'race, class and gender' have already deleted any reference to domination. No form of domination is acknowledged, however characterized (apart from passing, and increasingly rare, references to capitalism). There is no identifiable ruling class; the debate focuses exclusively on categories of the oppressed who are subjected to power relations which are never located in the vested interests of the powerful. If, in contrast, we enter the debate by recognizing the existence of male supremacy in the first place, then it is possible to identify the social system of meanings and values by which domination is maintained. While it is important to delineate the ways in which domination is resisted and the human spirit survives under even the most degrading conditions, it is also important to clarify the nature of the system which oppresses. It might be argued that this problem of the neutralization of political focus could equally well be addressed by entering the debate from the standpoint of resistance to capitalist domination or to racial supremacy. But both these forms of politics suffer from the so far insurmountable problem, from the feminist standpoint, of ignoring or subordinating the interests of women. It is only feminism, with its explicit acknowledgement of the ideological belief that only men are 'human', which promises to throw new light on those forms of domination which have traditionally focused only on the interests of men. Bringing feminist insights to bear on race and class domination keeps political attention focused on women, attention which is too easily diverted given the ongoing reality of the male monopolization of who counts as 'human'. But it also promises to illuminate the phenomenon of domination more generally, in ways in which confining attention to the interests of men, no matter how justified, does not.

One text which illustrates the problems with the 'race, class and gender' debate is Elizabeth Spelman's *Inessential Woman*. This is a brave attempt to fill out the details of a feminist anti-racist position. It ultimately fails, however, largely because feminism is defined only in terms of 'sexism' and 'gender' rather than in terms of the struggle against male domination. Typically, the book proceeds by way of a number of accusations that 'dominant Western feminist thought has taken the experiences of white middle-class women to be representative of, indeed normative for, the experiences of all women' (Spelman, 1988: ix). She does discuss the work of a number of feminist theorists, but she gives us no concrete examples from these writings of what might count as 'experiences of white, middle-class women'; nor does she tell us how these might differ from the experiences of those women who provide her main counter-example, that is, US black women. Moreover, since many of the targets of her criticism are not feminist on any criterion, those criticisms are irrelevant to her purported task of demonstrating the limitations of feminist theory. Her criticisms of the writings of Plato and Aristotle, for example, may be accurate and appropriate, but they hardly qualify as feminist thought; nor does the work of the other male writers she cites (for example, pp. 119–22); nor do the hypothetical examples which she devises for the purposes of her own argument (such as in Chapter 6, especially p. 140), but which she did not find in any feminist writings.

Spelman holds feminism responsible for the separation between 'race, class and gender':

> the attempt to isolate gender from other elements of human identity such as race and class, along with parallel attempts to isolate sexism from other forms of oppression such as racism and classism, has been instrumental in the preservation of white middle-class privilege in feminist theory. (Spelman, 1988: 16)

But it is the very setting up of the categories which keeps them distinct. In fact Spelman never manages to combine them. 'Class' is only ever mentioned as an occasional aside; and 'gender' becomes another aspect of 'race'. This usually involves defining 'gender' as 'different ways of being a man', and pointing out that black men are not superior to white women. In doing so, she not only misses the male supremacist connotations of her own examples, she also misses crucial aspects of the racism. To give just one example: she mentions that Emmet Till was 'murdered by white men for talking to a white woman'. This example occurs in the context of a discussion of 'the ideology of masculinity in the United States' which, Spelman says, 'hardly includes the idea that Black men are superior to white women'

(p. 89). But this interpretation misses the point. Till was not murdered by white women, and he was not murdered because he was 'inferior' to white women, but because, in the minds of his male racist murderers, he was 'inferior' to white men. In the evil logic of racism, he was murdered because he dared to behave like a white man towards a white woman, and because, as a black male, he did not have a white man's prerogatives. His status as male was crucial in his murderers' perception of him as 'above himself'. The question of his social ranking in relation to white women did not arise because the woman was no more than a pawn in a lethal white man's game.

Spelman gives us no information about the 'white woman' Till spoke to. Did this woman complain about his speaking to her, or did Till's murderers act without her knowledge or consent? Did she collude with the murderers, demanding that Till be punished because he dared to speak to her? Or was she horrified at the murder? Did she protest, or did she not know what was happening until it was all over? The answers to such questions are vital if what is at issue is the complicity of white women with racism. By deleting all reference to the woman in the case, Spelman is complicit with the male supremacist belief that women are unimportant. In Spelman's account, all the actors in the evil scenario were male. The woman had no moral agency. We are not told whether she consented or protested, nor whether her protests would have made any difference to the outcome. She is nothing but an icon of white supremacist masculinity, useful as a justification for murder in the racist male mind, but allowed no will of her own. The issue is not whether or not she was 'inferior' to Emmet Till; the issue is that she did not exist at all in her own right. That Spelman missed the point is a consequence of keeping the 'race' and 'gender' categories separate and distinct, and substituting the infinitely malleable concept of 'gender' for male supremacy.

Spelman does attempt to argue the case for the 'white, middle-class' nature of feminism in other ways than the 'women and other oppressed groups' argument (discussed above). She says that feminism's exclusive focus on 'gender' and its concomitant oppression, 'sexism', has meant that women's race and class identity, and 'the racism and classism some women face and other women help perpetuate' (pp. 112–13), have been peripheral to, or ignored by, feminist politics. As a consequence, the only kind of 'gender', that is, the only way of being a woman, which feminism has acknowledged, is that of women who are not subjected to racism and classism – 'namely, white middle-class women of Western industrialized countries' (p. 3). The solution, then, is to combine all three forms. We need to ask, she says, about the ways in which 'race and class identity may be intertwined with gender identity' (p. 112).

While Spelman is right about the need to combine the three great forms of oppression, her own attempt fails because she fails to get the feminism right. Feminism's main concern is not 'gender' or 'sexism', or even 'women' in the sense of what women 'are', but male supremacy. The question of 'women's identity' is problematic, not in and of itself, but because of the male supremacist requirement that the only 'human' identity permissible is male. That some men are more (and less) 'human' than other men is also an aspect of male domination. There is sufficient evidence for the domination of men by men in Spelman's own text, as well as for feminism's awareness of this. And yet she uses this evidence as a weapon against feminism, and argues against 'the common position of women' by pointing to relations of domination among men. As might be expected, the discussion then proceeds to focus on the oppression of men, with women cast in the role of oppressors of men. (One example of this is her reference to the murder of Emmet Till, discussed above.)

Another example occurs in her discussion of Simone de Beauvoir's *The Second Sex* (Spelman, 1988: pp. 63–4). She disagrees with Beauvoir's statements to the effect that the world belongs to men, and that everything in girls' experience confirms them in their belief in masculine superiority, by pointing out that some women hold positions of superiority over some men: 'a white girl [and] Black men ... girls of the upper classes [and] working-class men'. But Spelman herself has already located these oppressions of race and class in hierarchies among men – 'prince and pauper, master and slave ... are all male'. She also allows the same point by quoting without comment Beauvoir's statement: 'In the upper classes women are eager *accomplices* of their *masters*' (emphasis added). If women are accomplices rather than instigators, and men are masters, then what is at stake is primarily the interests of men. That class relations and racial domination are maintained at the expense of some men, makes them no less male interests. That these interests are also defended by women does not make them women's interests in any feminist sense, since they are based on women's subordination. Women benefit from class privilege only to the extent that they embrace their own subjugation to men. This does not mean that women are innocent of racism or class privilege. But it does mean that, to the extent that women defend race or class privilege, they are acting in complicity with male supremacist values.

There is a sense in which the demand that feminism address all forms of oppression is redundant. That is exactly what feminism is already doing because feminism is happening wherever women committed to feminism are situated. All feminists are already included because they are women struggling against male supremacy and for their own human dignity. The issues which feminism has placed on the public agenda are already relevant to all women. Exposing male violence, especially sexual violence, or asserting women's human right to control over the conditions of their own existence, including the secure integrity of their own bodies, for example, are not issues of concern only to relatively privileged women. Indeed, the less privileged women are, the fewer resources they have, economic or otherwise, the more pressing and vital such issues become. Feminism raises no barriers against the participation of any woman (or the understanding of any man) because all that is required for a feminist commitment is a feminist commitment. That is not to say that there are no barriers in the way of women's embracing of feminism. There are. Chief among those barriers are those distortions, largely purveyed by the mass media, but also exemplified by much of what I have identified as 'academic feminism', which alienate women from feminism by presenting it as something trivial, ridiculous, offensive or incomprehensible.

If, however, what is being demanded in the name of 'anti-racism' is that every feminist text without exception should include discussions of racism, that is unreasonable. Complying with that demand would be itself a form of racism. Unless the discussion of racism was intrinsic to the purpose of the text, to introduce it would be no more than a tokenistic using of women of colour to prove one's 'anti-racist' credentials. It also involves an impossibility. Once 'women' have been divided into a multiplicity of races, how many races, and which ones, must be cited if one is to avoid excluding someone? No one can cite them all, because no one can ever be in a position to know them all, even supposing there is an 'all' to know. And it threatens to establish a new hegemony, with 'white' being displaced from the dominant position in the same moment as it is recognized as such, and replaced with the most vocal, literate and published representatives of 'other' races.

As long as the debate remains confined within the terms of 'race, class and gender', no progress can be made in exposing the connections between all forms of domination. Not only are the categories as they stand too separated ever to be brought together, setting the debate up in this way puts difficulties in the way of recognizing domination at all, because it focuses attention on categories of the oppressed while leaving unspecified what it is that the oppressed are oppressed by. Just as the situations of women differ culturally and historically, so do the particular social problems which must be addressed in women's interests. But just as male domination is everywhere the same in its insistence that only men are 'human', so do women have a common interest in combating it. The forms that opposition takes may differ, but their meaning and value will be the same, a struggle for the human status of women at no one's expense.

A vivid sense of what is involved in the assertion that feminism is white and middle-class is conveyed by a cartoon in *The Sydney Morning Herald* on 8 March 2000, commenting on the fact that it is International Women's Day (IWD). Along the top of the drawing is written: 'International Women's Day – Somewhere in Ethiopia'. Four black women, one of them with two children, are depicted sitting around a small fire, with grass huts in the background and a couple of trees on the horizon. Each of the women is saying something. First woman: 'I just put my kids into child-care and enrolled in a business course'; second woman: 'I was glad to get my career off to a good start before I had my kids'; third woman: 'I told my husband, when we had kids, he had to share the load'; fourth woman: 'I've been so flat out enjoying my career, I haven't even thought of kids.'

At the risk of spoiling the fun, the anti-feminism of this piece of male supremacist propaganda needs to be spelled out. It says that the demands of Australian women are unimportant, even ludicrous, when we look at what Ethiopian women need. Women in Ethiopia, it says, do not even have basic necessities like adequate shelter (they are sitting on the ground in the open air and they only have grass huts to live in), food (there are six people but only two plates, and anyway this is Ethiopia, notorious for its famines), water (the trees are spindly and there is no other vegetation), cooking facilities (the camp fire), or any of the other benefits enjoyed by women in Australia. In comparison the IWD concerns of Australian women are trivial, it says, a mere matter of careers and getting husbands to help with the housework. Australian women (it is implied) are selfish and uncaring – either they see their careers as more important than their children whom they put into child-care, or they don't have children at all, thus ignoring what ought to be their primary mission in life. Either way, they are so privileged that they don't really have anything to complain about when other women are so deprived.

But there are other ways of looking at these issues. Wanting a career has nothing to do with women's selfishness. (The question of men's selfishness never arises unless the men are very, very rich, in which case it is called greed, and quite rightly so.) Women need to establish their own financial independence because being dependent on a man deprives a woman of the most basic form of control over her own life and, not incidentally, her control over the conditions her children live under. It is true that, once women have access to adequate resources, they have fewer children or none at all. But it is also true that over-population is a major world problem. In the light of that well-documented fact, it could even be said that having fewer children, far from being a selfish act, is an altruistic one, a contribution to world peace and security and sustainable development. As for the plight of Ethiopian women, that is the fault and responsibility of men: of the men who demand wives who are children in order to guarantee virginity; of the men of the Ethiopian ruling class (the detestable Mengistu is no longer dictator but he was neither the first, the last nor the only ruler of Ethiopia to keep the population in misery); of the men who control a world economic order which keeps nation states like Ethiopia beggared and poverty-stricken.

Whose interests are served by these invidious comparisons between women? It is certainly not the interests of Australian women whose concerns are distorted into something trivial and unimportant, and derided by being placed in the mouths of 'Ethiopian' women. But it is also not in the interests of Ethiopian women to be depicted as primitives living in grass huts and squatting on the ground. Comparing and contrasting categories of women is not in women's interests at all, as long as it deflects attention away from the real problem by disguising or ignoring the workings of male supremacy, or by reducing feminism to nothing but the trivial preoccupations of the privileged.

Notes

1   Daly made the same point in her autobiography where she said that she had pointed out in a conversation with Audre Lorde that *Gyn/Ecology* was not 'a

compendium of goddesses', but was intended as a discussion of 'those goddesses which were direct sources of christian myth' (Daly, 1993: 232).

2 For a similar argument to Mayo's, in relation to the British ruling class and its custom of 'the Nanny', see Gathorne-Hardy, 1972.

3 This is G.J. Barker-Benfield's *The Horrors of the Half-Known Life: Male Attitudes Toward Women in Nineteenth Century America*, published in 1976.

4 My judgement that Firestone's argument is wrong is confined to this particular aspect of it. Although this is her central argument, there is much more in her book which is eloquent and insightful about the workings of male supremacy.

5 Socialism is rarely mentioned within the 'race, class, gender' categories debate as the politics which is specific to class. This omission indicates that constructing the categories in this way is as inadequate for class politics as it is for feminist and anti-racist politics.

9 Masculinity
and dehumanization

The Radical Feminist Account

There is, however, another way to characterize a feminist account of 'race', which does not set up antagonistic categories of women, 'white and middle-class' and the rest, or an irresolvable distinction between 'gender', race and class, and which starts from the feminist problematic of male domination, or at least implicitly refers to it.

'Second-wave' radical feminism has from the beginning been concerned with all forms of oppression which affect the life chances and human dignity of women, that is, with all forms of oppression. By attributing all forms of oppression to male domination, the early radical feminist account linked them together, and provided the beginnings of a framework for understanding all forms of invidious hierarchical distinctions between categories of human beings. This early radical feminist account has never been challenged. It appears to have dropped out of the debate altogether and been forgotten. In what follows I take up this early radical feminist insight into the primacy of male domination, arguing that it was basically correct despite the problems.

One of those problems was a tendency to locate the primacy of male domination in 'history'. The oppression of women, it was argued, provided the model for all other forms of oppression because it happened first in human history. Women were the first social group to be enslaved. Once men learned that other human beings, namely women, could be enslaved, they applied that model to other groups of men. THE FEMINISTS, a group of radical feminists formed in New York in October 1968, said in their manifesto: 'Women, or "females", were the first class to be separated out from humanity and thus denied their humanity' (THE FEMINISTS, 1969: 360). The New York Redstockings said in 1970:

> Male supremacy is the oldest, most basic form of domination. All other forms of exploitation and oppression (racism, capitalism, imperialism, etc.) are extensions of male supremacy: men dominate women, a few men dominate the rest. All power structures throughout history have been male-dominated and male-oriented. (Redstockings, 1970: 599)

Ti-Grace Atkinson said:

> The oppression *of* women *by* men is the source of *all* the corrupt values throughout the world. ... Since the oppression of women is generally agreed to be the beginning of the class system and women the first exploited class, every culture or institution or value since that time contains that oppression as a major foundational ingredient and renders all political constructs after that initial model of human oppression at the very least suspect. (Atkinson, 1974: 5, 30 – her emphases)

Robin Morgan said:

> women ... comprise the oldest oppressed group on the face of the planet. ... [There is a] profoundly radical analysis beginning to emerge from revolutionary feminism: that capitalism, imperialism, and racism are *symptoms* of male supremacy – sexism. Racism as a major contradiction, for example, is surely based on the first 'alienizing' act: the basic primary contradiction that occurred with the enslavement of half the human species by the other half. (Morgan, 1970: xxiii, xxxix – her emphasis)

Shulamith Firestone said:

> the natural reproductive difference between the sexes led directly to the first division of labor at the origins of class, as well as furnishing the paradigm of caste (discrimination based on biological characteristics). ... [Radical feminism] sees feminist issues not only as *women's* first priority, but as central to any larger revolutionary analysis. ... the current leftist analysis ... does not relate the structures of the economic class system to its origins in the sexual class system, the model for all other exploitative systems, and thus the tapeworm which must be eliminated first by any true revolution. (Firestone, 1981: 9, 37 – her emphasis)

But locating the link in hypothetical accounts of the 'origins of patriarchy', in a distant past before the advent of written records, is not entirely satisfactory as a theoretical enterprise. It is more akin to myth-making than to historical research (Dunbar, 1970; for more recent and more convincing attempts, see Eisler, 1987; Lerner, 1986). The historical facts appealed to as evidence are few and far between. Given that the historical times referred to have left few traces, we cannot really know what happened thousands of years ago. Neither would the knowledge have much relevance for present purposes given that the conditions described no longer exist, that is, societies untouched by the rapacious demands of world-wide capitalism. However, the appeal to 'history' was not integral to the early radical feminist account. It need not be taken literally, but can be read as a metaphor for the pervasiveness and intransigence of domination, and as a genuine attempt to understand all forms of domination.

It can also be interpreted as no more than a necessary rejoinder to the male left insistence on putting socialism first. All feminists, including socialist feminists, were aware that socialism, as least as it had been traditionally defined by men, would not automatically lead to the liberation of women.

Feminists became tired of being told by male politicos that the liberation of women could wait until after the socialist revolution, that, because women's subordination was connected to the private ownership of the means of production, the abolition of that private ownership would automatically mean the abolition of women's subordination. Experiences in organizations of the male left, of being pushed into the background and used as domestic and sexual servicers, had led to a healthy scepticism on the part of politically committed women. Insisting on the primacy of women's oppression was a way of theorizing the need for women to organize independently.

But the radical feminist emphasis on the primacy of women's oppression, and hence the primacy of male domination, went further than this. It was not simply an organizational strategy for establishing political priorities, although it was certainly that. It was also a radically different way of looking at the world, different, that is, from the male dominant status quo. It placed the interests of women first, and from that standpoint spoke in the name of the universal human by asserting that the overcoming of women's subordination would mean the overcoming of all other forms of subordination as well. For Ti Grace Atkinson, for example, the oppression of women by men created a world where no one could be free:

> A human being is not born from the womb; it must create itself. It must be *free*, *self*-generative. A human being must feel that it can grow in a world where injustice, inequity, hatred, sadism are not directed at it. No person can grow into a life within these conditions; it is enough of a miracle to survive as a *functioning* organism. (Atkinson, 1974: 5 – her emphases)

On the radical feminist account, the struggle against male domination had political priority over other forms of politics, not only because of a pressing need to redress the harms done to women, but also because the liberation of women would mean the liberation of all. But although the early radical feminists saw all forms of domination as the result of male domination, they did not tell us how this was so, apart from the appeal to 'history'. They tended simply to assert a link without analysing it. The present task, then, is to extend this early radical feminist insight by identifying the links between male domination and social domination in general.

Racism, Masculinity and Dehumanization

There is some support in the anti-racist literature for the early radical feminist argument that all forms of domination are variations on the theme of male domination. It usually takes the form of asserting some kind of link between racism on the one hand, and masculinity and what is referred to as 'sexuality' but which is actually male sexuality, on the other. This link is not given a central emphasis. In fact it is not even a link at all except in the sense that both racism and masculinity/(male) sexuality are mentioned in the same breath. It is referred to only tangentially and briefly, as an addition to the main theme, an interesting by-product but never the crux of the matter. It would appear that the reason for this is, once again, the male supremacist belief that only men are 'human'. In other words, nothing very much has been said by connecting racism and masculinity, because all that has been said is that racism is part of being human, masculinity being 'humanity' *per se*. The implications for racism of the fact that women are not masculine remain undiscussed. What is also not discussed are the ways in which ideological justifications for the domination of men by men mimic those already operating in the domination of women by men.

Linking racism with masculinity does not mean that women have some special immunity to racism (or misogyny or any other form of elitist exclusion). Although women do not have the social power to wreak the havoc that men do, there have always been women who have supported men in their projects, no matter how evil, as well as identifying their own interests with those of men. Supporting and identifying with men is the only way women are permitted access to the 'human' under male supremacist conditions, although that does not mean that women are not responsible for what they do. Both sexes can fall into the easy automatic patterns of institutionalized racism. But it can be argued (although the anti-racist literature does not) that masculinity is the meaning of racism in the sense that it operates to render someone else subhuman in order to bolster one's own masculinity, or, in the case of women, the masculinity of the men they identify with or want to be recognized by. The link between masculinity and domination is dehumanization. Domination requires the dehumanization of those whose human rights cannot be allowed to stand in the way of the vested interests of the powerful, just as masculinity requires the dehumanization of women. But the parallel is not drawn in the anti-racist literature.

Ali Rattansi, for example, briefly mentions masculinity in the context of racism without drawing any inferences. He says:

> both working-class and middle-class masculinities are involved ... [in] racial harassment and violence ... with defences of the neighbourhood against racialized 'others' which Cohen refers to as the 'nationalism of the neighbourhood' ...; the proving of masculinity by beating up 'Pakis' ...; the sexual harassment of black women; and an aspect that deserves much greater research, in the middle-class and professional context, the complex intertwining of masculinity, class and racism in the exclusion of blacks from employment or promotion by white male managers. (Rattansi, 1992: 27)

Apart from a later brief discussion of 'the complex intertwining of racism with sexuality' (pp. 29–30), where he refers to the irrationality and intransigence of racism, Rattansi does not develop this theme any further. Although he appears to be suggesting here that the racism is in some sense a consequence of the masculinity and 'sexuality', he does not draw any implications. He does not say anything about the masculinity of black men. The 'masculinities' referred to are the prerogative of white males. But black men are masculine too. Does black male masculinity differ from white male masculinity, given that the proving ground of 'masculinity' is 'beating up "Pakis"'? What happens to black male masculinity in the context of racist dehumanization? And what are we to make of the inclusion in this list of the reference to the sexual harassment of black women? Black women are not sexually harassed only by white men, and neither are black women the only women to suffer sexual harassment. None the less, despite these problems, it is clear that Rattansi does perceive a link between masculinity and racism.

The link between masculinity and imperialism/racism wends a curious trajectory through Edward W. Said's *Orientalism* (1987). It is obvious from a number of references and discussions throughout the text that, for Said, there is a connection. What is less obvious is the exact nature of the connection and the importance Said assigns to it. It often appears in the text without his remarking on it, suggesting the possibility that on at least some occasions, he is not even aware the connection has been made.

It appears most frequently in the form of suggestive hints arising out of the connotations of the terms used. For example, Said characterizes Western Orientalism's own view of itself as involving a 'stripping [of the Orient] of its veils' (p. 76). He says that Western Orientalist scholars have a 'learned reliance on the Orient as a kind of womb out of which they were brought forth' (p. 88), that they 'survey[ed] ... the passive, seminal, feminine East' (p. 138), and that the colonizers 'poured out their exuberant activity onto the fairly supine, feminine Orient' (p. 220). He summarizes Orientalist assumptions about the East as involving 'the separateness of the Orient, its eccentricity, its backwardness, its silent indifference, its feminine penetrability, its supine malleability' (p. 206). He mentions a number of times that the Orient was 'penetrated and possessed' by the West. He quotes one Orientalist as saying, ' "A society colonizes when ... it brings to virility a new society to which it has given birth" ' (p. 219). And in a statement whose significance is obviously lost on him because he does not comment on it, he says that the effect of the new US social science on the Arab or Islamic Orient 'is to keep the region and its peoples *emasculated*, reduced to "attitudes", "trends", statistics: in short, *dehumanized*' (p. 291 – emphasis added).

But even when he discusses the connection in some detail, he fails to draw out the male supremacist implications. At one early point in the book, he illustrates the discourse of Orientalism, by which the West '*made* [the Orient] Oriental' (his emphasis), with a discussion of 'Flaubert's encounter with an Egyptian courtesan'. This account by Flaubert produced, he said, 'a widely influential model of the Oriental woman':

> she never spoke of herself, she never represented her emotions, presence, or history. *He* spoke for and represented her. He was foreign, comparatively wealthy, male, and these were historical facts of domination that allowed him not only to possess Kuchuk Hanem physically but to speak for her and tell his readers in what way she was 'typically Oriental'. My argument is that Flaubert's situation of strength in relation to Kuchuk Hanem was not an isolated instance. It fairly stands for the pattern of relative strength between East and West, and the discourse about the Orient that it enabled. (p. 6 – his emphasis)

He concludes a later, more detailed, discussion of the work of Flaubert by commenting:

> Woven through all of Flaubert's Oriental experiences, exciting or disappointing, is an almost uniform association between the Orient and sex. In making this association Flaubert was neither the first nor the most exaggerated instance of a remarkably persistent motif in Western attitudes to the Orient. And indeed, the motif itself is singularly unvaried. ... Why the Orient seems still to suggest not only fecundity but sexual promise (and threat), untiring sensuality, unlimited desire, deep generative energies, is something on which one could speculate. (p. 188)

Said himself, however, refrains from doing so. He ends the discussion by saying: 'it is not the province of my analysis here, alas, despite its frequently noted appearance' (p. 188). He did not comment on the fact that Flaubert's depiction of 'the Oriental woman' differed not at all from standard phallocratic depictions of any women anywhere. Neither did he comment on the fact that it was a text about a woman which so aptly illustrated Orientalism's approach to the East in general. If a text about a woman is typical of this approach, if it can 'stand for the pattern of relative strength between East and West', if it is an instance of a 'singularly unvaried' and 'remarkably persistent motif in Western attitudes to the Orient', then the fact that it *is* a text about a woman is not just an interesting side issue. It is a vital clue to the operation of that form of domination which is Western imperialism, of which Orientalism is one manifestation.

There emerges from Said's text a coherent constellation of themes which provides an unexpected substantiation of the early radical feminist insight that the domination of women by men is the model for all forms of domination. Within the discourse of Orientalism, 'the Orient' is feminized. It is made 'like a woman'.[1] It is given female characteristics and treated the way women are treated. It is never allowed to speak for or represent itself. He, the European male, speaks for 'her'. The differences between the West and 'the Orient' line up in the same way as male supremacist discourses construe the differences between the sexes. For example, Lord Cromer, Orientalist scholar and British governor of Egypt which he 'ruled almost single-handedly between 1883 and 1907', summed up the differences as follows: 'The European is a close reasoner; his statements of fact are devoid of any ambiguity; he is a natural logician, albeit he may not have studied logic; he is by nature sceptical and requires proof before he can accept the truth of any proposition; his trained intelligence works like a piece of mechanism' (Said, 1994: 239–40). Having delineated the supreme quality of the 'European' intellect to his own satisfaction, Cromer proceeded to contrast this with what he variously designated 'the mind of the Oriental', 'the Egyptian', and the present-day Arab. The thinking of this personage is, according to Cromer, 'eminently wanting in symmetry' and 'is of the most slipshod description'. He is 'singularly deficient in the logical faculty' and 'incapable of drawing the most obvious conclusions'. He is much given to 'lengthy' explanations which are 'wanting in lucidity', and 'will probably contradict himself half-a-dozen times before he has finished' (Said, 1978: 38). Substitute 'male' for 'European' and 'female' for 'Oriental' in this passage, and it could be transposed to any of a myriad of texts expatiating on the nature of the feminine.

But above all, in the discourse of Orientalism the East is there to be fucked. This is partly a figure of speech. The whole – 'the Orient' – is reduced to a part – the female part.[2] But in another sense it is not a figure of speech at all. European men actually went to the Orient to use their penises. Or rather, having feminized the Orient, they behaved towards it in the fashion appropriate to its feminine status. They imperialized and colonized the Orient, along with most of the rest of the non-European world, using their penises as well as other weapons of warfare. This is not surprising. Colonization is a kind of warfare, one in which there is a gross disparity of power, and men have always used their penises as weapons, that is, raped, in war (and not only in war). Neither is it surprising that this aspect of Western domination has received so little attention, given the continuing hegemony of male interests, and in particular the male interest in keeping sex out of the arena of public political debate and safely ensconced in the realm of the natural, the private, the pre-ordained and the unarguable, an interest which is not confined to white Western men. Even Said, who provides clear evidence of it, does not put it in such stark terms. Instead he refers to a non-specific 'sexuality', the meaning of which wavers between a licentiousness attributed to the Oriental male, a sensuality attributed to the whole Orient, and the actual sexual practices of European men. These are, of course, all aspects of the same thing, a male sexuality used to conquer and control, which is justified by projecting the responsibility for it on to the 'other' – it is the Orient which grabs the Western conqueror's penis and makes him use it, just as women do everywhere. But Said does not bring the strands together. Significantly, 'sexuality' does not appear as an entry in the index and hence cannot be traced throughout the text.

Once the suggestive hints are extricated and combined, however, the connection between masculinity and imperialism becomes clear. Imperialism, whether it takes the form of outright slavery, of the colonial dispossession of indigenous peoples, of the multinational control and exploitation of distant lands and their national economies, or of the forcible imposing of foreign cultures, requires the defining of subjugated populations as less than human. This removes all ethical barriers to exploitation since it characterizes people as not belonging to 'Mankind'. The abolition of moral restraint allows domination free rein to expand unchecked by any humanitarian consideration for those who are not entitled to human rights and dignity because their land and lives are forfeit in the interests of the dominators. Hence imperialism requires dehumanization. But so does masculinity in the sense that it is a 'human' status bought at someone else's expense. Domination already has a model of human beings who are not fully human – women.

Applying that model to other men does, of course, involve a contradiction – those men defined as 'inferior' are both men and not-men at one and the same time. The contradiction is managed by interpreting the maleness of 'racially inferior' men as a hyper-masculinity. Any maleness at all in men of the 'inferior races' is too much. Since it cannot be abolished despite the best efforts of the white dominators, it must have an intransigent power unavailable to the dominators, for whom masculinity is a precarious achievement constantly under threat from women who remain human despite the best efforts of the male supremacists. That intransigent masculinity of 'inferior' men functions as a repository for the worst excesses of the dominators' fantasies of phallic power. An apt depiction of this ideology of white male supremacy can be found in the work of Frantz Fanon. Speaking in the voice of the white supremacist ideologue, he said:

> As for the Negroes, they have tremendous sexual powers. What do you expect, with all the freedom they have in their jungles! They copulate at all times and in all places. They are really genital. They have so many children that they cannot even count them. Be careful, or they will flood us with little mulattos. (Fanon, 1952: 111)

Fanon accounted for beliefs of this kind in terms of the over-intellectualization of 'the civilized white man' who 'retains an irrational longing for unusual eras of sexual licence, of orgiastic scenes, of unpunished rapes, of unrepressed incest'. 'Every intellectual gain', he said, 'requires a loss in sexual potential' (p. 117). He also referred to an intrinsic link between sexuality and violence: 'We know how much of sexuality there is in all cruelties, tortures, beatings' (p. 113). These 'pre-logical' and infantile longings are projected on to 'the Negro' who, said Fanon, 'symbolizes the biological' (p. 118). Like sex, the Negro is uncivilized. His natural habitat is the jungle, and he lives in the open air unconfined by the rules and prohibitions of civilization. Like sex, he is wholly 'Nature'. Sex is 'Nature', the Negro is 'Nature', therefore the Negro is sex.

But although Fanon was right about the existential terror felt by the white male dominator faced with the man he has dehumanized, he failed to account for the fact that that terror took a sexual form. Certainly white supremacist ideology presents the Negro as 'Nature', but that can be accounted for by exposing the ideology of dehumanization: He is not 'Man', therefore he is animal-like. In itself, this provides no reason for the obsessive focus on sex. Fanon was right to perceive the problem in terms of the Negro's exclusion from a human status, and the solution in terms of a recognition of his right to human dignity. He was also right to expose the oppressiveness of whiteness as the model of the 'universal human'. However, he failed to see what was at stake in the link between racism and 'sex' because he too subscribed to a model of 'the human' which was only male. This is partly a consequence of the constant reiteration of the word 'man' throughout the text. (Presumably in the original French text, the word 'homme' was repeated as resoundingly.) What he said is sometimes relevant to women without qualification, for example: 'I find myself suddenly in the world and I recognize I have one right alone: that of demanding human behaviour from the other' (Fanon, 1952: 163). But at other times it is difficult or impossible to substitute 'woman' for 'man' and retain Fanon's meaning. When he said 'man' that was exactly what he meant, and not 'woman'. 'Man' is not the genuinely universal human, that is, including women too, in Fanon's text.

But the male interests of Fanon's text betray themselves in other ways as well. In his book, women appear only as the bearers of white supremacist ideology. They are white women who profess to be terrified of being raped by a black man, but whose noisy protestations he believed concealed an active desire for sexual degradation and violence at the hands of black men: 'Basically, does this *fear* of rape not itself cry out for rape? Just as there are faces that ask to be slapped, can one not speak of women who ask to be raped?' (p. 110 – his emphasis). Or they are light-skinned women of colour who scornfully reject black men as husbands, preferring degradation and maltreatment by a white man to marriage with a black man (Chapter 2). Or they are white prostitutes deluded by the myth of black male sexual potency. Of women of colour he 'knows nothing', apart from 'the all-but-whites' who regard black men as violent and inferior (p. 127).

Fanon did not completely ignore the possibility that men, too, could be bearers of white supremacist ideology, but he referred to white men in this context only fleetingly. At one point he raised the issue in a series of rhetorical questions suggesting that white men who hated black men were 'yielding to a feeling of impotence or of sexual inferiority', that they saw the Negro 'as a penis symbol', and used lynching as 'sexual revenge' (p. 113). But he did not discuss these issues any further. On another occasion he raised the issue in a statement which located the blame firstly with women, with men tacked on as an afterthought: 'One thing must be mentioned in this connection: a white woman who has had a Negro lover finds it difficult to return to white men. Or so at least it is believed, particularly by white men' (pp. 121–2).

Throughout his discussion of sexuality and race it is women who are primarily to blame for the ideology which connects sexual violence and black men. For Fanon, the link was deeply embedded in the white female psyche, and he made it clear that it was white women he was talking about, since he admitted he knew nothing about 'the woman of colour'. He took pains to argue the point at some length. Starting from a premise which he found in the work of Marie Bonaparte, he stated categorically that 'the desexualization of aggression in a girl is less complete than in a boy'. This might seem an odd assertion given that sexual aggression is typically male, but what he meant was that the aggression was turned inward. The girl directed it against herself. At between five and nine years of age, he said, the girl tries to get her father to respond to the aggression that her 'unconscious demands of him'. The father 'refuses in a way' (a significant qualification given the prevalence of father–daughter rape?), and so the girl looks around for another vehicle on which to project her desire to be subjected to sexual aggression. Since she is of an age to be aware of 'the folklore and culture' around her, it is the Negro, demonized by her culture, who 'becomes the predestined repository of this aggression', said Fanon. But because it is her own wish, it is a form of self-aggression. It is a well-known fact about women, 'commonplace', said Fanon, that they want to be hurt during the sex act. Hence, 'when a woman lives the fantasy of rape by a Negro ... it is the woman who rapes herself' (pp. 126–7).

This is vicious misogyny, and like all forms of woman-hating, it serves a purpose, that is, to absolve men of responsibility for the harm they do women. This discussion by Fanon occurred in the context of a chapter headed 'The Negro and Psychopathology'. But the psychopathology was simply a belief on the part of white women that they were more likely to be raped by black men. The desire to be raped was characteristic of all (white) women. It was only pathological when white women directed this desire exclusively towards black men who, according to Fanon, were no more sexual than white men. In fact, Fanon absolved all men, of whatever colour, himself included, of responsibility for rape. If women 'want it', then men who rape are merely complying with what women 'want'. Rapists are nothing but passive tools in the hands of avid women. Thus was Fanon complicit with the male supremacist ideology which holds women to blame for the depredations of men.

Fanon failed to identify the nature and origin of the ideology which attributed a hyper-sexuality to black men, because he failed to locate it first and foremost with racist white men. For Fanon, white men were brothers. True, they were deluded, and as genocidal colonizers and racist torturers and murderers, worse than deluded. But it was Fanon's belief and hope that black and white men would eventually be capable of mutual recognition and respect once the evils of European imperialism had finally been overcome. The white man was his chief interlocutor, his aim was 'to show the white man that he is at once the perpetrator and the victim of a delusion' (p. 160). It was to him that Fanon addressed his arguments. It was with the white man that Fanon claimed equality and with whom he shared a common humanity despite the terrible history of colonialism. Those who would eventually hold hands across the great chasm of colonialism and racism were all men, black and white together at last beyond hatred and contempt. The hero of his text was the black man. It was the black man who must learn to extricate himself from the psychological ravages of colonialism, who 'in a sense makes himself abnormal' (p. 160) by envying the white man and his culture, by trying to elicit guilt in the colonizer, by trying to ape the white man and his ways. And it is the black man who is the chief victim of the neurotic sexuality of white supremacy, who is dehumanized by being portrayed as nothing but a 'penis symbol', who is deprived of a sexuality by the woman of colour's dismissive scorn. The Negro who aspired to full human status despite the centuries of dehumanization was not a woman. Black women do not appear in Fanon's text at all, neither as those who need to be shown the ways in which black people can be unwittingly complicit with their own oppression, nor as those whose admission to full membership of the human race cannot be long delayed. But without women, how can men be human? Fanon did not ask the question.

Neither did Said. Although Said was more careful than Fanon to avoid the ritualistic repetition of the word 'man', and although he sporadically included references to work by women and to the importance of feminism, no more than Fanon did he show any awareness that the original model of dehumanization is male supremacy, the exclusion of women from 'human' status because we are not men.[3] Indeed, by equating 'dehumanization' with being 'emasculated' (see above) he is fully complicit with the ideological belief that only men are 'human'. If dehumanization means being deprived of masculinity ('emasculated'), only men can lose their 'human' status since women do not have any masculinity to lose. It is not in fact the whole 'region and its peoples' who are 'emasculated', conceptually or otherwise, by US social science, only the men, although all are dehumanized. It may be that this is merely a terminological quibble. It is not a term Said used frequently. But it is symptomatic of the continuing effectiveness of male supremacy's chief blind spot, namely the humanity of women. The solution is not to 'include' women while everything else remains the same. There is in fact no immediately obvious solution to the problem of women's exclusion from 'humanity'. But acknowledging that it is in fact the case in the ideological structures and processes of male supremacy, while insisting that it ought not to be and acting to change it, is a necessary first step towards ending domination.

A suggestive, if brief, account of the connections between masculinity and domination in all its forms is provided by Sandra Harding's description of the establishment, maintenance and reproduction of 'the stereotypically masculine personality ... the natures of the humans who design and control patriarchy and capital'. Harding went on to say:

> The frantic maintenance of dualisms between mind and body, between culture and nature, between highly-valued self and devalued others, take their first forms in the process of becoming a male person who must individuate himself from a devalued woman. Thus infant boys' psychological birth in families with our division of labor by gender produces men ... who will need to dominate. ... It produces misogyny and male-bonding as prototypes of appropriate social relations with others perceived to be respectively unlike and like themselves. ... From this perspective ... the vast panorama of the history of race relations becomes one more male drama in which the more powerful group of men works out its infantile project of dominating the other. (Harding, 1981: 152, 153)[4]

And, it might be added, the vast panorama of the history of capitalism, whose chief value is the accumulation of limitless hoards of wealth by greedy men obsessively proving to each other who has the biggest. The obscenity of capitalism is the concentration of the world's wealth in the hands of a few men, including those 'salaried employees' of capitalist enterprises, managers, entrepreneurs, skilled artisans of profit-producing technology, paid at grossly inflated rates because they keep the wealth coming, while a large proportion of the world's population, in every country but especially in the third world, lacks access to even the barest minimum of resources to ensure lives of comfort, happiness and dignity, and while the earth's resources are depleted and the biosphere polluted. The obscenity is compounded by the refusal or incapacity of national governments to tax the rich and redistribute wealth more equitably, a reluctance which is not confined to Western nations. Those men responsible for maintaining institutions of domination remain heedless of the horrendous consequences of their actions because they are committed to the values of dehumanization.

I am not arguing that racism, colonialism, imperialism or the worst aspects of capitalism can be wholly accounted for in terms of male supremacist masculinity. I do not know whether or not explaining masculinity will explain all forms of domination, whether, as Ti-Grace Atkinson put it, 'the oppression *of* women *by* men is the source of *all* the corrupt values throughout the world', or not (Atkinson, 1974: 5 – her emphases). What I am arguing is that no account of domination is adequate unless it is also seen in its male supremacist aspects. For whatever else those forms of domination are, they are also forms of masculinity, of that moral and political phenomenon whereby the male sense of self is maintained at the expense of someone else's human dignity. That someone else is always initially female. It is in this sense that male domination is the earliest and primary form of domination, not in the sense that it happened first in history, but in the sense that it happens first in the life of each individual and provides the mould from which all forms of dehumanization are cast. What links all forms of domination together is contempt. The holding of other human beings in contempt is what they all have in common, what gives domination its meaning and force. The first object of contempt is female, the mother who is 'contemptible' because she is a woman lacking the symbol of 'human' status, the penis. The primacy of male domination, chronologically and motivationally in the lives of individuals, is due to the fact that contempt is first learned in connection with the inculcation of masculinity. Contempt is the psychic mechanism which ensures that male infants will become men, and that women will have no alternative but to serve men because that is the only way they can get access to the 'human', a subsidiary and despised access though it might be.

Contempt is the chief meaning and value of a world ruled by men. Although all men have a special ontological status at women's expense under conditions of male supremacy because they bear emblazoned on their bodies the symbol of 'human' value, the world of men is not a realm of equality. Some men are less worthy than others because they occupy low positions in the hierarchies of power which organize the male world. Such men are both 'feminized' and 'hyper-masculinized'. They both partake of the devalued status accorded women, and continue to be men because they possess the penis. Lacking power, they become like women, without rights, without access to decision-making, without control over the conditions of their existence, without protection against exploitation, violence and murder. But as penis-bearers they are also 'human' in the only way recognized by the dominators. To the extent that men of the subordinated groups adhere to the belief that penis-possession signifies 'human' status, by ignoring the existence of women, by giving themselves permission to treat women with contempt, by demanding the same masculine prerogatives as the dominators, they remain complicit with the meanings and values of a world in which no one can be free.

Notes

1   There is one sentence in Said's text which, if read in a certain way, says exactly that. The full sentence reads: 'as early as Aeschylus's play *The Persians* the Orient is transformed from a very far distant and often threatening Otherness into figures that are relatively familiar (in Aeschylus's case, grieving Asiatic women)' (p. 21). If we read only the underlined words, the sentence becomes: 'the Orient is transformed into women'. But even taking the whole sentence into account, the meaning remains. The Orient is transformed from a threat into familiarity by being depicted as women. It is presumably irrelevant that the women are not in fact familiar, since they are 'Asiatics'. Obviously all women are the same in not posing any threat.

2   And sometimes boys too – a land 'of cut-rate boys and women', as Frantz Fanon once said (Fanon, 1952: 161).

3   In this context, it must be noted that Said did not receive any help from most of what has been published as 'feminism', as I have been at pains to point out throughout this present work. It must also be noted that these texts by Said and Fanon are no worse than any of a myriad of others I could have chosen to illustrate the ongoing hegemony of the male monopolization of 'human' status. The problem is not a personal deficiency of these two authors, but a social system of meanings and values with which individuals can be complicit but which they can also resist and challenge as long as they know about alternatives.

4   Unfortunately, Harding was later to repudiate this kind of insight, without, however, either acknowledging her own earlier embracing of it, or providing any reason for the shift in her point of view (Harding, 1986: 185).

Conclusion

My task throughout has been to argue that, without acknowledgement of the meanings and values of male supremacy which structure a reality where only men are 'human', feminism has no unifying point of reference. I have argued that feminism's obvious concern with women only makes sense as a concern to expose the ways in which women are dehumanized under conditions of male supremacy, while attempting to rectify that dehumanization through women taking our lives and destinies into our own hands by extricating ourselves from male-defined institutions, and by creating or reasserting our own meanings and values outside male control. I have also argued that that enterprise involves women striving for a human status which does not depend on the diminution of anyone else's human rights and dignities. I have suggested that that enterprise is already possible because it is in many ways already conceivable, although the task is by no means ended because male supremacy has not yet been overcome. Indeed the struggle has just begun. Despite the centuries of women's resistance to male definition and control, feminism has made little headway against the hydra-headed monster of male hegemony. None the less, the struggle must continue.

I began with an extended definition of feminism which detailed what is involved in the idea of 'social construction'. Although a 'social constructionist' perspective is central to feminist theorizing, it tends to be confined to challenging arguments appealing to 'nature', and hence to be too narrow in scope to allow other important implications of the concept of 'social construction' to be addressed. There is too little awareness of the extent to which the human individual is a social being all the way through, and of the implications of that for the feminist project of exposing and transforming the political dimensions of personal life. Taking seriously the idea that feminism's primary antagonist is a social system was necessary, I felt, if feminism was to resolve some of the contradictions into which it has been driven by a continuing covert adherence to a belief in the ontological primacy of 'individuals'. If the subject-matter of feminism is a social system rather than just 'women', it becomes possible to evaluate what is said by women in the name of feminism on moral and political criteria, rather than on the basis of the experiences or feelings of women as discrete individuals. It becomes possible to challenge anti-feminist positions which masquerade as 'feminism' simply because they are held by women who identify as feminist; and it becomes possible to keep feminist energy and attention focused on the main enemy rather than dissipated throughout a multitude of differences among women. If the subject-matter of feminism is a social system rather than a matter of female personal experience, it becomes possible to identify ways in which even women can consent to our own oppression and adhere to meanings and values which operate against our own best interests; and it becomes possible to hold men accountable for the wrongs they do to women, while still acknowledging that they have choices and can refuse to comply with male supremacist requirements that men treat women as less than human. Within the schema of a social system, individuals are *both* bearers of social relations *and* the loci of moral and political judgement, decision and action which can lead to resistance and refusal.

I went on to define what kind of social system it is that feminism is opposing, that is, the social system of male supremacy structured by meanings and values which maintain the male as the 'human' norm. I argued that feminism's undoubted concern for women arises out of the recognition that women are debarred from human status under conditions of male supremacy, and that that is the source of the atrocities against women identified by feminism. In other words, 'women' are problematic in feminist terms because the relations of ruling under which we live are maintained at our expense. Feminism is unquestionably concerned with the multitude of ways in which women are human too, including not only the various ways in which we live our lives, but also the very fact that we exist at all. But I also pointed out that, unless the feminist standpoint is acknowledged in the first place as the moral and political opposition to male supremacy, feminism loses its central unifying focus, and 'women' become nothing but the occupants of their present 'social locations', caught up in mutual antagonisms to the extent that some 'social locations' are more privileged than others. I argued that without the explicit identification of male supremacy as the problem, there is no feminist standpoint, that 'women's life activity' or 'women's experience' is not alone sufficient to define feminist politics.

In Part Two, I argued in some detail that there is much that is labelled 'feminism' which is complicit with male supremacist relations of ruling because it refuses, or neglects, to name them as such, or because it actively sets out to destroy the feminist standpoint which does. The academy is an important site for the formation and distribution of meaning, far too important to allow it to be turned against the ruling interests. The gates must be kept barred against the bad crazy women threatening to cut off the phallic source of all meaning and pleasure. Unfortunately for the success of this endeavour to exclude threats to phallic supremacy, the master needs 'trusties'. He needs discourses defending his interests visibly authored by women in order to demonstrate that his interests are women's too. But women are notoriously untrustworthy as defenders of phallocracy. There is no unequivocal sign marking off the reliable good women from the bad castrating ones. Sometimes the gatekeeping fails because the good woman and the bad woman are the same woman, struggling with the seductions and coercions of malestream thought, at one point losing her way in the tangled thickets of what counts as knowledge, at another point finding the way clearly marked by the interests of women in opposing male supremacy, only to lose it as the jungle closes in around her once again. Sometimes the gatekeeping fails because the master is fooled into believing that she is working in his interests because she is working in a traditional malestream discipline, whereas what she is actually doing is using her feminist insight to challenge and transform that discipline. Sometimes, sadly, it is the feminist who is deceived into believing that she is operating in women's interests by the mere fact that she is working in the field of Women's Studies, a self-deception which can only be exacerbated by the tendency to re-name Women's Studies 'Gender Studies'.[1] Sometimes the gatekeeping simply fails for no perceptible reason (apart, that is, from the general reason that no form of domination is inevitable).

I have said nothing in these pages about what is to be done in activist terms. My task has not been to address any of the various ways in which feminists in academe have struggled to place feminism on the intellectual agenda. Rather, my task has been to clarify what feminism is in the most general terms, to provide a number of illustrative examples of academic feminist writings which fall short of feminist aims, and to discuss some of the ways in which that happens. Certainly the theoretical schema I have outlined here has a multitude of practical implications. But decisions about what needs to be done, including what needs to be done within the academic domain, are the prerogative of those who are doing it. My own contribution to the struggle has been the clarification of feminist politics on the level of meaning. How that meaning translates into practical activism will depend on the particular problems and difficulties individual activists are faced with. How one engages with specific realities cannot be dictated beforehand. Each of us has to decide for herself (and himself) what is to be done, whether or not anything can be done, and how far one can go before the monstrous regime makes it too hard to go on. As Phyllis Chesler put it in the titles of the first and last chapters of her book: 'Heroism is our only alternative' and 'Sister, fear has no place here' (Chesler, 1994). Women are no strangers to heroism, despite its traditional monopolization by men; and although fear is an appropriate response to the Leviathan of male supremacy, we cannot allow fear alone to stop us.

Note

1 Jocelyn Pixley has suggested that 'Gender Studies' might have been justified originally as an improvement on 'Women's Studies', because the designation 'Women's Studies' implies that the problems are only women's, whereas 'Gender Studies' would facilitate dealing with men as well. But although the word 'gender' is sometimes used to mean male domination, its chief use and function is to deny it. And academic departments of 'Gender Studies' are in fact devoted to anti-feminist substitutions for feminism, of which the most fashionable at the moment is 'queer theory'.

References

Abbott, Sidney and Love, Barbara (1972) *Sappho Was a Right-On Woman: A Liberated View of Lesbianism*, New York: Stein & Day.

Abercrombie, Nicholas, Hill, Steven and Turner, Bryan S. (1980) *The Dominant Ideology Thesis*, London: George Allen & Unwin.

Aboriginal and Islander Women (1975a) 'Black women in society: discussion', in Department of the Prime Minister and Cabinet (ed.), *Women and Politics Conference 1975: Volume 2*, Canberra: Australian Government Publishing Service, 1977.

Aboriginal and Islander Women (1975b) 'Aboriginal women's speak-out', in Department of the Prime Minister and Cabinet (ed.), *Women and Politics Conference 1975: Volume 2*, Canberra: Australian Government Publishing Service, 1977.

Allen, Amy (1998) 'Rethinking power', *Hypatia*, 13 (1) (electronic version – 13 pages).

Andolsen, Barbara Hilkert, Gudorf, Christine E. and Pellauer, Mary D. (eds) (1987) *Women's Consciousness, Women's Conscience: A Reader in Feminist Ethics*, San Francisco: Harper & Row.

Atkinson, Judy (1990a) 'Violence against Aboriginal women: reconstitution of customary law – the way forward', *Aboriginal Law Bulletin*, 2 (46): 6–9.

Atkinson, Judy (1990b) 'Violence in Aboriginal Australia: colonisation and gender. Part I', *The Aboriginal and Islander Health Worker*, 14 (2): 5–21.

Atkinson, Judy (1990c) 'Violence in Aboriginal Australia: colonisation and gender. Part II', *The Aboriginal and Islander Health Worker*, 14 (3): 4–27.

Atkinson, Ti-Grace (1974) *Amazon Odyssey*, New York: Links Books.

Bacchi, Carol Lee (1990) *Same Difference: Feminism and Sexual Difference*, Sydney: Allen & Unwin.

Barrett, Michèle (1984) *Women's Oppression Today: Problems in Marxist Feminist Analysis*, London: Verso.

Barrett, Michèle (1991) *The Politics of Truth: From Marx to Foucault*, London: Polity Press.

Beal, Frances M. (1970) 'Double jeopardy: to be Black and female', in Robin Morgan (ed.), *Sisterhood is Powerful: An Anthology of Writings from the Women's Liberation Movement*, New York: Vintage Books.

Beechey, Veronica (1979) 'On patriarchy', *Feminist Review*, 3: 66–82.

Bell, Diane (1983) *Daughters of the Dreaming*, Melbourne: McPhee Gribble/George Allen & Unwin.

Bell, Diane (1987) 'The politics of separation', in Marilyn Strathern (ed.), *Dealing with Inequality: Analysing Gender Relations in Melanesia and Beyond*, Sydney: Cambridge University Press.

Bell, Diane (1991a) 'Intraracial rape revisited: on forging a feminist future beyond factions and frightening politics', *Women's Studies International Forum*, 14 (5): 385–412.

Bell, Diane (1991b) Letter to the Editors, *Women's Studies International Forum*, 14 (5): 507–13.

Bell, Diane and Klein, Renate (eds) (1996) *Radically Speaking: Feminism Reclaimed*, Melbourne: Spinifex Press.

Bell, Diane and Nelson, Topsy Napurrula (1989) 'Speaking about rape is everyone's business', *Women's Studies International Forum*, 12 (4): 403–16.

Benhabib, Seyla (1999) 'Sexual difference and collective identities: the new global constellation', *Signs*, 24 (2), Winter (electronic version – 17 pages).

Benhabib, Seyla and Cornell, Drucilla (eds) (1987) *Feminism as Critique: Essays on the Politics of Gender in Late-Capitalist Societies*, Cambridge: Polity Press.

Benjamin, Jessica (1989) *The Bonds of Love: Psychoanalysis, Feminism, and the Problem of Domination*, New York: Pantheon Books.

Black Women's Liberation Group (1970) 'Statement on birth control', in Robin Morgan (ed.), *Sisterhood is Powerful: An Anthology of Writings from the Women's Liberation Movement*, New York: Vintage Books.

Bligh, Vivian (1983) 'Study into the needs of Aboriginal women who have been raped or sexually assaulted', in Fay Gale (ed.), *We Are Bosses Ourselves*, Canberra: Australian Institute of Aboriginal Studies.

Bourdieu, Pierre (1990) 'La Domination masculine', *Actes de la recherche in sciences sociales*, no. 84, September.

Bourdieu, Pierre (1998) *La Domination masculine*, Paris: Seuil.

Bulkin, Elly (1991) [1980] 'Racism and writing: some implications for white lesbian critics', *Sinister Wisdom*, 43/44: 114–34.

Butler, Judith (1987) 'Variations on sex and gender: Beauvoir, Wittig and Foucault', in Seyla Benhabib and Drucilla Cornell (eds), *Feminism as Critique: Essays on the Politics of Gender in Late-Capitalist Societies*, Cambridge: Polity Press.

Butler, Judith (1990) *Gender Trouble: Feminism and the Subversion of Identity*, London: Routledge.

Caine, Barbara, Gatens, Moira, Grahame, Emma, Larbalestier, Jan, Watson, Sophie and Webby, Elizabeth (eds) (1998) *Australian Feminism: A Companion*, Melbourne: Oxford University Press.

Campioni, Mia (1987) 'Bringing it all back home: love and hate in lesbian relationships', *Gay Information*, 17–18 – Lesbian Issue.

Campioni, Mia (1991) 'Women and otherness', *Journal of Australian Lesbian Feminist Studies*, 1 (1): 49–57.

Campioni, Mia (1997) 'Revolting women, women in revolt', in Paul Komesaroff, Philipa Rothfield and Jeanne Daly (eds), *Reinterpreting Menopause: Cultural and Philosophical Issues*, New York: Routledge.

Carby, Hazel (1982) 'White women listen! Black feminism and the boundaries of sisterhood', in Centre for Cultural Studies (eds), *The Empire Strikes Back: Race and Racism in 70s Britain*, London: Hutchinson.

Chesler, Phyllis (1994) *Patriarchy: Notes of an Expert Witness*, Monroe, ME: Common Courage Press.

Chodorow, Nancy (1978) *The Reproduction of Mothering: Psychoanalysis and the Sociology of Gender*, Berkeley, Los Angeles and London: University of California Press.

Chodorow, Nancy (1989) *Feminism and Psychoanalytic Theory*, New Haven and London: Yale University Press.

Cohen, Joshua, Howard, Matthew and Nussbaum, Martha (eds) (1999) *Is Multiculturalism Bad for Women?* Princeton, NJ: Princeton University Press.

Coward, Rosalind (1978) 'Re-thinking Marxism', *m/f*, 2: 85–96.

Dalston Study Group (1978) 'Was the Patriarchy Conference "patriarchal"?', in Patriarchy Conference, *Papers on Patriarchy: London, 1976*, Brighton: Women's Publishing Collective.

Daly, Mary (1978) *Gyn/Ecology: The Metaethics of Radical Feminism*, London: Women's Press.

Daly, Mary (1993) *Outercourse: The Be-Dazzling Voyage*, Melbourne: Spinifex Press.

de Beauvoir, Simone (1970) [1949] *The Second Sex*, trans. H.M. Parshley, Harmondsworth: Penguin Books.

de Lauretis, Teresa (1987) *Technologies of Gender: Essays on Theory, Film, and Fiction*, Bloomington and Indianapolis: Indiana University Press.

Delmar, Rosalind (1986) 'What is feminism?', in Juliet Mitchell and Ann Oakley (eds), *What is Feminism?* New York: Pantheon Books.

Delphy, Christine (1996) ' "French feminism": an imperialist invention', in Diane Bell and Renate Klein (eds), *Radically Speaking: Feminism Reclaimed*, Melbourne: Spinifex Press.

Dinnerstein, Dorothy (1976) *The Mermaid and the Minotaur: Sexual Arrangements and Human Malaise*, New York: Harper Colophon Books.

Dunbar, Roxanne (1970) 'Female liberation as the basis for social revolution', in Robin Morgan (ed.), *Sisterhood is Powerful: An Anthology of Writings from the Women's Liberation Movement*, New York: Vintage Books.

Dworkin, Andrea (1974) *Woman Hating*, New York: E.P. Dutton.

Dworkin, Andrea (1981) *Pornography: Men Possessing Women*, London: Women's Press.

Eagleton, Terry (1991) *Ideology: An Introduction*, London and New York: Verso.

Eisenstein, Hester (1984) *Contemporary Feminist Thought*, London and Sydney: Unwin Paperbacks.

Eisenstein, Hester (1985) 'Introduction', in Hester Eisenstein and Alice Jardine (eds), *The Future of Difference*, New Brunswick, NJ: Rutgers University Press.

Eisenstein, Hester and Jardine, Alice (eds) (1985) *The Future of Difference*, New Brunswick, NJ: Rutgers University Press.

Eisenstein, Zillah (ed.) (1979) *Capitalist Patriarchy and the Case for Socialist Feminism*, New York and London: Monthly Review Press.

Eisler, Riane (1987) *The Chalice and the Blade: Our History, Our Future*, New York: HarperCollins.

Fanon, Franz (1970) [1952] *Black Skin White Masks*, London: Paladin.

Fesl, Eve (1984) 'Eve Fesl', in Robyn Rowland (ed.), *Women Who Do and Women Who Don't Join the Women's Movement*. London: Routledge & Kegan Paul.

Firestone, Shulamith (1981) [1970] *The Dialectic of Sex: The Case for Feminist Revolution*, New York: Bantam Books.

Flax, Jane (1990) *Thinking Fragments: Psychoanalysis, Feminism, and Postmodernism in the Contemporary West*, Berkeley, Los Angeles and Oxford: University of California Press.

Foucault, Michel (1980) *Power/Knowledge: Selected Interviews and Other Writings 1972–1977*, edited by Colin Gordon, New York: Pantheon Books.

Foucault, Michel (1985) *The Use of Pleasure: The History of Sexuality*, vol. 2, New York: Vintage Books.

Fraser, Nancy and Nicholson, Linda J. (1990) 'Social criticism without philosophy: an encounter between feminism and postmodernism', in Linda Nicholson (ed.), *Feminism/Postmodernism*, London and New York: Routledge.

Freud, Sigmund (1977a) [1925] 'Some psychical consequences of the anatomical distinction between the sexes', in *On Sexuality*, Pelican Freud Library, vol. 7, Harmondsworth: Penguin Books.

Freud, Sigmund (1977b) [1927] 'Fetishism', in *On Sexuality*, Pelican Freud Library, vol. 7, Harmondsworth: Penguin Books.

Gatens, Moira (1983) 'A critique of the sex/gender distinction', in Judith Allen and Paul Patton (eds), *Beyond Marxism: Interventions After Marx*, Leichhardt, Sydney: Intervention Publications.

Gatens, Moira (1991) *Feminism and Philosophy: Perspectives on Difference and Equality*, Bloomington and Indianapolis: Indiana University Press.

Gathorne-Hardy, Jonathan (1972) *The Rise and Fall of the British Nanny*, London: Hodder & Stoughton.

Giddens, Anthony (1984) *The Constitution of Society: Outline of the Theory of Structuration*, London: Polity Press.

Grieve, Norma and Grimshaw, Patricia (eds) (1981) *Australian Women: Feminist Perspectives*, Melbourne: Oxford University Press.

Grimshaw, Jean (1981) 'Aboriginal women: a study of culture contact', in Norma Grieve and Patricia Grimshaw (eds), *Australian Women: Feminist Perspectives*, Melbourne: Oxford University Press.

Grosz, Elizabeth (1989) *Sexual Subversions: Three French Feminists*, Sydney: Allen & Unwin.

Gunew, Sneja and Yeatman, Anna (eds) (1993) *Feminism and the Politics of Difference*, Sydney: Allen & Unwin.

Hamilton, Annette (1975) 'Aboriginal women: the means of production', in Jan Mercer (ed.), *The Other Half: Women in Australian Society*, Victoria: Penguin Books.

Hamilton, Annette (1981) 'A complex strategical situation: gender and power in Aboriginal Australia', in Norma Grieve and Patricia Grimshaw (eds), *Australian Women: Feminist Perspectives*, Melbourne: Oxford University Press.

Harding, Sandra (1981) 'What is the real material base of patriarchy and capital?' in Lydia Sargent (ed.), *Women and Revolution: A Discussion of the Unhappy Marriage of Marxism and Feminism*, Boston: South End Press.

Harding, Sandra (1983) 'Why has the sex/gender system become visible only now?' in Sandra Harding and Merrill B. Hintikka (eds), *Discovering Reality: Feminist Perspectives on Epistemology, Metaphysics, Methodology, and Philosophy of Science*, Dordrecht, Boston and London: D. Reidel.

Harding, Sandra (1986) *The Science Question in Feminism*, Ithaca and London: Cornell University Press.

Harding, Sandra (1991) *Whose Science? Whose Knowledge? Thinking from Women's Lives*, Ithaca, NY: Cornell University Press.

Harding, Sandra (ed.) (1987) *Feminism and Methodology: Social Science Issues*, Indiana and Milton Keynes: Indiana University Press.

Hartsock, Nancy C.M. (1974) 'Political change: two perspectives on power', *Quest*, 1 (1), Summer.

Hartsock, Nancy (1985) *Money, Sex, and Power: Toward a Feminist Historical Materialism*, Boston: Northeastern University Press.

Hartsock, Nancy (1987) 'The feminist standpoint: developing the ground for a specifically feminist historical materialism', in Sandra Harding (ed.), *Feminism and Methodology*.

Hawkesworth, Mary E. (1989) 'Knowers, knowing, known: feminist theory and claims of truth', *Signs*, 14 (3): 533–57.

Hoagland, Sarah Lucia (1988) *Lesbian Ethics: Toward New Value*, Palo Alto, CA: The Institute of Lesbian Studies.

Hole, Jacquelyn (1994) 'Women victims denied help by Black legal centre', *Sydney Morning Herald*, 5 April.

hooks, bell (1981) *Ain't I a Woman? Black Women and Feminism*, London: Pluto Press.

hooks, bell (1984) *Feminist Theory: From Margin to Centre*, Boston: South End Press.

Huggins, Jackie (1994) 'A contemporary view of Aboriginal women's relationship to the white women's movement', in Norma Grieve and Ailsa Burns (eds), *Australian Women: Contemporary Feminist Thought*, Melbourne: Oxford University Press.

Huggins, Jackie, Willmot, Jo and Tarrago, Isabel (1991) Letter, *Women's Studies International Forum*, 14 (5): 506–7.

Hull, Gloria T., Scott, Patricia Bell and Smith, Barbara (eds) (1982) *All the Women are White, All the Blacks are Men, But Some of us are Brave: Black Women's Studies*, New York: Feminist Press.

Humm, Maggie (1989) *The Dictionary of Feminist Theory*, Hemel Hempstead: Harvester Wheatsheaf.

Jaggar, Alison M. (1983) *Feminist Politics and Human Nature*, Brighton: Harvester Press.

Jaggar, Alison M. (1990) 'Sexual difference and sexual equality', in Deborah Rhode (ed.), *Theoretical Perspectives on Sexual Difference*, New Haven and London: Yale University Press.

Jardine, Alice (1985) *Gynesis: Configurations of Woman and Modernity*, Ithaca and London: Cornell University Press.

Jeffreys, Sheila (1990) *Anticlimax: A Feminist Perspective on the Sexual Revolution*, London: Women's Press.

Jeffreys, Sheila (1992) 'Lesbian sex therapy and the lesbian sexual revolution', *Journal of Australian Lesbian Feminist Studies*, 2 (1), June.

Jeffreys, Sheila (1993) *The Lesbian Heresy: A Feminist Perspective on the Lesbian Sexual Revolution*, Melbourne: Spinifex Press.

Johnson, Miriam M. (1988) *Strong Mothers, Weak Wives*, Berkeley and London: University of California Press.

Joseph, Gloria I. and Lewis, Jill (eds) (1981) *Common Differences: Conflicts in Black and White Perspectives*, Boston: South End Press.

Keller, Evelyn Fox (1983) *A Feeling for the Organism: The Life and Work of Barbara McClintock*, New York: W.H. Freeman and Company.

Keller, Evelyn Fox (1985) *Reflections on Gender and Science*, New Haven and London: Yale University Press.

Kennedy, Florynce (1970) 'Institutionalized oppression vs. the female', in Robin Morgan (ed.), *Sisterhood is Powerful: An Anthology of Writings from the Women's Liberation Movement*, New York: Vintage Books.

Kramarae, Cheris and Treichler, Paula A. (1985) *A Feminist Dictionary*, Boston, London and Henley: Pandora.

Kumar, Mina (1994) 'Bringing class out of the closet: Book Review', *Ms*, V (3): 75–6.

Lake, Marilyn (1998) 'A history of feminism in Australia', in Barbara Caine et al. (eds), *Australian Feminism: A Companion*, Melbourne: Oxford University Press.

Langton, Marcia (1989) 'Feminism: what do Aboriginal women gain?' *Broadside: Newsletter of the National Foundation for Australian Women*, 1 (1), November: 3.

Larrain, Jorge (1979) *The Concept of Ideology*, London: Hutchinson.

Lerner, Gerda (1986) *The Creation of Patriarchy*, New York and Oxford: Oxford University Press.

Lerner, Gerda (1993) *The Creation of Feminist Consciousness: From the Middle Ages to Eighteen-Seventy*, New York and Oxford: Oxford University Press.

Lesbian Ethics (1991) vol. 4, no. 2.

Lloyd, Genevieve (1984) *The Man of Reason: 'Male' and 'Female' in Western Philosophy*, London: Methuen.

Lorde, Audre (1978) 'Scratching the surface: some notes on barriers to women and loving', in Lorde, 1984.

Lorde, Audre (1979a) 'Sexism: an American disease in Black face', in Lorde, 1984.

Lorde, Audre (1979b) 'An open letter to Mary Daly', in Lorde, 1984.

Lorde, Audre (1984) *Sister Outsider: Essays and Speeches*, Freedom, CA: Crossing Press.

Lugones, Maria (1987) 'Playfulness, "World"-travelling and loving perception', *Hypatia*, 2 (2), Summer: 3–20.

Lukes, Steven (1974) *Power: A Radical View*, London and Basingstoke: Macmillan.

Lukes, Steven (1977) *Essays in Social Theory*, London and Basingstoke: Macmillan.

Maccoby, Eleanor Emmons and Jacklin, Carol Nagy (1974) *The Psychology of Sex Differences*, Stanford, CA: Stanford University Press.

MacKinnon, Catharine (1982) 'Feminism, Marxism, method and the state: an agenda for theory', in Nannerl O. Keohane, Michelle Z. Rosaldo and Barbara C. Gelpi (eds), *Feminist Theory: A Critique of Ideology*, Brighton: Harvester Press.

MacKinnon, Catharine (1987) *Feminism Unmodified: Discourses on Life and Law*, Cambridge, MA: Harvard University Press.

MacKinnon, Catharine (1990) 'Legal perspectives on sexual difference', in Deborah Rhode (ed.), *Theoretical Perspectives on Sexual Difference*, New Haven and London: Yale University Press.

MacKinnon, Catharine (1991) *Toward a Feminist Theory of the State*, Cambridge, MA and London: Harvard University Press.

Marx, Karl and Engels, Frederick (1974) [1846] *The German Ideology*, edited and abridged by C.J. Arthur, New York: International Publishers.

Mathieu, Nicole-Claude (1999) 'Bourdieu ou le pouvoir auto-hypnotique de la domination masculine', *Les Temps Modernes*, no. 604 (mai-juin-juillet): 286–324.

McNay, Lois (1992) *Foucault and Feminism: Power, Gender and the Self*, London: Polity Press.

Mies, Maria (1982) *The Lace Makers of Narsapur: Indian Housewives Produce for the World Market*, London: Zed Press.

Millett, Kate (1970) *Sexual Politics*, London: Rupert Hart-Davis.

Mills, C. Wright (1970) [1959] *The Sociological Imagination*, Harmondsworth: Penguin Books.

Mitchell, Juliet (1984) [1974a] 'On Freud and the distinction between the sexes', in *Women: The Longest Revolution – Essays in Feminism, Literature and Psychoanalysis*, London: Virago.

Mitchell, Juliet (1974b) *Psychoanalysis and Feminism*, Harmondsworth: Penguin Books.

Mohanty, Chandra Talpade (1988) 'Under Western eyes: feminist scholarship and colonial discourse', *Feminist Review*, 30: 61–88.

Molyneux, Maxine (1981) 'Socialist societies old and new: progress towards women's emancipation?' *Feminist Review*, 8, Summer: 1–34.

Montefiore, Alan (1990) 'The political responsibility of intellectuals', in Ian Maclean, Alan Montefiore and Peter Winch (eds), *The Political Responsibility of Intellectuals*, Cambridge: Cambridge University Press.

Morgan, Robin (ed.) (1970) *Sisterhood is Powerful*, New York: Vintage Books.

Moses, Claire Goldberg (1998) 'Made in America: "French feminism" in academia', *Feminist Studies*, 24 (2) (electronic version – 20 pages).

Mosey, Anne (1994) *Central Australian 'Remote Area Aboriginal Night Patrols': A Review*, Alice Springs: Drug and Alcohol Services Association.

Myron, Nancy and Bunch, Charlotte (eds) (1975) *Lesbianism and the Women's Movement*, Baltimore: Diana Press.

New Republic, The (1999) 'Martha C. Nussbaum and her critics: an exchange', *The New Republic*, 19 April (electronic version – 4 pages).

Ng, Roxana (1993) 'Sexism, racism and Canadian nationalism', in Sneja Gunew and Anna Yeatman (eds), *Feminism and the Politics of Difference*, Sydney: Allen & Unwin.

Nicholson, Linda J. (ed.) (1990) *Feminism/Postmodernism*, London and New York: Routledge.

Noddings, Nell (1984) *Caring: A Feminine Approach to Ethics and Moral Education*, Berkeley: University of California Press.

Norton, Eleanor Holmes (1970) 'For Sadie and Maude', in Robin Morgan (ed.), *Sisterhood is Powerful: An Anthology of Writing from the Women's Liberation Movement*, New York: Vintage Press.

Nussbaum, Martha (1999) 'The professor of parody: the hip defeatism of Judith Butler (Review)', *The New Republic*, 22 Feb. (electronic version – 12 pages).

Oakley, Ann (1972) *Sex, Gender and Society*, Melbourne: Sun Books.

Offen, Karen (1988) 'Defining feminism: a comparative historical approach', *Signs*, 14 (1), Autumn: 119–57.

Omolade, Barbara (1985) 'Black women and feminism', in Hester Eisenstein and Alice Jardine (eds), *The Future of Difference*, New Brunswick, NJ: Rutgers University Press.

Phillips, Anne (1987) *Divided Loyalties: Dilemmas of Sex and Class*, London: Virago.

Poole, Linda J. (1993) 'Legal developments and reform in the inter-American system', in Joanna Kerr (ed.), *Ours by Right: Women's Rights as Human Rights*, London: Zed Books.

Queensland Domestic Violence Task Force (1988) *Report: Beyond These Walls*, Brisbane: Queensland Domestic Violence Task Force.

Rattansi, Ali (1992) 'Changing the subject? Racism, culture and education', in James Donald and Ali Rattansi (eds), *'Race', Culture and Difference*, London: Sage.

Redstockings (1970) 'Redstockings Manifesto', in Robin Morgan (ed.), *Sisterhood is Powerful: An Anthology of Writing from the Women's Liberation Movement*, New York: Vintage Press.

Refractory Girl (1974a) no. 5, Summer.

Refractory Girl (1974b) no. 6, Autumn.

Rhode, Deborah L. (ed.) (1990) *Theoretical Perspectives on Sexual Difference*, New Haven and London: Yale University Press.

Rose, Hilary (1987) [1983] 'Hand, brain, and heart: a feminist epistemology for the natural sciences', in Sandra Harding and Jean O'Barr (eds), *Sex and Scientific Inquiry*, Chicago and London: University of Chicago Press.

Rowland, Robyn (ed.) (1984) *Women Who Do and Women Who Don't Join the Women's Movement*, London: Routledge & Kegan Paul.

Rubin, Gayle (1984) 'Thinking sex', in Carole S. Vance (ed.), *Pleasure and Danger: Exploring Female Sexuality*, London: Routledge & Kegan Paul.

Said, Edward (1987) [1978] *Orientalism*, London: Peregrine Books.

Said, Edward (1994) *Culture and Imperialism*, London: Vintage Books.

Saunders, Hilary (1975) 'Women hold up half the sky', *Aboriginal and Islander Identity*, 2 (6), October: 28.

Schor, Naomi (1992) 'Feminism and George Sand: Lettres à Marie', in Judith Butler and Joan Scott (eds), *Feminists Theorize the Political*, London and New York: Routledge.

Sculthorpe, Heather (1990) 'Review of domestic violence resource materials', *Aboriginal Law Bulletin*, 2 (46), October: 15–16.

Segal, Lynne (1984) *Is the Future Female? Troubled Thoughts on Contemporary Feminism*, London: Virago.

Smith, Dorothy E. (1987) [1972] 'Women's Perspective as a Radical Critique of Sociology', in Sandra Harding (ed.), *Feminism and Methodology: Social Science Issues*, Indiana and Milton Keynes: Indiana University Press.

Smith, Dorothy E. (1987) *The Everyday World as Problematic: A Feminist Sociology*, Boston: Northeastern University Press.

Smith, Dorothy E. (1990) *The Conceptual Practice of Power: A Feminist Sociology of Knowledge*, Boston: Northeastern University Press.

Spacks, Patricia Meyer (1976) *The Female Imagination*, New York: A Discus Book.

Spelman, Elizabeth (1988) *Inessential Woman: Problems of Exclusion in Feminist Thought*, London: Women's Press.

Spender, Dale (1987) [1980] *Man Made Language*, London and New York: Routledge & Kegan Paul.

Spender, Dale (1982) *Women of Ideas (and What Men Have Done to Them): From Aphra Behn to Adrienne Rich*, London: Ark Paperbacks.

Stanley, Liz and Wise, Sue (1993) *Breaking out Again: Feminist Ontology and Epistemology*, London and New York: Routledge.

Stimpson, Catharine R. (1988) *Where the Meanings Are: Feminism and Cultural Spaces*, New York and London: Routledge.

Summers, Anne (1975) *Damned Whores and God's Police: The Colonization of Women in Australia*, Ringwood, Victoria: Penguin Books.

Sykes, Bobbi (Roberta) (1975) 'Black women in Australia: a history', in Jan Mercer (ed.), *The Other Half*, Victoria: Penguin Books.

Sykes, Bobbi (Roberta) (1984) 'Bobbi Sykes', in Robyn Rowland (ed.), *Women Who Do and Women Who Don't Join the Women's Movement*, London: Routledge & Kegan Paul.

THE FEMINISTS (1973) [1969] 'THE FEMINISTS: a political organization to eliminate sex roles', in Anne Koedt, Ellen Levine and Anita Rapone (eds), *Radical Feminism*, New York: Quadrangle Books.

Thompson, Denise (1991) *Reading Between the Lines: A Lesbian Feminist Critique of Feminist Accounts of Sexuality*, Sydney: Gorgon's Head Press (self-published).

Thompson, Denise (1994) 'Retaining the radical challenge: a reply to Wendy Hollway', *Feminism and Psychology*, 4 (2): 326–9.

Thompson, Denise (1995) 'Theory and its discontents: another reply to Wendy Hollway', *Feminism and Psychology*, 5 (4): 531–3.

Trebilcot, Joyce (1991) 'Ethics of method: greasing the machine and telling stories', in Claudia Card (ed.), *Feminist Ethics*, Lawrence, KS: University Press of Kansas.

Tucker, Margaret (1977) *If Everyone Cared*, Sydney: Ure Smith.

United Nations (1995) *Human Rights: Harmful Traditional Practices Affecting the Health of Women and Children*, Fact Sheet no. 23, Geneva and New York: United Nations Centre for Human Rights.

United Nations (1996) *The United Nations and the Advancement of Women 1945–1996*, New York: Department of Public Information, United Nations.

Venceremos Brigade (1975) 'Black women's statement', *Aboriginal and Islander Identity*, 2 (6), October: 18.

Walker, Alice (1982) 'One child of one's own: a meaningful digression within the work(s) – an excerpt', in Gloria T. Hull, Patricia Bell Scott and Barbara Smith (eds), *All the Women are White, All the Blacks are Men, But Some of us are Brave: Black Women's Studies*, New York: Feminist Press.

Wallace, Michele (1982) 'Black feminists search for sisterhood', in Gloria T. Hull, Patricia Bell Scott and Barbara Smith (eds), *All the Women are White, All the Blacks are Men, But Some of us are Brave: Black Women's Studies*, New York: Feminist Press.

Wallace, Michele (1990) *Black Macho and the Myth of the Superwoman*, New York and London: Verso.

Ward, Glenyse (1987) *Wandering Girl*, Broome, Western Australia: Magabala Books.

Ware, Celestine (1970) *Woman Power: The Movement for Women's Liberation*, New York: Tower Publications.

Washington, Mary Helen (1982) 'Teaching *Black Eyed Susans*: an approach to the study of Black women writers', in Gloria T. Hull, Patricia Bell Scott and Barbara Smith (eds), *All the Women are White, All the Blacks are Men, But Some of us are Brave: Black Women's Studies*, New York: Feminist Press.

Weedon, Chris (1987) *Feminist Practice and Poststructuralist Theory*, Oxford and New York: Basil Blackwell.

Winter, Bronwyn (1997) '(Mis)Representations: what French feminism isn't', *Women's Studies International Forum*, 20 (2): 211–24.

Wittgenstein, Ludwig (1951) [1922] *Tractatus Logico-Philosophicus*, London: Routledge & Kegan Paul.

Woolf, Virginia (1946) [1929] *A Room of One's Own*, London: The Hogarth Press.

Woolf, Virginia (1952) [1938] *Three Guineas*, London: The Hogarth Press.

Index